TEACHING CONTENT AREA READING SKILLS

A Modular Preservice and Inservice Program

THIRD EDITION

Harry W. Forgan
Charles T. Mangrum II

University of Miami

WITHDRAWN

Charles E. Merrill Publishing Company
A Bell & Howell Company
Columbus Toronto London Sydney

To Ruth Ann and Jane
Whose encouragement, help, and loyalty make every
undertaking—and all of life—a joyous pursuit.

Published by
Charles E. Merrill Publishing Company
A Bell & Howell Company
Columbus, Ohio 43216

Photo Credits: Cover — © Terry Wild, DPI; pages 7, 14, 67, 103, 131, 199, 261,
287 — Jean Greenwald; page 165 — Strix Pix; page 229 — © C. Quinlan.

Library of Congress Catalog Card Number: 84-71915
International Standard Book Number: 0-675-20308-2
1 2 3 4 5 6 7 8 9—89 88 87 86 85
Printed in the United States of America

PREFACE

You may find this book different from textbooks you have used in college courses or inservice programs. It is not a research textbook, with summaries of knowledge organized by chapter and subsections. Although there is a definite need for the research textbook, there is also a need for an alternative text—the *applied textbook*. An applied textbook combines experience with information from research to supply the reader with a way of performing. This applied textbook helps content area teachers develop the basic competencies for helping students read the written materials that are used in subject areas.

We think the competencies that content area teachers need for helping students read materials are best developed through the use of a *modular* format such as the one in this book. A module is a self-instructional package designed to help the user accomplish certain objectives. An objective consists of those things you will be able to do, know, and/or feel after instruction that you may not have done, known, and/or felt before instruction. The ten modules in this book will help you enable your students to read the materials you use in your content area classes.

In this third edition, we have made changes to make this modular program more readable and useful to students. The changes were suggested by the many university and college professors and inservice directors who have used the textbook since it was first published. Despite our changes, we have maintained the basic theme and format of the original textbook. This third edition will help content area teachers acquire the competencies they need to effectively and efficiently help students read their textual materials.

We extend a special note of appreciation to Edward Fry for developing the Graph for Estimating Readability (extended form), to Alton Raygor for developing The Raygor Readability Estimate, and to Nativadad Santos for developing the Classification Scheme for Reading Questions—all three of these devices should prove valuable to content area teachers. We appreciate the opportunity to share with our readers the devices and the suggestions for their effective use. We also acknowledge our present and past University of Miami students and inservice teachers who gave us with many excellent suggestions for this edition. Their comments and suggestions keep us thinking about the practical aspects of reading instruction. We also acknowledge the many students of Southwood Junior High School in Miami, Florida, with whom our University of Miami undergraduate students worked to develop the competencies explained in these modules.

Finally, we appreciate the continued support of our families as we proceed with our writing projects. Our children, Jennifer, Jimmy, Mykel, and Mark, have continued to show patience while their dads worked hard to prepare the third edition. At the same time, they helped us release our anxieties by going for bicycle rides and walks to help us keep our sense of reality and perspective on children. Most important, we continue to receive and appreciate the necessary encouragement and support of our wives, Ruth Ann and Jane.

Harry Forgan
Charles Mangrum

CONTENTS

Contents

OVERVIEW

There are three reasons you need to acquire the competencies in this modular program. First, there is dissatisfaction with the present reading achievement levels of secondary students. Second, it is impossible for elementary school teachers to help students develop *all* the necessary reading skills for different types of content area materials. Elementary school children are incapable of developing some of the higher level reading skills and the specialized vocabulary required for reading content area materials. Third, it is generally agreed that the teachers who are most effective in helping students read specialized content materials are the teachers of the content areas.

The purpose of this modular program is to enable you to help students read content area materials. As content area teachers, you are not expected to teach beginning reading skills. Content teachers are mainly responsible for helping students meet the objectives of particular subject areas. The competencies stressed in these modules do not give you additional responsibilities; rather, they enable you to be more effective as you execute your present responsibilities.

TEN BASIC COMPETENCIES

This program will help you accomplish the ten reading competencies required of content area teachers. When you perform them, you will be doing your part to help students read content area materials and thus be more likely to succeed in your classes. Specifically, you are expected to help students read content area materials by performing the following tasks:

1. Students cannot be expected to read materials written above their reading levels. Therefore, you must be able to determine the readability of written material to avoid frustrating students with reading requirements they cannot handle.
2. You will frequently need to supplement the available materials by preparing written materials for your students. To do this you must be able to write and alter materials at specified readability levels. This will increase your teaching resources and make them more appropriate for your students.
3. Often a variety of reading materials are used to teach basic concepts in content area courses. Before assigning materials,

you must be sure the materials are suitable in reading level and determine which materials are suitable for particular students.

4. All content areas have specialized vocabulary. Teachers are expected to help students develop and expand word meanings at different levels. To do so, you will need guidelines and activities for teaching the specialized vocabulary of your area.

5. A student is not reading unless she is comprehending. Students often need help in comprehending subject area materials. You must be able to help students develop comprehension strategies for the specialized reading materials in your content area.

6. Different types of study strategies are appropriate for different content areas. Since content area teachers have themselves employed study strategies, they are the most qualified persons to help students develop appropriate strategies for the specific area. You must be aware of your strategies and share them with your students.

7. Students often encounter long and difficult words in content area materials. You are not expected to teach beginning word-recognition skills, but you should be able to help students develop a strategy for pronouncing multisyllable words that may at first appear unfamiliar to them.

8. Many reading skills are needed to read specialized materials. After becoming aware of the necessary reading skills in your content area, you must determine which reading skills students have or have not acquired. You need reading skills tests to diagnose the needs of students.

9. Many students know how to read, but are reluctant to read. You should be able to use a strategy to increase motivation.

10. Just because students are reluctant to read does not mean they are reluctant to learn. Some students are far behind in reading and need assistance to succeed in content areas. Every content teacher is responsible for identifying and referring problem readers, and for adapting instruction so problem readers can succeed. You are expected to help problem readers survive—and learn—in your classroom while they are overcoming their reading problems.

THE MODULAR FORMAT

You will probably notice that the format of this book is different from other textbooks you have used. The title states that this is a *modular program.* A module is a self-instructional package designed to help the learner accomplish certain objectives. An objective consists of what you are able to do, know, and/or feel after instruction that you may not have done, known, and/or felt before instruction. The ten modules in this book are self-instructional packages whose purpose is to enable you to achieve the ten basic tasks required of content area teachers. There is a separate module for each of the ten major competencies you need to help students read content materials.

In examining the modules, you will notice that each includes the following components: Prospectus, Pretest, Branching Program Alternatives for Pretest Responses, several Enabling Elements, Posttest, Posttest Answers, and References. Since you may be expected to complete the modules independently, let us take a closer look at each of these parts.

The *Prospectus* provides an overview of the module. It includes the rationale for the objectives of the module. After reading the rationale, you will understand why the module might be of value to you as a content area teacher. Terminal and specific objectives are also listed in the Prospectus. The terminal objective indicates the behavior you are expected to perform in the classroom. This behavior is indicated in more detail by the precisely defined specific objectives. The Prospectus also includes a description of the resources and time required to do the module so you will be able to plan its completion. Materials that may be required for completing the module are specified, along with an estimated completion time for the most important activities.

After reading the Prospectus, turn to the Pretest to determine if there are any objectives you have accomplished. The Pretest is a simple yes–no checklist for self-evaluation. If you think you can perform the behavior asked for in the Pretest, choose YES; if you have any doubt, choose NO.

The *Branching Program Alternatives for Pretest Responses* provides the direction you need to go through the modules. The Branching Program tells you which Enabling Elements will help you accomplish specific objectives. The Branching Program tells you what to do for each response you made on the Pretest. The modules then take into account your individual differences; you work only to accomplish the objectives you have not yet developed.

The major parts of the modules are *Enabling Elements.* Each Enabling Element restates the specific objective and offers Enabling Activities to help you accomplish that specific objective. Some of the activities in every Enabling Element suggest that you read a study guide. Study guides include the background information you need to accomplish the objectives. In addition to the background information, many of the study guides include practicum exercises to help you put your new skills to work. The study guides make the modules relatively self-contained, since you need not refer to other resources to accomplish the objectives.

A *Posttest* is included for each of the ten modules. The Posttest items are based on the objectives and are used to determine whether or not you have accomplished the objectives. Posttest items vary in format. Some of the items require you to list or describe, and others are simulation-type activities requiring you to apply your newly developed skills.

Posttest answers are provided in each module, so you can check your responses as a method of self-evaluation. The results of your self-evaluation determine if you have accomplished the objectives. If so, you can go on to the next module. If not, you may want to return through some of the Enabling Elements, as directed.

References are included after each module. In some cases you may want more information or may wish to consult other sources for different ideas. The references have been selected because we think they are the most helpful and readily available to content area teachers.

INSTRUCTIONS AND FLOWCHART FOR COMPLETING THE TEN MODULES

Your instructor may have specific suggestions for completing the modules in this book. If not, we suggest beginning with Module 1. The following instructions and flowchart explain the recommended procedure for completing each module. After completing Module 1, complete the remaining modules in any sequence, according to your needs as a content area teacher.

INSTRUCTIONS

1. Read the Prospectus to determine if the module meets your specific professional needs. If the module meets your specific needs, continue reading.
2. Self-administer the Pretest and follow the Branching Program to complete the objectives you have not accomplished.
3. Complete the Enabling Elements in sequence. Use the study guides and activities as appropriate.
4. When you have completed all activities for your selected objectives, take the Posttest to determine if you have met the evaluative criteria.
5. If performance was not satisfactory, return to previous Enabling Activities as needed, or consult your instructor. Retake the appropriate Posttest items.
6. When the module has been completed, you may wish to examine the References for additional information or study.

You can keep records for your progress with this checklist of terminal objectives.

CHECKLIST OF TERMINAL OBJECTIVES

_____ *Module 1.* You will determine the readability level of passages selected from major reading sources in your content area.

_____ *Module 2.* You will write materials at specified readability levels and alter the readability levels of passages related to your content area.

_____ *Module 3.* You will use an Informal Suitability Survey to determine the suitability of content area materials.

_____ *Module 4.* You will be able to introduce and expand word meanings in your subject area.

_____ *Module 5.* You will prepare a lesson plan to improve the comprehension achievement of students in your subject area.

_____ *Module 6.* You will specify the major study skills from your content area, prepare a plan for teaching a study skill, and apply three study strategies.

_____ *Module 7.* You will determine the word-pronunciation strategies used by students and help them use a strategy for pronouncing multisyllable words.

_____ *Module 8.* You will use reading skills tests to determine if students have acquired the reading skills related to your content area.

_____ *Module 9.* You will acquire and use the provided strategy for motivating reluctant readers.

_____ *Module 10.* You will identify problem readers and factors that may be interfering with their responsiveness to reading tasks and adapt your instructional procedures to help problem readers succeed in your content areas.

M O D U L E   1

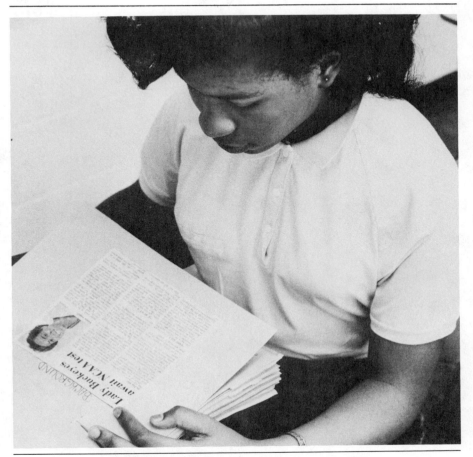

DETERMINING
READABILITY
LEVELS

CONTENTS

PROSPECTUS

RATIONALE

As a teacher you will need to select materials for your students to read in conjunction with course assignments. These materials may include textbooks, newspapers, magazines, and pamphlets. One criterion you should use for selecting materials is readability. *Readability* concerns the difficulty of materials to be read. This module will help you use Fry's Graph for Estimating Readability to determine the difficulty of reading materials. Its use will help you find appropriate materials for the range of reading levels in your classes. You will learn how to use Fry's graph to find the reading levels of textbooks, newspaper articles, magazines, and pamphlets. Fry's graph can also be used to determine the readability levels of the test items you prepare. This module is extremely important for you, the content area teacher, since you will want to be able to provide students with materials appropriate to their reading levels.

OBJECTIVES

Terminal Objective
You will determine the readability level of passages selected from major reading sources in your content area.

Specific Objectives

1. You will list the two major factors that influence the readability of material and the two major uses of readability formulas.
2. You will state the five steps for using Fry's Graph for Estimating Readability to determine the reading level of specified passages.

3. You will use Fry's graph to estimate readability levels of (a) textbooks, (b) articles, and (c) selections with fewer than 100 words.

RESOURCES AND TIME REQUIRED

Most of the materials required for completing this module are provided. You will also need textbooks, newspaper or magazine articles, and those other written materials, such as handouts, that you commonly use in teaching. The estimated time to complete the core Enabling Activities* is three to four hours.

PRETEST

Directions: For each question, choose the word that indicates your belief regarding your competency. If you are in doubt, choose NO.

1. There are two major factors that influence the readability of written material and two major uses of readability formulas. Can you state the two major factors influencing the readability of written material and list the two major uses of readability formulas?   YES   NO

2. Edward Fry developed the Graph for Estimating Readability. Do you know how to use Fry's graph to determine the readability level of written material?   YES   NO

3. Have you used Fry's graph to estimate readability levels of (a) textbooks, (b) articles, and (c) selections with less than 100 words?   YES   NO

BRANCHING PROGRAM ALTERNATIVES FOR PRETEST RESPONSES

1. If you can state the two major factors that influence the readability of written material and list the two major uses of readability formulas, you are ready for Enabling Element 2. If not, Enabling Element 1 will provide you with this information.

2. If you know how to use Fry's Graph for Estimating Readability, you are ready for Enabling Element 3. If not, Enabling Element 2 is designed to develop this competency.

3. If you are skillful in using Fry's graph to estimate readability levels of (a) textbooks, (b) articles, and (c) selections with

---

*Core Enabling Activities are marked with an asterisk.

less than 100 words, you have completed the objectives of this module and are ready for the Posttest. If you need to practice, or use Fry's graph to estimate readability levels of different types of written materials such as textbooks, articles, *or* other selections with fewer than 100 words, do the appropriate sections in Enabling Element 3.

ENABLING ELEMENT 1
FACTORS INFLUENCING READABILITY

SPECIFIC OBJECTIVE 1

You will list the two major factors that influence the readability of material and the two major uses of readability formulas.

ENABLING ACTIVITIES

*1. Read Study Guide 1. Identify the two factors that influence readability and the two major uses of readability formulas.

2. Reflect upon your own reading and ask, "What makes some selections more difficult for me to comprehend?"

3. Ask your students, "Why are some materials easier to read than others?" Have you identified other factors that may make some material more difficult than others?

4. Why should you learn about the factors that influence readability and the formulas that are available to determine it? How can this information help you as a teacher? Discuss these questions with your colleagues.

5. Most readability formulas are for the English language; however, applications are growing. Locate the Klare article, "Assessing Readability," in the References for this module if you want to learn about formulas available to measure materials in any of these foreign languages: French, Dutch, Spanish, Hebrew, German, Hindi, Russian, and Chinese.

STUDY GUIDE 1

Readability is the objective measure of the difficulty of a book or article. Readability levels are generally reported in terms of grade level. Therefore, one might find a textbook written at the ninth-grade level, fourth-grade level, and so forth. The readability of texts and supplementary reading materials should be of great concern to teachers, because students are expected to gather information and develop new

---

*Indicates core Enabling Activity.

skills through reading. Teachers thus need to know what factors influence readability and how to determine readability.

History

Factors that influence readability have been the subject of scholarly study for thousands of years. According to Klare, "Lorge tells of word and idea counts made by Talmudists in 900 A.D. so that they could use frequency of occurrence to distinguish from usual senses (meanings)" (1963, p. 30).

Although the study of readability has been under way for many years, little progress was made until statistical techniques were developed. Such techniques made it possible to identify important readability factors and to construct formulas for estimating passage difficulty. According to Klare (1963), early studies revealed many factors related to readability. Gray and Leary, for example, had identified 289 factors influencing readability, 20 of which were significant.

Several dozen readability formulas have been developed over the years. Many of the earlier formulas were complex and required the user to count a number of variables. Later research revealed that the two most important factors influencing readability are *sentence length* and *word difficulty*. In general, the longer the sentences and the longer the words, the more difficult the material is to read. Conversely, if sentences and words are short, the material is easier to read.

Today, the more commonly accepted and widely used formulas use sentence length and word difficulty for estimating reading level. Examples of this method are the Spache Readability Formula (1953) for primary grade materials and the Dale-Chall Readability Formula (1947, 1948) for materials in grades four through sixteen. Because the Spache and Dale-Chall formulas require considerable time, researchers have developed shortcut tables or charts, that facilitate the use of the Spache and Dale-Chall formulas. Others, such as Edward Fry (1968, 1977), have developed alternative formulas based upon the same factors that can be more simply and quickly applied. Of the less time-consuming formulas, Fry's Graph for Estimating Readability is one of the most commonly accepted.

Uses of Readability Formulas

One use of a readability formula is to estimate the reading difficulty of printed materials. Estimates of reading level are especially useful to the teacher interested in making reading assignments or in selecting textbooks and other commonly used written materials. Teachers who have the opportunity to participate in textbook selection should consider how difficult the textbooks are to read. Likewise, many content area teachers are not bound to one textbook, but rather develop a collection of resource materials to use in teaching their classes. They use newspaper clippings, articles from journals or magazines, pamphlets, and other printed materials that correlate with the objectives of their content area classes. Before asking students to read these materials, teachers should determine just how difficult their reading levels are.

The second major use of the readability formula is to guide the teacher in preparing or altering reading levels of materials. All teachers must be writers as they prepare tests, study guides, course outlines, letters to parents, and other materials. In writing materials for others to read, it is important that the content area teacher write at a readability level within the reading level range of the students and/or parents. Likewise, some teachers like to alter materials by raising or lowering the reading level to go along with the capabilities of students. For example, if you find a very technical article with a readability level above your students' level, yet desire to use this article because of its content, you may want to lower the reading level.

Limitations of Readability Formulas

Even though readability formulas are useful, there are some limitations. First, most readability formulas do not take into consideration the concepts presented in the materials. As mentioned earlier, the two most common criteria used in readability formulas are sentence length and word difficulty. However, some materials that are within the students' reading level according to the readability formulas may be more difficult to read than other materials because they deal with concepts that are beyond the students' understanding.

Another limitation of readability formulas is that they do not consider the use of slang, satire, multiple meanings, or the interest of the reader. Likewise, readability formulas cannot be used with certain types of material such as poetry in which the sentence structure is different. These limitations must be kept in mind when applying the formulas to reading materials.

Common Formulas

For use in the primary grades, the Spache Readability Formula is the most commonly accepted formula. Developed in 1953, the formula uses two factors to estimate reading level: average sentence length and percentage of difficult words. Through use and study, this formula has been demonstrated to be valid and reliable for estimating reading level of written material; however, it is complex and time-consuming.

For grades four through sixteen, the Dale-Chall Readability Formula is widely used. This formula first appeared in 1947. Like the Spache, it uses sentence length and word difficulty for estimating reading level. While it is considered one of the more accurate readability formulas, it is also complex and time-consuming.

Fry's Graph for Estimating Readability is an outgrowth of the need for a simple and efficient technique for estimating reading difficulty. Fry's graph uses the traditional factors of sentence length and word

difficulty to determine readability; however, word difficulty is estimated by counting syllables rather than by the cumbersome and lengthy
technique of comparing every word to a list of words to determine its
difficulty. Fry (1969, pp. 534–38) reports that the Fry Graph for Estimating Readability correlates 0.90 with the Spache Readability Formula and 0.94 with the Dale-Chall Readability Formula. These high
correlations indicate considerable consistency between formulas and
support the wide acceptance and use of Fry's graph.

You are ready to learn how to use Fry's Graph for Estimating
Readability. The graph you are going to use is the most recent one
developed by Edward Fry. This graph, which first appeared in the
Journal of Reading in December 1977, is an extended version of Fry's
original graph, which appeared in 1968. If you know how to use Fry's
extended graph, go directly to Enabling Element 3. If not, or if you
need practice with the procedure, Enabling Element 2 will teach you
how to use Fry's newer graph for estimating readability.

ENABLING ELEMENT 2
HOW TO USE FRY'S GRAPH FOR
ESTIMATING READABILITY

SPECIFIC OBJECTIVE 2

You will state the five steps for using Fry's Graph for Estimating
Readability to determine the reading level of specified passages.

ENABLING ACTIVITIES

*1.   Read Study Guide 2, "How to Use Fry's Graph for Estimating
      Readability," and familiarize yourself with the procedures for
      estimating readability.
*2.   List the five steps for using Fry's graph.
*3.   Do you need more practice in counting syllables? If so, read
      these words aloud and count the number of sound units you
      hear. Check your responses with those listed on page 24 of
      this Enabling Element.

a.	very	**i.**	matches
b.	telephone	**j.**	Washington
c.	¢	**k.**	seventeenth
d.	environment	**l.**	1961
e.	drenched	**m.**	any
f.	basketball	**n.**	$4.98
g.	hopeful	**o.**	let's
h.	ERA		

*Indicates core Enabling Activities.

*4. When counting the number of sentences in a 100-word passage, the hundredth word is often not the last word in a sentence. The proportion of the last sentence must be determined if this is the case. What proportion (in a decimal) is each of the following sentences?

  a. The last sentence contains 8 words, 4 of which are in the 100-word count.

  b. The last sentence is 15 words, and 4 of the words are part of the 100-word selection.

  c. The last sentence includes 32 words, and 9 of these are in your 100-word passage.

  Check your responses with those listed on page 24 of this Enabling Element.

*5. Let us suppose you find that the readability estimate of a selection is tenth grade. What is the range of the true estimate of readability? Check your response with the answer on page 00.

*6. According to Fry's graph, what are the readability levels of selections with the following counts?

  a. 128 syllables in five sentences

  b. 156 syllables in seven sentences

  c. 160 syllables in ten sentences

  Check your response with the answers on page 24 of this Enabling Element.

*7. Do the three Practicum Exercises to see if you can follow the directions for using Fry's graph.

STUDY GUIDE 2

Fry's graph was developed as a quick, easy, usable technique for estimating the reading difficulty of written material for grade one through graduate school. The graph incorporates two factors to use in estimating reading level: average sentence length and total number of syllables. Examine Fry's graph in Figure 1.1.

The top heading in Fry's graph is "average number of syllables per 100 words." The numerals at the top of the graph, then, refer to the number of syllables contained in a 100-word selection. A 100-word selection with short words may contain as few as 108 syllables; thus, each word is only about one syllable long. A 100-word selection with long words may contain more than 182 syllables. If a 100-word selection contains 182 syllables, most of the words are more than one syllable.

Now look at the left side of the graph and notice the statement, "average number of sentences per 100 words." As you examine the left

---

*Indicates core Enabling Activities.

Determining Readability Levels

Average number of syllables per 100 words

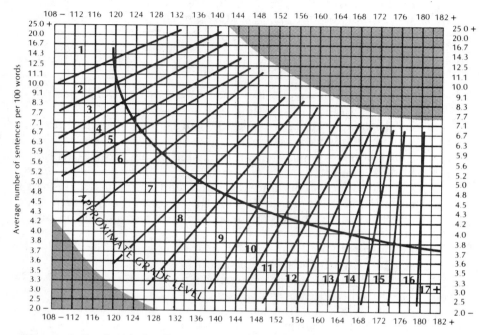

Figure 1–1 Graph for Estimating Readability—Extended

Expanded Directions for Working Readability Graph

1. Randomly select three (3) sample passages and count out exactly 100 words each, beginning with the beginning of a sentence. Do count proper nouns, initializations, and numerals.
2. Count the number of sentences in the hundred words, estimating length of the fraction of the last sentence to the nearest one-tenth.
3. Count the total number of syllables in the 100-word passage. If you don't have a hand counter available, an easy way is to simply put a mark above every syllable over one in each word: then when you get to the end of the passage, count the number of marks and add 100. Small calculators can also be used as counters by pushing numeral 1, then push the + sign for each word or syllable when counting.
4. Enter graph with *average* sentence length and *average* number of syllables: plot dot where the two lines intersect. Area where dot is plotted will give you the approximate grade level.
5. If a great deal of variability is found in syllable count or sentence count, putting more samples into the average is desirable.
6. A word is defined as a group of symbols with a space on either side: thus, *Joe, IRA, 1945,* and *&* are each one word.
7. A syllable is defined as a phonetic syllable. Generally, there are as many syllables as vowel sounds. For example, *stopped* is one syllable and *wanted* is two syllables. When counting syllables for numerals and initializations, count one syllable for each symbol. For example, *1945* is four syllables, *IRA* is three syllables, and *&* is one syllable.

Note: This "extended graph" does not outmode or render the earlier (1968) version inoperative or inaccurate; it is an extension.

Source: By Edward Fry. Reprinted from *The Journal of Reading,* December 1977. Reproduction permitted. No copyright.

side of the graph, you will notice that the number of sentences ranges from two (long sentences) to twenty-five sentences (short sentences). If there are only two sentences in 100 words, each sentence is about 50 words long. Likewise, if there are twenty-five sentences in 100 words, each sentence is about 4 words long. If a 100-word selection has fewer than two sentences or more than twenty-five sentences, Fry's graph cannot be used.

As you look at the center of the graph, you will notice that grade-level bands range from first grade to seventeenth grade. Of course, thirteenth grade is the freshman year of college; the fourteenth year is the sophomore; the fifteenth is the junior year of college; and the sixteenth is the senior year of college. The seventeenth+ grade level indicates the readability would be at a level appropriate for a graduate student.

You will notice that some areas of the graph are gray. Grade-level scores in these areas are invalid because the lines converge or diverge. Readability estimates are most valid when they are near the center line on Fry's graph.

Now that you have carefully examined Fry's Graph for Estimating Readability, you are ready for directions on how to use the graph. Refer to the graph as you read these directions.

Directions for Using Fry's Graph

Fry (1977, pp. 242–52) gives the following directions (which we have partially adapted) for obtaining reading level estimates:

1. *Select a representative passage from written material for which you wish to know the reading level.* Since you use only a sample from the printed material for which you want to determine readability, it is essential that the material you select is representative of the entire article or book. After you find a representative selection, count 100 words in the sample, beginning with the first word of a sentence. Do not count the words in titles or headings. Be sure to count all the words, including initials and numerals. A word is defined as a group of symbols with a space on each side of the group; thus, *Charles, USA, 1980,* and + are each one word.

2. *Count the number of sentences in the 100-word passage.* This procedure is rather simple since you just go through the passage and look for sentences ending with a period, question mark, or exclamation mark. If the final sentence does not stop at the end of the 100 words, determine what proportion of this last sentence you are including in the 100-word count. Estimate the last sentence to the nearest tenth. For example, if the final sentence in a 100-word count has 16 words, and 8 of these are in the 100-word count, the final sentence would be

counted as 0.5 sentences. (For additional practice, see Enabling Activity 4.)

3. *Count the number of syllables in the 100-word passage.* You do not need to decide where syllable breaks occur in each of the words. Rather, you simply read the selection aloud and put a slash above each syllable you hear in the words. For example, the word *though* has one syllable, *counted* has two syllables, *determine* has three syllables, and *appropriate* has four syllables. For our purposes, a *syllable* is a phonetic syllable that you actually hear. A word usually has as many syllables as there are vowel sounds. When counting syllables for numerals and initializations, count one syllable for each symbol. For example, *1980* would be counted as four syllables, *USA* has three syllables, and + has one syllable. (For additional practice see Enabling Activity 3.)

4. *Refer to Fry's graph* (see Figure 1.1). Notice the grid of intersecting lines. The vertical lines represent the average number of syllables per 100 words. The horizontal lines represent the average number of sentences per 100 words. Where any vertical and horizontal lines intersect, approximate grade levels are indicated. Record the level of your selection at this time. According to Fry, most of the intersecting points will fall near the curved line. If the intersecting point falls in the gray area, conclude that the results are invalid, select another 100-word sample, and refigure.

5. *Remember that these are estimates of readability.* Fry (1977) states that these estimates are probably within plus or minus one year of the true estimates of readability.

Illustrations of Each Step

Suppose you wish to use the following selection, "Teachers Don't Want to Be Labeled," with your students to help them realize that each person has strengths and weaknesses rather than being totally gifted, average, or slow. You want to know at what reading level it is written to determine whether you can require your students to read it.

Step 1: Select a Representative 100-word Selection. Usually, the first 100 words in an article are useful if they are fairly representative of the selection. You count every word, including small words such as *a* and *the,* as well as proper nouns, numerals, and initializations. If you use the first 100 words of "Teachers Don't Want to Be Labeled," you will find that the one-hundredth word is *number,* which is in the first sentence of the second paragraph. Remember not to count titles in your word count.

Step 2: Count the Number of Sentences. The second step in using Fry's graph is to count the number of sentences in the 100-word selection. The one-hundredth word does not always end the selection; therefore, it is necessary to determine the proportion of the last sentence that falls within the word count. Estimate to the nearest one-tenth the fraction of the last sentence that is within the 100-word count.

Our 100-word sample has three complete sentences and part of another sentence. The fourth sentence contains a total of 31 words, of which 24 are in our 100-word count. The fraction of the fourth sentence to be used is $^{24}/_{31}$. The fraction $^{24}/_{31}$ can be changed to a decimal by dividing 31 into 24. The result is the decimal 0.77, which we round to the nearest tenth—0.8. Thus, our sentence count for the 100-word selection is 3.8. You need not do the division when you can estimate the fraction to the nearest tenth.

Teachers Don't Want to Be Labeled*
(*Harry W. Forgan*)

When teaching a course on tests and measurements at Kent State University recently, I decided to administer an adult group intelligence test to the class. I wanted the students to "feel" what it was like to take such a test and realize what items we use to measure intelligence. I also thought they might be more aware of the short time it takes to obtain a number which is regarded as very important by many educators.

The students were told not to write their names on the test papers, but rather to use a code such as their house number, physical measurements, or any less obvious symbol. I explained that I really didn't have faith in IQ scores; therefore, I didn't want to know their IQs.

The administration of the test required only 50 minutes. The students seemed to enjoy taking it and chuckled at some of the tasks they were expected to perform. I had to laugh myself when I saw some of them looking at their hands and feet when responding to items concerning right and left.

Upon scoring the test I found that the lowest IQ was 87 and the highest 143. The mean IQ for the 48 students was 117. I was not astonished by the 87, even though all of the students had successfully completed the general education course and student teaching at Kent State and were ready to graduate by the end of the term. After all, IQ tests have many limitations.

Then I got an idea. I decided to prepare a report for each student, writing his code on the outside and "IQ 87" on the inside of each. I folded and stapled each paper—after all, an IQ is confidential information!

At the next class period I arranged all of the folded papers on a table at the front of the room. I wrote the range and the average IQ on the chalkboard. Many students snickered at the thought of somebody getting an 87. The students were eager and afraid as I began by explaining the procedures for picking up their papers. I made a point of telling them not to tell others their IQ score, because this would make the other person feel as if he too had to

*Reprinted with permission from the *Phi Delta Kappan*, vol. LV. no. 1. September 1973, p. 98.

divulge his "total endowment." The students were then directed to come up to the table, row by row, to find their coded paper. I stood sheepishly—ready to laugh out loud as I watched the students carefully open their papers and see "IQ 87." Many opened their mouths with astonishment and then smiled at their friends to indicate they were extremely happy with their scores.

There was dead silence when I began to discuss the implications of the IQ scores. I explained that in some states a person who scores below 90 on an IQ test is classified as a slow learner. The fact that group intelligence tests should not be used to make such a classification was stressed. I also emphasized the fact that *someone* in this class could have been classified as a slow learner and placed in a special class on the basis of this test.

I told how many guidance counselors would discourage a child with an 87 IQ from attending college. Again I emphasized the fact that one person in this room was ready to graduate from college having passed several courses in history, biology, English, and many other areas.

I then went on to explain that the majority of elementary and secondary school teachers believe in ability grouping. This is usually done on the basis of intelligence tests, so I explained that I would like to try ability grouping with this class—again to see "how it feels." Some students objected right away, saying that "I did not want to know their IQ scores." I calmed them by saying it would be a worthwhile learning experience and assured them that I really didn't believe in IQ scores.

I told the students not to move at this time, but I would like all of those with an IQ below 90 to come to the front so they could sit nearer to me for individual help. I told the students who had an average IQ (between 90–109) to go to the back of the room and then take the seats in the middle of the class. The students with an above average IQ were asked to go to the side of the room and take the seats in the back because they really didn't need much extra help.

"O.K., all those who got an IQ below 90 can come to the front of the room." The students looked around to find those who scored below 90. I said that I knew there was an 87 and maybe a couple of 89's. Again, there was dead silence.

"O.K., all those students whose IQ is between 90–109 go to the back of the room." Immediately, to my amazement, 8 or 10 students picked up their books and headed for the back of the room. Before they could get there I said, "Wait a minute! Sit down! I don't want to embarrass you, but you would lie and cheat—the same way we make our students lie and cheat—because you don't want to be classified as 'slow.' I wrote 'IQ 87' on every paper!"

The class erupted. It was in an uproar for about five minutes. Some of the students cried. Some indicated that they needed to use the restroom. All agreed it was a horrifying and yet valuable experience.

I asked them to do one thing for me: Please don't label kids because we are all "gifted," "average," and "slow," depending on the task at hand. They promised.

Determining Readability Levels

Step 3: Count the Number of Syllables. We illustrate two procedures, choose the one that is easier for you.

Procedure A. Read the selection subvocally and make a slash to indicate the number of syllables in each word. Remember that it is not necessary to divide the words into syllables. Simply note how many syllables you hear in each word. After making slashes for each syllable, count the number of syllables in each line, and record this number at the right. Add the number of syllables in each line to determine the total number of syllables in the 100-word selection, as you see here:

	Syllables
When teaching a course on tests and measurements at Kent	13
State University recently, I decided to administer an adult group	22
intelligence test to the class. I wanted the students to "feel" what	17
it was like to take such a test and realize what items we use to	18
measure intelligence. I also thought they might be more aware of	17
the short time it takes to obtain a number which is regarded as very	19
important by many educators.	10
The students were told not to write their names on the test	13
papers, but rather to use a code such as their house number, [100 words] physical	15
measurements, or any less obvious symbol.	
Total	144

Procedure B. Assume each word in the 100-word selection has one syllable (that's true!) and simply make slashes for or count the second, third, fourth syllable in each word. Remember to add your subtotal to 100 to determine the total number of syllables in the 100-word selection. An illustration follows:

	Syllables
When teaching a course on tests and measurements at Kent	3
State University recently, I decided to administer an adult group	12
intelligence test to the class. I wanted the students to "feel" what	5
it was like to take such a test and realize what items we use to	3
measure intelligence. I also thought they might be more aware of	6
the short time it takes to obtain a number which is regarded as very	5
important by many educators.	6
The students were told not to write their names on the test	1
papers, but rather to use a code such as their house number, [100 words] physical	3
measurements, or any less obvious symbol.	
Subtotal	44
+ 100 =	144

Step 4: Refer to Fry's Graph. Locate the number at the top of Fry's graph that indicates the number of syllables. For our sample, look at 144. Place your right index finger on the vertical line under 144. Lo-

cate the number at the left side of Fry's graph that indicates the number of sentences. Our selection has 3.8 sentences, so place your left index finger on 3.8. Move both fingers along the appropriate lines until they meet. Notice the grade level band within which the two lines intersect. For this selection, the reading level estimate is between ninth and tenth grade. Remember that lines intersecting in the gray areas always reveal invalid scores.

Step 5: Remember, this is an estimate! Because the estimate for readability using Fry's graph is within one year of the true estimate, our sample has a true range of ninth or tenth grade, since it is right in the middle. If the estimate were eighth grade, the true range would be seventh, eighth, or ninth.

PRACTICUM EXERCISE 1

You learn by doing! Now that you know how to use Fry's Graph for Estimating Readability, try it on a passage. The following selection contains exactly 100 words, so the first step has been done for you. Second, count the number of sentences in the 100 words. Third, count the number of syllables in the 100 words. Next, refer to Fry's graph to determine the readability. Finally, consider the estimates you obtain to be within plus or minus one year of the true estimate of readability. Do this Practicum Exercise, then compare your results with ours at the end of this Enabling Element.

Selection for Practicum Exercise 1
Using a Card Catalog

	Syllables
If you wish to see if the library has a book you want and	_____
where to find it, you will use the card catalog. The card catalog is a	_____
cabinet with small drawers containing alphabetically arranged cards.	_____
Each card tells the title of the book and its classification number.	_____
To find a book, copy the call number on a slip of paper. The	_____
same call number you copy will be printed on the spine of the	_____
book near the bottom. You will have to find the call number on the	_____
stack of shelves which will lead you to your book. (100 words)	_____
	Total _____

1. Number of Sentences   _____
2. Number of Syllables   _____
3. Estimate of Readability _____

PRACTICUM EXERCISE 2

The second exercise to help you become skillful in using Fry's Graph is "The Conductor." This article was adapted from a music book and contains more than 100 words. Remember, your first step is always to count out 100 words. Follow the five steps for using Fry's Graph, then check your answers with the answers for Practicum Exercise 2 at the end of this Enabling Element.

Selection for Practicum Exercise 2
The Conductor

Syllables

    The orchestra is on stage, the house lights have been dimmed, _____
and the audience waits with great anticipation. Soon a person _____
emerges from the wings, walks to the middle of the stage in front _____
of the orchestra and bows to acknowledge the applause of the _____
audience. This person is a conductor who is about to lead the _____
orchestra in an exciting concert of symphonic music. _____
    An orchestra did not need a conductor until it began to in- _____
crease in size. Beginning in the early nineteenth century, during _____
Beethoven's time, the orchestra increased to such a size that a _____
conductor was needed. This was the beginning of the art of con- _____
ducting as it is known and practiced today.

Total _____

1. Number of Sentences   _____
2. Number of Syllables   _____
3. Estimate of Readability   _____

PRACTICUM EXERCISE 3

The final Practicum Exercise, entitled "Fry's Graph," includes numerals and symbols as well as words. It contains more than 100 words, so make sure to begin by counting exactly 100 words. Again, remember to count each date as a word and symbols such as + as separate words. After you complete this Practicum Exercise 3, go to the end of this Enabling Element to check your responses with ours.

Selection for Practicum Exercise 3
Fry's Graph

Syllables

    The purpose of this selection is to provide you with practice in _____
using Fry's Graph for Estimating Readability. The first edition of _____
Fry's graph came out in 1968, and Fry extended his graph in 1977. _____
The extended graph continues through the seventeenth + grade _____
level. This extended graph was published in an IRA publication enti- _____
tled *Journal of Reading* in December 1977. _____
    Because Fry did not obtain a copyright for his graph, reproduc- _____
tion is permitted. Personally, we feel that Fry has made a worth- _____

Determining Readability Levels

while contribution to the field of reading, and we thank him for it. ⎯⎯⎯
    We believe you will find Fry's graph easy to use and, after ⎯⎯⎯
practice, will be able to determine readability levels of printed mate- ⎯⎯⎯
rials within a few minutes. This new competency will enable you to ⎯⎯⎯
select materials that are appropriate for the ranges of reading levels ⎯⎯⎯
found among your students. ⎯⎯⎯

Total ⎯⎯⎯

1. Number of Sentences   ⎯⎯⎯
2. Number of Syllables   ⎯⎯⎯
3. Estimate of Readability   ⎯⎯⎯

ANSWERS

Enabling Activities 3–6

3.   **a.** very (2)   **i.** matches (2)
      b. telephone (3)   **j.** Washington (3)
      c. ¢ (1)   **k.** seventeenth (3)
      d. environment (4)   **l.** 1961 (4)
      e. drenched (1)   **m.** any (2)
      f. basketball (3)   **n.** $4.98 (4)
      g. hopeful (2)   **o.** let's (1)
      h. ERA (3)
4.   **a.** $4/8 = 0.5$
      b. $4/15 = 0.3$
      c. $9/32 = 0.3$
5. The true estimate is ninth-, tenth-, or eleventh-grade reading level.
6.   **a.** Seventh grade
      b. Ninth grade
      c. Invalid estimate (Another sample would have to be used to find the reading level.)

PRACTICUM EXERCISE 1

Using a Card Catalog

Syllables

    If you wish to see if the library has a book you want and   16
where to find it, you will use the card catalog. The card catalog is a   19
cabinet with small drawers containing alphabetically arranged cards.   19
Each card tells the title of the book and its classification number.   18
    To find a book, copy the call number on a slip of paper. The   17

same call number you copied will be printed on the spine of the   _16_
book near the bottom. You will have to find the call number on the   _16_
stack of shelves which will lead you to your book. (100 words)   _10_

Total   _131_

1. Number of Sentences   _6_
2. Number of Syllables   _131_
3. Estimate of Readability   _7ᵗʰ grade_

PRACTICUM EXERCISE 2

The Conductor

Syllables

The orchestra is on stage, the house lights have been dimmed,   _13_
and the audience waits with great anticipation. Soon a person   _17_
emerges from the wings, walks to the middle of the stage in front   _16_
of the orchestra and bows to acknowledge the applause of the   _16_
audience. This person is a conductor who is about to lead the   _18_
orchestra in an exciting concert of symphonic music.   _16_
An orchestra did not need a conductor until it began to in-   _18_
crease in size. Beginning in the early nineteenth century, during   _17_
Beethoven's time, the orchestra increased to such a size that a   _16_
conductor was needed. (100 words) This was the beginning of the   _6_
art of conducting as it is known and practiced today.

Total   _153_

1. Number of Sentences   _5_
2. Number of Syllables   _153_
3. Estimate of Readability   _10ᵗʰ grade_

PRACTICUM EXERCISE 3

Fry's Graph

Syllables

The purpose of this selection is to provide you with practice in   _17_
using Fry's Graph for Estimating Readability. The first edition of   _20_
Fry's graph came out in 1968, and Fry extended his graph in 1977.   _21_
The extended graph continues through the seventeenth + grade   _15_
level. The extended graph was published in an IRA publication enti-   _21_
tled *Journal of Reading* in December 1977.   _14_
Because Fry did not obtain a copyright for his graph, reproduc-   _17_
tion is permitted. Personally, we feel that Fry has made a worth-   _17_
while contribution to the field of reading, and we thank him for it.   _17_

Determining Readability Levels

We believe you will find /*100 words*/ Fry's graph easy to use and, after ___6___

practice, will be able to determine readability levels of printed mate- _____

rials within a few minutes. This new competency will enable you to _____

select materials that are appropriate for the ranges of reading levels _____

found among your students.

Total __165__

1. Number of Sentences   *6.2*
2. Number of Syllables   *165*
3. Estimate of Readability   *11ᵗʰ grade*

Go to Enabling Element 3 to locate specific directions and practice activities for estimating readability levels of (1) textbooks, (2),
articles, and (3) selections with fewer than 100 words. After using Fry's
graph several times, you will be able to determine the readability of a
selection within five to ten minutes.

ENABLING ELEMENT 3
USING FRY'S GRAPH TO
DETERMINE READABILITY

SPECIFIC OBJECTIVE 3

You will use Fry's graph to estimate readability levels of (1)
textbooks, (2) articles, and (3) selections with fewer than 100 words.

ENABLING ACTIVITIES

*1. Read Study Guide 3. It is designed to acquaint you with the
   specific directions necessary to use Fry's graph with different
   types of written materials.

*2. Do Practicum Exercises 1 and 2 to develop skill in determin-
   ing readability levels of textbooks. This skill will help you
   evaluate textbooks for use and determine the readability levels of your present texts. Check your response for Practicum
   Exercise 1 with the answers listed on page 34 of this Enabling Element.

*3. Do Practicum Exercise 3 and 4 to practice evaluating the read-
   ability levels of articles. Check your answers for Exercise 3
   with those on page 36 of this Enabling Element.

*4. Do Practicum Exercises 5 and 6 to develop skill in using Fry's
   graph to estimate the readability of selections that have fewer

---

*Indicates core Enabling Activities.

than 100 words. Check your response for Exercise 5 on page 37 of the Enabling Element.

5. You may want to duplicate Fry's graph for your students and teach them how to use the graph. Many secondary students can learn to use Fry's graph and thus help you determine the readability of many of your written materials. Of course, you will want to check their work.

STUDY GUIDE 3

You can use Fry's graph to estimate the readability of several types of written materials. This Study Guide provides specific directions and practice activities for using Fry's graph to estimate readability of (1) textbooks, (2) articles, and (3) selections with less than 100 words. Refer to Enabling Element 2 for general directions.

Using Fry's Graph with Textbooks

To determine the readability level of a textbook, you will need to select a minimum of three 100-word passages. One selection should be from the beginning of the book, one from the middle, and one from the last third of the book. Be sure to choose self-contained selections that do not refer to charts or illustrations.

Follow the directions in Enabling Element 2 to determine the number of syllables and sentences in each selection. After doing so, find the *average* number of syllables and sentences by adding the three passages together and dividing by three; for example:

100-Word Passages	Syllables	Sentences
First 100 Words	124	6.6
Second 100 Words	141	5.5
Third 100 Words	158	6.8
Totals	423	18.9
Averages	141	6.3

Plot on the graph the average number of sentences and syllables to estimate readability. (The average readability in this example is seventh grade.)

PRACTICUM EXERCISE 1

Determine the average readability of the following three passages, randomly selected from the beginning, middle, and end of a hypothetical basic health book.

1. Count 100 words in each representative passage. Always start counting at the beginning of a sentence and *do* count the proper nouns, numerals, and initializations.

2. Count the number of syllables in each passage.
3. Count the number of sentences in each passage.
4. Determine the reading level of each passage.
5. Determine the average reading level of the health textbook by finding the average number of syllables and sentences in the three selections, then using these averages as you refer to Fry's graph.
6. Check your answers with the answers on page 34 of this Study Guide.

Rabies

Syllables

      Since bites by cats, dogs, or any wild animal always present _____
the danger of infection with rabies, a biting animal should never be _____
killed unless unavoidable as a matter of safety. It should be caught _____
and held for observation for at least fifteen days, in order to deter- _____
mine whether it develops rabies. _____
      If it is necessary to kill the animal at the time of the biting, the _____
carcass should be sent to the state public health laboratory for an _____
examination of its brain. If the laboratory finds the animal was rabid, _____
it is essential that treatment be initiated at once. _____

Total _____

Headache

Syllables

      The term *headache* is such a part of our everyday vocabulary _____
that it has become almost synonymous with any unpleasant situa- _____
tion or problem. But in a medical sense the term quite literally _____
means a head pain or an aching head and is a symptom rather than _____
itself an actual disease condition. _____
      Hence, headache can suggest the possibility of a great many _____
underlying conditions. Perhaps one of the better known types is the _____
throbbing, devastating headache that sometimes accompanies a _____
hangover. This differs from the type known as tension headache, _____
associated with figuring out one's income tax, since they arise from _____
different causes. _____

Total _____

Determining Readability Levels

Heatstroke

Syllables

    The most important feature of heatstroke, which is some-   _____
times also referred to as sunstroke, is the extremely high body   _____
temperature that accompanies it. It is a far more serious condition   _____
than heat exhaustion.   _____
    Heatstroke occurs more often in males than in females and is   _____
more common in elderly people and in those addicted to alcohol.   _____
Physical exertion is a definite contributing factor; and an attack is   _____
much more likely to occur when the humidity is high than when it is   _____
low, even at the same temperature.   _____
    The underlying cause of heatstroke is intimately connected   _____
with a cessation of sweating, accounting for the excessive rise in   _____
body temperature.   _____

Total _____

	Number of Sentences	*Number of Syllables*	*Reading Level*	*True Estimate Range*
"Rabies"	____	____	____	____
"Headache"	____	____	____	____
"Heatstroke"	____	____	____	____
Sums	____	____		
Averages	____	____	____	____

The answers are at the end of Enabling Element 3. If your answers are correct, continue reading. If not, repeat steps 1 through 6 and determine why not. Your syllable count may vary by a few syllables because of dialect differences.

PRACTICUM EXERCISE 2

Now try a real exercise. Randomly select at least three 100-word passages from a textbook in your teaching area. Determine the average grade level reading ability necessary for reading this material. A chart may be helpful.

	Number of Sentences	*Number of Syllables*	*Reading Level*	*True Estimate Range*
First 100-word Passage	____	____	____	____
Second 100-Word Passage	____	____	____	____
Third 100-Word Passage	____	____	____	____
Sums	____	____		
Averages	____	____	____	____

Here are some follow-up questions you may want to ask yourself. Does the readability estimate match the reading levels of my students? If yes, then you have chosen textual material suitable for your students. If no, you may want to consider changing textual material. Is the readability range among passages less than two years for grades seven through nine and three years for grades ten through twelve? If yes, the range of reading levels should not overtax your students' reading ability. If not, many passages may frustrate your students, and it may be advisable to consider changing the textual material.

A *word of caution:* sometimes a book shows great variability either in sentence length or syllable count for all passages. If this is the case, randomly select additional sample passages; average the number of syllables and sentences, and plot as before. If the same variability occurs, conclude that the book has uneven readability and consider changing texts. This type of material is the most frustrating for students.

Now you know how to determine the readability level of textbooks in your subject area. Read on to learn how to evaluate journal articles.

Using Fry's Graph with Articles

Teachers often wish to use articles from magazines, newspapers, or other sources, and need to know if the reading levels are appropriate for their students.

The directions for using Fry's graph in Study Guide 2 can be followed exactly if the articles contain at least 100 words. One representative 100-word selection is sufficient to determine the readability, unless the article is unusually long. For longer articles, two or three randomly selected passages provide a more valid estimate.

Practice your skill in using Fry's graph by determining the readability of the following article.

PRACTICUM EXERCISE 3

1. Count the number of sentences per 100 words.
2. Count the number of syllables per 100 words, including proper nouns, numerals, and initializations.
3. Refer to Fry's graph.
4. Check your answers on the last page of this Study Guide. If you have the correct answer, go to the next Practicum Exercise. If not, check to see if your numbers for syllables and sentences match ours; if they don't, recount your syllables and sentences and repeat step number 3. Your syllable count may differ from ours because of dialect differences; however, the count should vary by only a few syllables.

New Target for Feminists: TV Kiddie Cartoons

Syllables

Women's liberation may have a new battle to fight—Saturday _____
morning cartoon shows. According to researchers at the University _____
of Michigan, cartoons still are entrenched firmly in traditional male- _____
female sex roles. _____

This conclusion was drawn by analyzing twenty programs from _____
such series as "Fat Albert," "Underdog," and "The Flintstones." _____
Males were seen in forty-two job roles, while females appeared in _____
only nine. Only six of the thirty-one cartoon women had jobs out- _____
side the home; whereas in reality, 50 percent of all American women _____
are in the labor force. _____

Perhaps the time has come for feminists to analyze all televi- _____
sion shows to determine if this is how children develop stereotypes _____
of sex roles. _____

Total _____

PRACTICUM EXERCISE 4

Select an article you have used or would like to use with your classes and follow the directions to estimate the readability level.

Selections with Fewer Than 100 Words

Sometimes teachers want to evaluate selections with fewer than 100 words, such as essay test questions, math problems, directions to an activity, or brief articles. Fry's graph can still be useful; however, the directions must be adapted because the graph is based on 100-word selections. Use the following procedures:

1. Count the total number of words in the selection and round down to the nearest ten. For example, if there are forty-four words in your selection, use only the first forty to count the number of syllables and sentences.
2. Count the number of syllables and sentences in the selected words.
3. Multiply the total number of sentences and syllables by the number in the Conversion Chart that corresponds with the number of words in your selection.

Conversion Chart for Fry's Graph
For Selections with Fewer Than 100 Words

If the number of words in the selection is:	Multiply the number of syllables and sentences by:
30	3.3
40	2.5
50	2.0
60	1.67
70	1.43
80	1.25
90	1.1

4. Refer to Fry's graph to find the grade level band that indicates the readability level. The following essay questions demonstrate these directions.

Essay Questions

Syllables

1. To what extent do you believe it is possible for people of different races, religions, or political beliefs to live together in harmony? What suggestions can you make to help people become more tolerant?   _19_ _22_ _14_ _3_

2. It is often said that communism develops fastest in those countries where people do not have the basic necessities of life. Why do you think this might be possible? _18_ _17_ _4_

160 words   Total _97_

Counting the words, you will find a total of 62. Rounding down to the nearest ten, you will use 60 words in our sample. There are 97 syllables and 3.8 sentences in the 60 words. Both numbers are then multiplied by 1.67 to convert them to a scale of 100 words. Thus, we have 162 syllables and 6.3 sentences, indicating readability at the eleventh-grade level.

PRACTICUM EXERCISE 5

A sample math problem follows. Notice there are only 83 words in this selection. Estimate the readability by following these directions:

1. Count the number of words and round down to the nearest ten.
2. Count the number of syllables and sentences in the selected words.
3. To base your estimate on a 100-word passage, find the appropriate number on the Conversion Chart.

Determining Readability Levels

4. Multiply the appropriate number times the number of sentences and syllables.
5. Plot these numbers on Fry's graph to obtain an estimate of readability. Check your answers at the end of this Study Guide.

Math Problem

Syllables

Nancy got a job working at a local store. She makes $4.12 an _____
hour. She is to report to work after school each afternoon and work _____
for three hours. On Saturdays and Sundays, she works eight hours. _____
She wanted this job so she could save money to buy a car. She _____
hopes to be able to get a used MG car for $4000. Assuming that _____
she does not have to pay her own taxes, how long will it take her to _____
earn $4000? _____

Total _____

Record your answers and check them with the answers at the end of the Study Guide.

_____ Nearest ten (number of words used in determing readability)
_____ Number of syllables × _____ = _____ syllables
_____ Number of sentences × _____ = _____ sentences
_____ Estimate of readability

PRACTICUM EXERCISE 6

Don't lose your new skill—retain it by determining the readability of selections from textual material in your content area. Find the readability levels of essay questions and other material containing fewer than 100 words. Students often fail tests simply because the questions are written at reading levels that are too difficult.

Applying the Concept of Fry's Graph for Estimating Readability

As a content area teacher, you probably use many printed materials to help students accomplish the objectives of your course. We realize there is not enough time in the day to determine the readability of every single newspaper article, magazine article, pamphlet, or other written material you want to use.

But after you have completed this module on using Fry's Graph for Estimating Readability, you will have a better concept of readability, to apply informally when you select printed materials. In other words, you will be aware that sentence length and word length make the biggest difference in readability levels. When you consider using an article with your students, you can simply glance at sentence length and word length to get a feel for the level of difficulty of the material. If the sentences in the passages are extremely long and have many difficult words, you know the readability level may be beyond many of your students. Now that you have this competency, you can apply it informally in making reading assignments and selecting reading materials for your students.

Fry recently published the computerized Fry Readability Program (Jamestown Publishers, P. O. Box 6743, Providence, RI 02940) to calculate reading levels of materials. To use this computer program, simply type your selections on the computer. The video screen of the computer displays syllable and sentence count as you keyboard each 100-word entry. Of course you will want at least three 100-word selections to determine the readability of a book; however, the computer program can accommodate and average up to 100 passages from a single source. With this computer program, school office personnel can determine the readability of the written materials you are thinking of using.

Competency in using Fry's graph will be most useful when you participate in textbook selection, or when you select articles to prepare and duplicate for your students. Otherwise, you will apply the concept of readability informally as you peruse the reading assignments you are asking students to complete.

If you can use Fry's graph to determine the readability levels of textbooks, articles, and selections of fewer than 100 words, you are ready for the Posttest. You have acquired some new skills that will help you select appropriate materials for your students. You will also be able to use this information to write and alter reading levels of different materials. Module 2 will show you how to do this. Pass the Posttest and go on to Module 2.

ANSWERS

Practicum Exercise 1

The average reading level of the three health book selections, "Rabies," "Headache," and "Heatstroke," is 13th level (freshman). This was found by finding the average number of sentences (4.5) and the average number of syllables (167), and then locating the intersecting point on the graph.

Determining Readability Levels

	Number of Sentences	*Number of Syllables	Reading Level	True Estimate Range
"Rabies"	4.0	161	12th grade	11–13
"Headache"	4.9	170	14th level	13–15
"Heatstroke"	4.7	169	14th level	13–15
Sums	13.6	500		
Averages	4.5	167	13th level	12–14
(sums divided by 3)				

Rabies

Syllables

Since bites by cats, dogs, or any wild animal always present   _16_
the danger of infection with rabies, a biting animal should never be   _20_
killed unless unavoidable as a matter of safety. It should be caught   _19_
and held for observation for at least fifteen days, in order to deter-   _19_
mine whether it develops rabies.   _9_

     If it is necessary to kill the animal at the time of the biting, the   _21_
carcass should be sent to the state public health laboratory for an   _18_
examination of its brain. If the laboratory finds the animal was rabid,   _23_
it is essential that treatment be initiated at once. /100 words   _16_

Total   _161_

Headache

Syllables

The term *headache* is such a part of our everyday vocabulary   _19_
that it has become almost synonymous with any unpleasant situa-   _20_
tion or problem. But in a medical sense the term quite literally   _18_
means a head pain or an aching head and is a symptom rather than   _17_
itself an actual disease condition.   _11_

     Hence, headache can suggest the possibility of a great many   _16_
underlying conditions. Perhaps one of the better known types is the   _18_
throbbing, devastating headache that sometimes accompanies a   _16_
hangover. This differs from the type known as a tension headache,   _16_
associated with figuring out one's income tax, since they arise from/   _19_
different causes.   100 words   _0_

Total   _170_

---

*Caution: Remember that dialects make a difference in syllable counts. Check your syllable counts with those listed below if there is a great variance.

Determining Readability Levels

Heatstroke

Syllables

The most important feature of heatstroke, which is some- _13_
times also referred to as sunstroke, is the extremely high body _16_
temperature that accompanies it. It is a far more serious condition _21_
than heat exhaustion. _5_

Heatstroke occurs more often in males than in females and is _15_
more common in elderly people and in those addicted to alcohol. _19_
Physical exertion is a definite contributing factor; and an attack is _22_
much more likely to occur when the humidity is high than when it is _19_
low, even at the same temperature. _10_

The underlying cause of heatstroke is intimately connected _17_
with a cessation of sweating, accounting for the excessive rise in _11_
body temperature. *100 words*

Total _169_

Practicum Exercise 3

The article, "New Target for Feminists: TV Kiddie Cartoons," contains 5.4 sentences and 163 syllables in the first 100 words of the passage; therefore, the readability is twelfth-grade level. The true estimate of readability is from eleventh grade to thirteenth level. If your syllable count total is different, check it line by line with the following.

New Target for Feminists: TV Kiddie Cartoons

Syllables

Women's liberation may have a new battle to fight—Saturday _17_
morning cartoon shows. According to researchers at the University _19_
of Michigan, cartoons still are entrenched firmly in traditional male- _18_
female sex roles. _4_

This conclusion was drawn by analyzing twenty programs from _16_
such series as "Fat Albert," "Underdog," and "The Flintstones." _14_
Males were seen in forty-two job roles, while females appeared in _15_
only nine. Only six of the thirty-one cartoon women had jobs out- _18_
side the home; whereas, in reality, 50 percent of all American _20_
women are in the labor force. _8_

Perhaps the time has come for feminists to analyze all televi- _14_
sion shows to determine if this is how children develop stereotypes
of sex roles.

Total _163_

Practicum Exercise 5

__80__ Nearest ten

__104__ Number of syllables × __1.25__ = __130__ syllables

__6.8__ Number of sentences × __1.25__ = __8.6__ sentences

__4-5__ Estimate of readability

If your syllable count is extremely different, check it line by line with the one below.

Math Problem

	Syllables
Nancy got a job working at a local store. She makes $4.12 an	__19__
hour. She is to report to work after school each afternoon and work	__17__
for three hours. On Saturdays and Sundays she works eight hours.	__14__
She wanted this job so she could save money to buy a car. She	__16__
hopes to be able to get a used MG car for $4000. Assuming that she	__23__
does not have to pay her own taxes, how long will it take her to	__15__
earn $4000?	_80 words_
	Total __104__

POSTTEST

Directions: Read each of the following statements and complete each Posttest item.

1. State the two most important factors that influence the readability of written material.
2. List the two major uses of readability devices such as Fry's Graph for Estimating Readability.
3. Write the five steps for estimating readability when using Fry's Graph for Estimating Readability.
4. Use Fry's graph to determine the reading level of the following selection. "The International Date Line."

The International Date Line

	Syllables
The International Date Line is often referred to as the Sunday-	_____
Monday line. It follows approximately the 180th meridian, on oppo-	_____
site sides of which the reckoning of the date differs by one complete	_____
day. If you travel from west to east, standard time advances one	_____
hour for each fifteen degrees, which is one twenty-fourth of a circle	_____
of longitude around the earth. In passing around the earth completely,	_____

Determining Readability Levels

you gain twenty-four hours, or one complete day. If you travel from   ———
east to west, it is necessary to turn your clock back one hour for   ———
each fifteen degrees of longitude; thus, you lose twenty-four hours   ———
in passing completely around the earth.   ———

Total ———

——— Number of sentences
——— Number of syllables
——— Readability level

5. Decide if the following directions for using Fry's graph are true or false.
   ——— a. Skip all proper nouns when selecting a 100-word passage.
   ——— b. The estimate of readability is probably within one-half year of the true estimate of readability.
   ——— c. Syllable counts by various people may differ slightly.
   ——— d. If the intersecting points fall in the gray areas of the graph, the results are invalid.
   ——— e. Count only complete sentences when counting the number of sentences in the 100-word count.
6. What adaptations would you make to use Fry's graph with selections containing fewer than 100 words?
7. What adaptations are necessary when using Fry's graph to determine the readability levels of textbooks?

POSTTEST ANSWERS

1. The two most important factors that influence the readability of written material are:
   a. sentence length
   b. vocabulary (or word difficulty)
2. The two major uses of readability formulas such as Fry's Graph for Estimating Readability are:
   a. estimating reading level
   b. preparing or rewriting material
3. To estimate the reading level of any material when using Fry's Graph for Estimating Readability:
   Step 1. Select a representative 100-word passage.
   Step 2. Count the number of sentences.
   Step 3. Count the number of syllables.
   Step 4. Plot the number of sentences and syllables on Fry's graph to obtain an estimate of readability.

Step 5. Remember that the true estimate is in a range of one
year in either direction.
4. The selection, "The International Date Line" has:

_____ Number of sentences
_____ Number of syllables
_____ Readability level

Check your syllable count by comparing it line by line
with the sample:

The International Date Line

	Syllables
The International Date Line is often referred to as the Sunday-	18
Monday line. It follows approximately the 180th meridian, on oppo-	23
site sides of which the reckoning of the date differs by one complete	17
day. If you travel from west to east, standard time advances one	16
hour for each fifteen degrees, which is one twenty-fourth of a circle	17
of longitude around the earth. In passing around the earth completely,	18
you gain twenty-four hours or one complete day. If you travel from	16
east to west it is necessary to turn your clock back one hour for	17
each fifteen degrees of longitude; thus, you lose twenty-four hours	6
in passing completely around the earth.	
	Total 148

(handwritten note over text: 100 words)

5. a. false
   b. false
   c. true
   d. true
   e. false
6. Count the words and round down to the nearest ten. To base
   your selection on a scale of 100 words, find the appropriate
   number on the Conversion Chart. Multiply this number by
   the number of syllables and sentences.
7. Make sure you include a minimum of three 100-word selections randomly selected from the beginning, middle, and end
   of a textbook. The readability level is found by averaging the
   number of syllables and sentences in the selections.

If you have completed all Posttest items with 100 percent accuracy,
you are ready for another module. If not, refer to the appropriate
Study Guides for clarification of your difficulty. If you cannot clarify
the difficulty, contact your instructor.

Final Comment

If you have completed this module with 100 percent accuracy, congratulations! You have acquired a set of skills that will enable you to more adequately meet the needs of the students you teach. One word of caution, however. Your new knowledge is of no value unless you use it to help students cope with their reading assignments. This module does not test your intentions or application of readability skills; these qualities depend on your professional and ethical responsibility.

REFERENCES

Anderson, J. "Lix and Rix: Variations on a Little-known Readability Index." *Journal of Reading* 26, no. 6 (1983): 490–96.

Dale, E. and J. S. Chall. "A Formula for Predicting Readability." *Educational Research Bulletin* 27, no. 1 (1947): 11–20.

_____, and J. S. Chall. "A Formula for Predicting Readability: Instructions." *Educational Research Bulletin* 27, no. 2 (1948): 37–54.

Fry, E. "A Readability Formula that Saves Time." *Journal of Reading* 11, no. 4 (1968): 513–16, 575–78.

_____. "The Readability Graph Validated at Primary Levels." *The Reading Teacher* 22, no. 3 (1969): 534–38.

_____. "Fry's Readability Graph: Clarifications, Validity, and Extension to Level 17." *Journal of Reading* 21, no. 3 (1977): 242–52.

_____. *Fry's Readability Program.* Providence, R.I.: Jamestown Publishers, 1983.

Johnson, R. E., and E. B. Vardian. "Reading, Readability, and Social Studies." *The Reading Teacher* 26, no. 2 (1973): 483–88.

Kennedy, K. "Reading Level Determination for Selected Texts." *The Science Teacher* 41 (1974): 26–27.

Klare, G. R. "Assessing Readability." *Reading Research Quarterly* 10 (1974): 62–102.

_____. *The Measurement of Readability.* Ames, Iowa: Iowa State University, 1963.

Lorge, I. "Readability Formulas—An Evaluation." *Elementary English* 36, no. 2 (1949): 86–95.

Maxwell, M. J. "Readability: Have We Gone Too Far?" *Journal of Reading* 21, no. 6 (1978): 525–30.

Pyrczak, F. "Readability of Directions on Potentially Hazardous Household Products." *Reading Improvement* 14, no. 2 (Summer 1977): 77–81.

Schuyler, M. R. "A Readability Formula Program for Use on Microcomputers." *Journal of Reading* 25, no. 6 (1982): 560–91.

Spiegel, D. L., and J. D. Wright. "Biology Teachers' Use of Readability Concepts When Selecting Texts for Students." *Journal of Reading* 27, no. 1 (1983): 28–34.

MODULE 2

PREPARING MATERIALS AT SPECIFIED READABILITY LEVELS

CONTENTS

PROSPECTUS

RATIONALE

Teachers often select reading material from magazines, newspapers, pamphlets, and other materials for their students. The materials are usually valuable, but sometimes the readability level is above the students' reading level. To make this material useful, skill in altering readability is necessary.

Over the school year, teachers prepare many tests, course syllabi, worksheets, summaries, and other instructional aids for their students. It is essential for these materials to be prepared at the reading level suitable for most, if not all, students. Therefore it is necessary when teachers write material that they be able to control readability. This module is designed to help you write and alter materials to make them appropriate for your students.

OBJECTIVES

Terminal Objective

You will write materials at specified readability levels and alter the readability levels of passages related to your content area.

Specific Objectives

1. You will state the two major reasons for writing and altering materials for specified readability levels.
2. You will take a specified passage at the twelfth-grade reading

level and alter the passage for a student with a sixth-grade reading level.

3. You will select a topic from your content area and write a 100-word passage at the fifth-grade reading level.

RESOURCES AND TIME REQUIRED

Most of the materials required for completing this module are provided; however, it will be valuable to have some content area materials available. Gather sample test items, handouts you have prepared, magazine or newspaper articles, and various content area textbooks so they are ready for use. You should complete Module 1 before beginning this module. Since skill in finding readability is a prerequisite for completing this module, we provide an alternative technique, Raygor's graph, for determining readability for those who found it difficult to use Fry's graph. The estimated time for completing the core Enabling Activities* in this module is three to four hours.

PRETEST

Directions: For each question, determine the word that indicates your belief regarding your competency. If you are in doubt, choose NO.

1. Many educators believe it is important for teachers to be able to write and alter materials for specified reading levels. Can you state two reasons why these skills are necessary?   YES NO

2. Readability formulas can be used to alter the reading level of materials. Can you alter materials in your content area to change the reading level?   YES NO

3. Content teachers must frequently write test items and handouts for their students. Can you use Fry's graph to write materials at specified reading levels?   YES NO

BRANCHING PROGRAM ALTERNATIVES FOR PRETEST RESPONSES

1. If you can state the rationale that explains why teachers should be able to write and alter materials for specified readability levels, you are ready for Enabling Element 2. If not, Enabling Element 1 will provide you with this information.

---

*Core enabling activities are marked with an asterisk.

2. If you can alter materials to lower reading levels, you do not need to complete Enabling Element 2. Enabling Element 2 is helpful if you do not know how to rewrite materials to change reading levels.

3. If you can use Fry's graph for preparing materials at specified readability levels, you are ready for the Posttest. If not, Enabling Element 3 is designed to help you develop this competency.

ENABLING ELEMENT 1
REASONS FOR PREPARING MATERIALS FOR SPECIFIED READING LEVELS

SPECIFIC OBJECTIVE 1

You will state the two main reasons for writing and altering materials for specified readability levels.

ENABLING ACTIVITIES

*1. Read Study Guide 1. Identify the main reasons teachers must be able to develop skill in writing and altering materials for particular reading levels.

2. Talk with some of your students and colleagues. Do they believe it is necessary for teachers to write materials at specified readability levels? Is Raths (1964) correct in saying that one responsibility assumed by good teachers is that of preparing curriculum materials?

3. Hold a discussion with one of your classes. Ask the students why they sometimes fail tests or neglect to complete assignments. See if anyone mentions not understanding the test items or directions. Probe to determine what caused the lack of understanding. Is the readability level one of the factors?

*4. Teachers are often cautioned to avoid "talking over the heads" of their students. Likewise, students do not like teachers who "talk down" to them. Discuss the implications for preparation of materials.

5. Some teachers believe standards are lowered when reading levels of materials are lowered. Evaluate this statement.

6. A prerequisite for successfully completing this module is skill in determining readability levels. If you have not completed Module 1, "Determining Readability," do so now. If you at-

*Indicates core Enabling Activities.

tempted Module 1 but failed to develop competency in using Fry's graph to estimate readability levels, we provide an alternative technique at the end of Study Guide 1. Be sure to pay attention to "Prerequisites for Preparing Materials for Specified Readability Levels" in Study Guide 1 if you want to learn another—perhaps easier—technique for determining readability levels.

STUDY GUIDE 1

Effective Communication

According to Raths, one responsibility of a good teacher is preparing materials. All teachers recognize the inadequacies of available materials for meeting individual needs of each student, so they prepare supplemental materials—handouts, review sheets, test items, directions for assignments and activities, and summaries from magazines and newspaper articles. Since students must be able to read these materials, it is imperative that teachers be able to write them at appropriate reading levels.

Teachers often cannot understand why their students fail an examination after hours of teaching and reviewing. Some teachers claim the students knew the answers the day before the test, but on the day of the test they did not seem to know a thing! When one examines the test items, it is relatively easy to understand why students failed.

The same problem arises if assignment sheets, course outlines, summaries, or other handouts are too difficult for students. Both teachers and students become frustrated because they are not communicating. Teachers are often warned about talking above the levels of their students, and should take equal caution with written communication.

We are not suggesting that content teachers should lower their course standards; rather, they should do a more effective job of communicating so the students can achieve high standards. Just as students do not like teachers to talk down to them, neither do they enjoy materials that insult their reading capabilities, nor do they want to be confused by materials that are too difficult to understand. Somewhere between these two extremes, clear communication is possible. Clear communication makes it possible to achieve subject area objectives. Teachers are advised to identify appropriate objectives and then prepare effective handouts, course outlines, assignment sheets, and so forth. Also, if test items for evaluating student knowledge are appropriate for the students' reading levels, tests will evaluate course objectives rather than students' reading abilities. The level of written communication should be adapted to help students attain standards appropriate to their capabilities.

Alteration of Texts and Other Resources

In addition to developing skill in writing materials, teachers should develop competency in altering valuable materials that are above the students' reading levels. For example, you may find interesting articles in current journals or magazines that are written far above the reading levels of your students. If you believe the concepts in these articles are extremely important, you may want the students to have copies. With competency in altering materials, you will have more resources to use with your classes.

At times it may be necessary to alter the readability level of textual materials, also. Since textbooks are often written by more than one author, you have probably found that some parts of the textbooks are more difficult to read. We do not suggest that you rewrite all your textbooks at lower readability levels; however, until more authors and publishers begin to evaluate textbooks and make them more readable, teachers must be able to alter some of the textual materials if they want to use them.

Letters to Parents

Teachers are frequently asked to write letters to parents. If you know how to write materials at specified readability levels, you will do a better job making the letters readable for parents. Sometimes lack of communication between teachers and parents results from the use of educational jargon and/or technical language, which many parents do not understand. Awareness of how to write materials at specified readability levels will help you choose appropriate words for letters and notes to parents.

In summary, if you develop skill in writing at specified readability levels, you will be confident that your students can read the materials you prepare. If you develop skill in altering readability, you will have more resources for your classes. Use of these skills will result in more appropriate reading materials in your classroom, enabling more of your students to accomplish content area objectives.

Prerequisites for Preparing Materials for Specified Readability Levels

To complete this module successfully, you will need competency in using Fry's Graph for Estimating Readability. We hope you have completed Module 1 and passed the Posttest to demonstrate your skill in applying this competency. If you have not completed Module 1, you should go back to it now before attempting to complete this module.

If you experienced difficulty in learning how to use Fry's graph and were not able to develop this competency, we suggest that you consider another technique for determining readability. Alton L. Raygor developed a graph for estimating readability that is similar to the Fry graph. The major difference in the techniques is that word difficulty is estimated by counting long words (words of six or more letters), rather than by counting syllables. Raygor's graph also takes sentence length into consideration. Thus, Raygor's graph is also based on the two major factors that influence readability: sentence length and word difficulty.

Raygor's Graph

According to our experience in working with content area teachers, if you were unable to develop proficiency in using Fry's graph, chances are you had difficulty counting syllables. If you did have difficulty counting syllables, you will probably prefer using the Raygor graph. Rather than counting syllables to determine word difficulty, you simply circle and count the words in the 100-word passage that have six or more letters. The other procedures for determining readability are the same, except you do not count numerals when using Raygor's graph.

If you look at Raygor's graph in Figure 2-1, you will notice many similarities between the Fry and Raygor graphs. First, the number of sentences is indicated on the left side of the graph, as on the Fry graph.The major difference is that the longer sentences (3.2 sentences in 100 words) are indicated at the top of the graph and the shorter sentences (28 sentences in 100 words) are indicated at the bottom of the graph. Now look at the bottom of the graph, where the number of long (hard) words is indicated. Notice that the number of long words ranges from 6 to 44. As you look at the grade level bands in the center of the graph, you will notice that the Raygor graph can be used to estimate the readability of materials from third grade through professional or graduate-school level.

These are the directions for using the Raygor graph:

1. Count out three 100-word passages at the beginning, middle, and end of a book. Be sure to include proper nouns in your word count, but do not count numerals.
2. Count the number of sentences in each passage, estimating to the nearest tenth.
3. Circle and count the words having six or more letters. Words having six or more letters are defined as *long* (hard) *words*.
4. Average the sentence length and the number of long (hard) words over the three samples, and plot the average on the graph.

The directions for using the Raygor graph are exactly the same as for the Fry graph, except that (1) you skip the numerals when you count the 100-word passages, and (2) rather than counting syllables, you determine word difficulty by circling and counting words of six or more letters.

Figure 2-1 The Raygor Readability Estimate

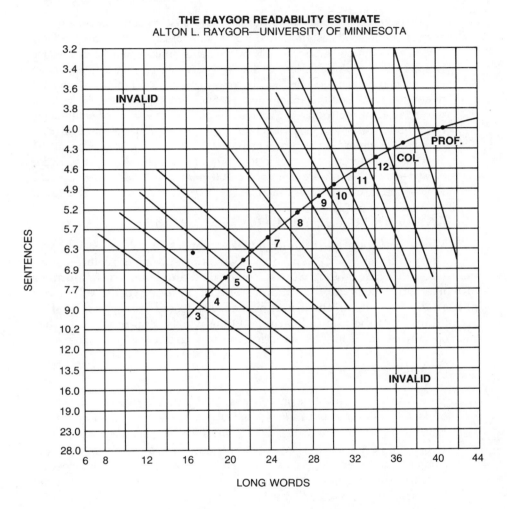

THE RAYGOR READABILITY ESTIMATE
ALTON L. RAYGOR—UNIVERSITY OF MINNESOTA

PRACTICUM EXERCISE

You can use the Raygor graph on the following selection, "A Positive Use of Fire." Follow these directions:

1. Count the first 100 words in the selection (skip numerals.)
2. Count the number of sentences to the nearest tenth.
3. Circle and count those words that have six or more letters.
4. On Raygor's graph, plot a line across from the number of sentences and a line up from the number of hard or difficult words. The grade-level band in which the lines intersect is the estimate of readability.

A Positive Use of Fire

> If you look around, signs of fires, long past or quite recent, will be evident. In the southeastern United States, pine forests are a product of fires. If they were not burned periodically by natural or artificial means, hardwoods would replace the pines. Here in the Sanctuary, fire is used carefully under controlled conditions to maintain the pines and keep a proper balance between the pines and the undergrowth. If fire were kept out for a long time, the undergrowth would gain considerable height; then if wildfire swept through, even the fire-resistant pines would be in danger. All of the plants that grow here are "fireproof," coming back rapidly after a burn.
>
> How many sentences are there in the 100-word sample?   _____
> How many hard words are there in the 100 words?   _____
> What is the readability of this sample?   _____

ANSWERS TO THE PRACTICUM EXERCISE

When you counted the number of sentences in this selection, you found approximately 5.1 sentences. Words of six or more letters are defined as *difficult* or *long* words. You circled and counted the number of words with six or more letters, a total of 30 long words. When you plotted these points on the graph, you came across from approximately 5.2 and up from the line indicating 30 long words. You thus found that the readability level for the selection is ninth grade.

A Positive Use of Fire

> If you look around, signs of fires, long past or quite recent, will be evident. In the southeastern United States, pine forests are a product of fires. If they were not burned periodically by natural or artificial means, hardwoods would replace the pines. Here in the Sanctuary, fire is used carefully under controlled conditions to maintain the pines and keep a proper balance between the pines and the undergrowth. If fire were kept out for a long time, the undergrowth would gain considerable height; then if wildfire swept through, even the fire-resistant pines would be in danger. All of the plants that grow here are "fireproof," coming back rapidly after a burn.

If you prefer Raygor's graph to Fry's graph because you find it easier to count words with six or more letters than to determine the number of syllables in each word, you may wonder why we did not include this graph in Module 1, "Determining Readability Levels of Content Area Materials." We used Fry's Graph for Estimating Readability because there have been more research studies comparing its results to the most respected readability formulas, Dale-Chall and Spache. There have been only a limited number of research studies concerning the validity of Raygor's Graph for Estimating Readability. According to the preliminary studies, the results obtained with the Raygor graph are similar to the results obtained with the Fry graph. For example, Baldwin and Kaufman (1979) found the correlation between the Raygor and Fry readability estimates to be .87. Comparing the results obtained with the Raygor and Fry methods for 100 different reading materials, they found that the estimates for 50 of the materials were exactly the same according to both graphs. For 25 of the books, the Raygor graph indicated estimates one grade level above the results of the Fry graph and one grade level below on 19 of the materials. The mean grade level of all the reading passages was ninth grade according to both Raygor and Fry graphs.

Baldwin and Kaufman also found it faster to determine readability using the Raygor graph; however, there was no significant difference between the Raygor and Fry groups in the errors made using the graphs.

As more research studies are done, we may come to recommend Raygor's graph; however, at this time we feel more comfortable recommending Fry's graph, since it is based on more research. For the present, we encourage you to use the Fry graph unless you have experienced much difficulty counting syllables.

Now that you have the prerequisite skill for completing this module, go to Enabling Element 2 to find out how to alter reading levels of subject area materials.

ENABLING ELEMENT 2
ALTERING READING LEVELS OF
SUBJECT AREA MATERIALS

SPECIFIC OBJECTIVE 2

You will take a specified passage at the twelfth-grade reading level and alter the passage for a student with a sixth-grade reading level.

ENABLING ACTIVITIES

*1.   Read Study Guide 2 and identify the steps in the altering procedure.
*2.   Do the Practicum Exercise, which asks you to rewrite the twelfth-grade passage, "Barracudas," for a student with a sixth-grade reading level. Check your response with the one at the end of this Enabling Element.
3.   Select a passage from a magazine or newspaper article in your subject area, and alter the passage for a student who reads two years below the level of the material.

---

*Indicates core Enabling Activities.

4. Select an editorial from the newspaper or a short selection from a magazine and rewrite the selection to a lower or higher reading level.
5. Check the reading level of your essay test items. Alter them if necessary.
6. Try this if you have problems communicating with your students. Record one of your lectures. Select a 100-word unit and use Fry's or Raygor's graph to determine the listening level. Is it necessary to alter your oral communication?
7. You probably have a particularly good pamphlet you have not shared with your students because you thought it was too difficult for them. Select some 100-word passages and rewrite them to lower reading levels. Ask your students to read the rewritten passages. If the material is now readable, you may want to rewrite the rest of the pamphlet and some of the other materials you have been storing simply because they are too difficult for your students to read in their present form.

STUDY GUIDE 2

Readability level can be altered by increasing or decreasing the reading difficulty of the material. This Study Guide emphasizes lowering the readability levels because, although many content area resource materials are available for students who read above grade level, the supply of lower-level material is limited.

It is easy to rewrite materials to a lower reading level by changing sentence length and word difficulty as necessary. Remember, sentence length and word difficulty are the two most important factors influencing readability of materials.

Read the following selections. The first was written at the eighth-grade level, the second at the fourth-grade level. Notice that the content is the same. Try to determine what changes were made to lower the second selection to a fourth-grade reading level.

Selection 1: Eighth-Grade Reading Level

A glance at the advertisements in magazines leaves no doubt as to the interest of people in their weight. The dictators of fashion have made us weight conscious. And now the writers of advertisements are trying to convince the thin and fat alike that if they will only buy this exercising machine, this or that drug, or eat certain foods, a beautiful figure will result. They promise to make us look like, or at least desire to be like, the model who is pictured in the advertisement. They usually fail to point out that each person is different.

Selection 2: Fourth-Grade Reading Level

Do you ever read magazines? If so, you have probably noticed all the advertisements about weight. Most people are interested in their weight. The people who determine what is in style make us attach importance to weight. Now advertisers are doing the same thing. Some will tell you to buy an exercise machine. Others try to sell drugs to reduce or gain weight. Special food or liquid diets are often suggested, too. All of the advertisements try to make us want to be like the model in the picture. Yet each person is different. The advertisements do not say this.

What are the differences in the two selections?

1. _____
2. _____

If you look closely at the two selections, you will notice one difference is that there are more sentences in the last selection. The fourth-grade selection has eleven sentences, compared to five sentences in the eight-grade selection. Adding more sentences and decreasing the length of the existing sentences reduces the number of complex ideas per sentence. Understanding is facilitated because the ideas are offered in smaller doses.

Another difference is that the fourth-grade selection includes fewer difficult words. The words *conscious, dictators, fashion,* and *pictured* have been replaced by shorter synonyms. This generally reduces the number of syllables and thereby lowers the reading level. The fourth-grade selection has 137 syllables; the eighth-grade selection has 140 syllables.

How to Alter Readability of Written Materials

Revising sentence structure is perhaps the easier of two ways to alter readability level. Good materials often include long sentences with many details to express the thought or idea. Consider the following descriptive sentence:

In general, each flower consists of a floral axis upon which are borne the necessary organs of reproduction (stamen and pistils) and usually accessory organs (sepals and petals), which may serve both to attract pollinating insects and to protect the essential organs.

When reading this sentence, one must process and organize many different facts:

1. Each flower consists of a floral axis.
2. The necessary organs of reproduction are borne on the floral axis.
3. The necessary organs of reproduction are stamens and pistils.
4. Sepals and petals are also borne on the floral axis.

5. Sepals and petals are accessory organs.
6. Sepals and petals attract pollinating insects.
7. Sepals and petals protect the essential organs.

To lower readability, it is necessary to introduce the facts in many sentences rather than in one long complex sentence. This helps the reader organize facts and usually improves comprehension, because the facts are introduced in shorter doses. The example might be rewritten this way:

> In general, each flower consists of a floral axis. The necessary organs of reproduction, stamens and pistils, are borne upon the floral axis. The floral axis also contains sepals and petals. Sepals and petals are important because they attract pollinating insects and protect the essential organs.

Did you find this easier to understand? Probably so, because the information is presented in four sentences rather than in one. You had an opportunity to process each fact in a separate sentence rather than having to separate the complex sentence to notice each fact. The need to "run that by again" does not occur.

The second method of lowering readability is to decrease the number of syllables by substituting shorter words for longer words. A dictionary or thesaurus will help you change words in the selection; however, it will be hard to find synonyms for some basic words. For example, stamens and pistils do not have easier synonyms. The emphasis in such a case should be on changing the sentence length rather than the vocabulary. This is not to say that it is unnecessary to change some vocabulary words, but overall, it is easier to lower readability level by increasing the number of sentences.

Procedure for Altering Readability to a Lower Level
Follow these directions to change a selection to a specified readability level.

1. Look for difficult words in the selection. Usually, the longer the word, the more difficult it is for students to read. Identify multisyllabic words or words of six or more letters.
2. Change some of the harder words to easier words. See if you can substitute synonyms for the difficult words. If so, change some of the difficult words by substituting shorter and easier words.
3. Reread the sentences to determine if you can divide some of them into two or three shorter sentences. Remember that it is easier to change readability by increasing the number of sentences, thus presenting the thoughts in shorter doses.
4. Rewrite the selection using shorter sentences and easier words.
5. Determine the readability of the altered selection to see if you have lowered its reading level.

Note: When altering the readability of a selection, it is not essential that the word count remain exactly the same. Often the word count increases or decreases when changing vocabulary and sentence length. The goal is to alter the selection so your students can read and understand it, not to have an exact number of words. If the word count in the altered selection is less than 100 words, simply follow the directions for using Fry's graph with selections containing fewer than 100 words (Enabling Element 3, Module 1).

Illustrations of the Steps for Altering Materials to a Lower Readability Level

Now that you know the procedure for altering reading levels, let us demonstrate with the following selection entitled "Florida." In its present form, we know the selection is at the twelfth-grade level because it contains 7.2 sentences and 168 syllables. Let us see if we can reduce the selection so children with a ninth-grade reading level can learn more about Florida. Remember, it is not essential to keep the word count exactly the same when changing readability; the word count can increase or decrease when changing vocabulary and sentence length. Our goal is to alter the selection so students can read and understand it. If the word count in your altered selection is fewer than 100 words, simply follow the directions for using Fry's graph with selections containing fewer than 100 words (Enabling Element 3, Module 1) to determine the new readability level.

Florida

In 1565 the Spanish founded St. Augustine, the oldest permanent European settlement on the North American mainland. Most of Florida is young even though the state contains the country's oldest city. Cape Canaveral, a symbol of the space age, is the launching site of space vehicles. Walt Disney World is changing the rolling, citrus-clad hills around Orlando and attracting tens of thousands of tourists. Miami Beach entertains thousands of visitors.

Annually the woodlands of northern Florida are a rich resource of pulpwood. The orange groves of central Florida produce much of the country's orange crop. The vegetable fields of southern Florida produce fresh vegetables— corn, beans, and tomatoes—which are sent to the colder parts of the country in the winter.

This is how to rewrite "Florida."

Step 1: Look for difficult words in the selection. As you read "Florida," you will notice several difficult words such as *permanent, settlement, symbol, launching, vehicles, citrus, annually,* and *woodlands.*

Step 2: Change some of the harder words to easier words. It is not possible to change every difficult word in a selection, but you can make the selection easier to read by using synonyms for some of them. For example, you can use the synonym *yearly* for *annually, lasting* for *permanent, sign* for *symbol, woods* for *woodlands,* and *blast-off* for *launching.*

Step 3: Reread the sentences to see if you can divide some of them into two or three shorter sentences. Most of the sentences in the selection are about ten to fifteen words long; you can divide some into two sentences. For example, the first sentence could be rewritten to read, "In 1565 the Spanish founded St. Augustine. This is the longest-lasting European settlement on the mainland of North America." By dividing long sentences into shorter ones, we control the number of thoughts introduced at one time.

Step 4: Rewrite the selection using shorter sentences and easier words. This is one possible revision of the selection.

Florida

In 1565 the Spanish founded St. Augustine. This is the longest lasting European settlement on the mainland of North America. Most of Florida is young, even though it has the country's oldest city. Cape Canaveral, a sign of the space age, is the blast-off site of space vehicles. Walt Disney World is changing the rolling, citrus-clad hills around Orlando. Disney World is getting tens of thousands of tourists now. Miami Beach entertains thousands of visitors.

Yearly the woods of northern Florida are a rich source of pulpwood. Orange groves of central Florida produce much of the country's orange crop. Vegetable fields of southern Florida produce fresh vegetables. Corn, beans, and tomatoes are sent to colder parts of the country in the winter season.

Step 5: Determine the readability of the altered selection to see if you have lowered its reading level. If you use Fry's Extended Graph, you will find the readability level for this selection to be ninth-grade, because it now contains 9.1 sentences and 159 syllables.

PRACTICUM EXERCISE 1

Now it is time to try your skill at altering readability to a lower level. Here is a selection about barracudas, adapted from a textbook for marine biology. Presently, the exercise is written at the twelfth-grade level, because it contains five sentences and 162 syllables. Your task is to rewrite the selection to the sixth-grade reading level. Begin by reading the selection. Then complete the five steps necessary to lower readability to a sixth-grade level.

Barracudas

Barracudas are predatory fish that range in length from three to ten feet and have long, pointed jaws filled with teeth of razorlike sharpness. Large barracudas are, for the most part, solitary as they lurk about tropical reefs or are seen stationary, alert and watchful in the water.

Barracudas fearlessly approach anything moving in the water. Because they are not easily exhausted and spring about in a very reckless fashion, barracudas do not have a difficult time seizing small fishes. Fish is their normal food and the risk to bathers from their attack is doubtless exaggerated in the popular mind.

Rewrite "Barracudas."

Step 1: Look for the difficult words in the selection. As you read "Barracudas," you will probably find several difficult words. List those words here.

Step 2: Change some of the harder words to easier words. At this time, go back to your list of words and write synonyms that are shorter and easier to read.

Step 3: Reread the sentences to determine if you can divide some of them into two or three shorter sentences. Perhaps you will notice that the first, second, and fourth sentences contain 24 words each. Concentrate on dividing these sentences into two or three smaller and easier-to-read sentences.

Step 4: Rewrite the selection using shorter sentences and easier words. Write your revised selection here.

Step 5: Determine the readability of the altered selection to see if you have lowered its reading level.

Number of sentences: _____

Number of syllables: _____

Readability level: _____

ANSWERS TO PRACTICUM EXERCISE 1

Answers to this practicum exercise will vary, because people will have chosen different words and sentences to lower the readability level. The following selection is written at the sixth-grade level, since it has 11 sentences and 144 syllables. Notice the word substitutions: "eat other fish" for "predatory"; "alone" for "solitary"; "still" for "stationary"; "not true" for "exaggerated"; "not afraid" for "fearlessly"; "tired" for "exhausted"; "getting" for "seizing."

Notice how the longer sentences have been divided into two or three separate sentences; instead of five sentences, the selection now has 11 sentences.

Revised Selection on Barracudas

Barracudas are fish that have long, pointed jaws. Their teeth are as sharp as razors. Barracudas are about a yard long but may grow to be about 10 feet. They like to eat other fish. Most times barracudas swim alone. Sometimes they are very still watching for fish to eat.

Barracudas are not afraid. They move very fast toward anything moving in the water. Barracudas do not get tired fast so they can swim around getting lots of fish to eat. Barracudas will attack swimmers, but they usually don't. The stories you hear about these fish biting people are most often not true.

PRACTICUM EXERCISE

Now you need to practice changing the readability level of content material. You may want to choose test items, letters to parents, study or listening guides you have developed, or articles you frequently use with your classes. Follow the five steps illustrated above. After doing this several times, you will be able to change a 100-word selection in approximately ten minutes. As we said earlier, we are not implying that you should rewrite all your textbooks and supplemental materials, but skill in altering reading levels is useful. After completing this Practicum Exercise successfully, go on to Enabling Element 3 to develop another skill that will prove extremely helpful—writing materials at specified readability levels.

ENABLING ELEMENT 3
WRITING MATERIALS AT SPECIFIED
READABILITY LEVELS

SPECIFIC OBJECTIVE 3

You will select a topic from your content area and write a 100-word passage at the fifth-grade reading level.

ENABLING ACTIVITIES

*1. Read Study Guide 3. It provides detailed directions and examples of writing materials at particular reading levels.
*2. Use Fry's or Raygor's graph to check a few of your test items. At what readability levels did you write them? If the readability level is too high, prepare new questions at a lower readability level. You may administer both forms of the test and compare the results.

*Indicates core Enabling Activities.

3. Work with fellow content area teachers to identify important concepts, ideas, or other knowledge. Have each one select a few topics and prepare a handout at a low reading level. If the members of your department cooperate, you will have many low-level reading materials on your most important topics.

4. Check the readability levels of some of the items on a standardized test in your area. Could the reading level be one reason some students do poorly on standardized tests?

5. The next time you prepare a course outline or assignment sheet, follow the directions for writing materials at specified readability levels. Observe and compare the reactions of your students.

*6. Do the two Practicum Exercises to develop skill in writing materials.

STUDY GUIDE 3

Teachers have the responsibility of preparing specialized material such as test items, assignments, and supplementary handouts. Since students must be able to read these prepared materials, it is essential that the reading levels be appropriate.

How to Write at Particular Readability Levels

Perhaps the easiest step in the procedure for writing materials at specified readability levels is to write as if you were talking to your students. Then use Fry's graph to check the readability. If the readability level is appropriate, there is no need to alter the material. If the reading level is too difficult, you can follow the procedure suggested in Study Guide 2 for altering materials. Let us examine these steps in greater depth.

Step 1: Write the materials as if you were talking to your students. When writing materials at specified readability levels, begin by writing down the information as if you were talking to your students. If you are trying to write low level materials, use shorter sentences and shorter words. At this point, be more concerned about expressing your ideas than about the reading level. After the ideas are well organized, you can go back to change the difficult words and the longer sentences. First say what you want to say.

Step 2: Check the reading level against Fry's graph. Follow the directions in Module 1 to find the readability level of what you have written. After you use Fry's graph several times, you will develop a sense of the level of difficulty of written materials and a sense for the necessary adjustments. If you are not proficient with Fry's graph, use Raygor's graph.

Step 3: Alter the readability level if necessary. If adjustments are necessary, follow the procedures in Study Guide 2 of this module for altering the readability level of materials: (1) look for difficult words in the selection; (2) find synonyms for these difficult words; (3) identify the longer and more complex sentences; (4) change the complex sentences into simple sentences; (5) determine the readability of the rewritten selection. Remember, it is not essential to have the same word count in your altered selection as in the original.

Illustrations of the Steps

Step 1. Suppose you teach social studies and must prepare an examination. Your first step is to write the questions as if you were talking to your students (as in giving an oral examination). Your test items might read as follows:

Sample Test Items

Essay Questions
1. What effects do you think Europe's great population growth in the nineteenth century had on the population growth of the United States during the same period?
2. What are the Soviet planners doing to overcome the hazards of the droughts that are so prevalent throughout the grassland areas of southern USSR?

True and False
1. Penetration of the interior of Africa was a relatively easy matter for the explorers because of the continent's many navigable rivers.

Short Answer
1. Name an area in northern Eurasia where farming is not an important occupation because there is no month that is free of frost, hence, where it is too cold for food crops to be grown except in sheltered places.

Step 2. The next step is to use Fry's graph to determine the readability of the questions. In determining the readability levels of the test items, you find a total of 110 words. Use the first 100 words to determine the number of syllables and sentences. You find 168 syllables and 3.7 sentences in the first 100 words; thus, the readability level is at the fourteenth-grade level on Fry's graph.

Step 3. Suppose most of your students read at the ninth-grade level. This means you must alter the readability level by changing some of the longer words and longer sentences. Your newly rewritten questions might read as follows:

Rewritten Test Items

Essay Questions
1. Europe had a great population growth in the nineteenth century. What effects do you think Europe's growth had on the population growth of the United States in the same period?

2. Droughts are common throughout the grassland areas of southern USSR. What are Soviet planners doing to overcome the hazards of the droughts?

True and False
1. Getting to the interior of Africa was pretty easy for the explorers because there are so many rivers the explorers were able to use to get there.

Short Answer
1. In some places the weather is too cold to grow food crops except in sheltered places. Name an area in northern Eurasia where farming is not an important occupation because there is no month that is free of frost.

The reading level of your revised questions is now at the ninth-grade level, because there are seven sentences and 156 syllables. You changed the number of sentences from four to seven and decreased the syllable count by 12, by changing words like *prevalent* and *penetration*.

PRACTICUM EXERCISE 1

The following five social studies questions are written at the fifteenth or sixteenth grade level (college), because they have 176 syllables and 5.6 sentences. The teacher who wrote them was not aware they were written at such a high level. She wrote them as if she were talking to the students. She suspected they were at a much higher level than she had anticipated when many of the students had difficulties trying to answer the questions. Alter the readability of the questions by changing some of the longer words and longer sentences.

Social Studies Questions

1. Explain whether or not you would agree or disagree with the following information: "In working to achieve ratification of the Constitution, the Federalists should have appealed only to reason and not to emotion."
2. Would it be better for us today if the Founding Fathers had provided for a majority vote, rather than a two-thirds vote for ratification of treaties?
3. Do you feel the delegates who feared "excess of democracy" were justified in their fear?
4. What actions did Britain take immediately after the Revolution that antagonized the Americans?
5. Concerning Shay's Rebellion, tell why Shay's supporters felt that Massachusetts was unfair to them and why the uprising alarmed people in many states.

Write your revised questions here:

1.

2.

3.

4.

5.

ANSWERS TO PRACTICUM EXERCISE 1

Your answers to the Practicum Exercise will vary, of course, because there are many different ways to rewrite the questions. The following examples are written at the seventh-grade level; they contain 8.9 sentences and 143 syllables.

1. Do you agree or disagree with this statement: "When people were trying to get the Constitution accepted, they should have just laid out the facts. They should not have appealed to emotion to get others to accept the Constitution." Explain your answer.
2. To get a treaty approved, a two-thirds vote is needed. Would it be better for us today if the Founding Fathers agreed to a majority vote?
3. Some delegates thought we were planning too much democracy. Do you think they should have been concerned about this?
4. What did Britain do right after the Revolution that made the Americans angry?
5. Why did people who liked Shay think Massachusetts was unfair to them?
6. Why did Shay's Rebellion alarm people in many states?

PRACTICUM EXERCISE 2

You learn by doing. Write some test items or directions for an assignment, or prepare a handout. Try to write the material at the most appropriate grade level for most of your students. You may want to work with a colleague to develop a series of handouts on important topics.

Final Comment

The new skills you have developed will enable your students to learn more in your content area. If you practice altering and writing materials, the procedures will become automatic. We believe you will find this competency most useful when preparing test questions, study guides, listening guides, articles that are "too good for the student to miss," and handouts explaining assignments and requirements. After you use the procedure several times, you will not have to determine the readability levels of altered selections because you will have a sense for readability.

POSTTEST

Directions: Read each of the following statements and complete each Posttest item. One hundred percent accuracy is expected.

1. State the two major reasons why teachers should be able to write and alter materials for specified readability levels.
2. Rewrite the following selection, "The Comma," so it has sixth-grade readability. In its present form, "The Comma" contains 100 words, 6 sentences, 166 syllables, and has twelfth-grade readability according to Fry's graph.

The Comma

When speaking to someone, you are communicating information or ideas from your mind to his. If you communicate effectively, you control the flow of information and ideas in such a way that the listener can follow you easily. You do this by using changes in stress and pitch and by using pauses. Likewise, you use punctuation to control the flow of information in writing. Punctuation separates one sentence or thought from another, thus keeping the relationships among parts of the sentence clear and distinct. The comma is especially useful for this purpose, so remember to use commas to separate thoughts.

3. Describe the three steps for writing materials at the fifth-grade readability level.

POSTTEST ANSWERS

1. One responsibility of teachers is to prepare written materials such as tests, handouts, and directions to assignments. If students are to read the materials, teachers must write them at appropriate reading levels to enhance communication. Teachers should be able to alter selections so they will have more resources available for teaching their classes.
2. If you have written "The Comma" on a sixth-grade reading level and can substantiate the reading level using Fry's or Raygor's graph, you have successfully completed Posttest item

number 2. Remember that your selection need not contain exactly 100 words, but it must be at the sixth-grade level. The following is a sample revision of the selection on a sixth-grade level according to Fry's graph (9 sentences and 139 syllables).

The Comma

When speaking to someone, you are relaying ideas and information. The ideas go from your mind to his. If you are communicating well, you control the flow of thoughts in such a way that the listener can follow easily. You can do this by using changes in stress and pitch. Pauses can be used, too. When you write, you use commas to control the flow of thoughts. Commas are used to separate one thought from another in a sentence and thus make the sentence clear. The comma is really useful for this purpose. You can use commas to separate thought units.

3. Three steps for writing materials at the fifth-grade level are to

   a. Write the selection as if you are talking to your students.
   b. Use Fry's or Raygor's graph to check the readability level.
   c. Alter the selection, if necessary, by changing the number of sentences and syllables. At the fifth-grade level, you can have approximately five to twelve sentences (depending upon the number of syllables) and approximately 108 to 146 syllables (depending upon the sentence length).

REFERENCES

Baldwin, R.S., and R. K. Kaufman. "A Concurrent Validity Study of the Raygor Readability Estimate." *Journal of Reading* 23, no. 2 (1979): 148–53.

Craig, L. C. "If It's Too Difficult for the Kids to Read—Rewrite It!" *Journal of Reading* 21, no. 3 (1977): 212–14.

Endicott, A. L. "A Proposed Scale for Syntactic Complexity." *Research in the Teaching of English* 7 (1973): 5–12.

Flesch, R. *The Art of Readable Writing.* New York: Collier Books, 1951.

Klare, G. R. "The Role of Word Frequency in Readability." *Elementary English* 45 (1968): 12–22.

Koenke, K. "Another Practical Note on Readability Formulas." *Journal of Reading* 15 (1971): 203–8.

Kulm, G. "Sources of Reading Difficulty in Elementary Algebra Textbooks." *The Mathematics Teacher* 66 (1973): 649–52.

McCuaig, S. M., and B. Hutchings. "Using Fry's Graph to Describe the Variation of Readability." *Journal of Reading* 18 (1975): 298–300.

Raths, L. E. "What Is a Good Teacher?" *Childhood Education* 40 (1964): 451–56.

Raygor, A. L. "The Raygor Readability Estimate: A Quick and Easy Way to Determine Difficulty." *Reading: Theory, Research, and Practice.* Edited by P. David Pearson. Twenty-sixth Yearbook of the National Reading Conference, 1977, 259–63.

Shepherd, J. W., and F. E. Dickerson. "A Fry Graph Wakes up Student Writers." *Journal of Reading* 20, no. 4 (1977): 292–94.

Spache, G. D. *Good Reading for Poor Readers.* 9th ed., rev. Champaign, Ill.: Garrard, 1974.

Trapini, F., and S. Walmsley. "Five Readability Estimates: Differential Effects of Simplifying a Document." *Journal of Reading* 24, no. 5 (1981): 398–403.

M O D U L E   3

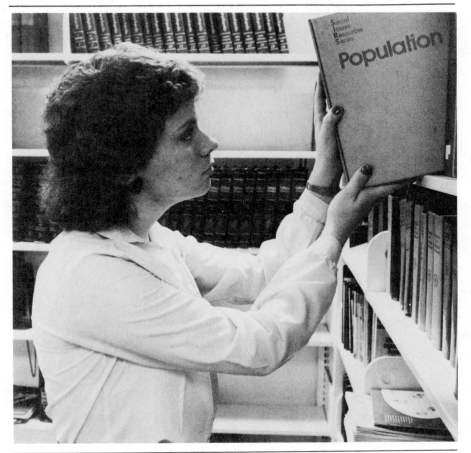

DETERMINING
SUITABILITY
OF MATERIALS

CONTENTS

PROSPECTUS

RATIONALE

One factor that influences student achievement in content areas is the suitability of the textbooks or other required written materials. Materials can be classified as suitable if the student can recognize 95 percent of the words and comprehend 75 percent of what he or she reads. Just as one golf club is not suitable for all the various shots on a golf course, neither is one textbook suitable for all the students in a typical class. One task of the content teacher is to determine the suitability of available materials so that pupils are capable of handling assignments.

The easiest way to determine whether the books you plan to use are suitable is to have the students attempt to read a selection from the book. Your students can try reading selections from the various content area materials to find those that correspond to their capabilities. Some printed materials will be too difficult, some will be too easy, and others will be just right.

This module is designed to teach you how to construct, administer, score, and interpret an Informal Suitability Survey for your content classes. An Informal Suitability Survey consists of (1) a sample reading selection, (2) an accompanying motivation statement to provide a purpose for reading, and (3) comprehension questions to check understanding. The Informal Suitability Survey can help determine the suitability or appropriateness of the available materials and help you match these to your students. The result should be that students can read their assignments and therefore succeed in content areas.

Determining Suitability of Materials

Terminal Objective

You will use an Informal Suitability Survey to determine the suitability of content area materials.

Specific Objectives

1. You will describe an Informal Suitability Survey and state the major purpose for using one with your class.
2. You will construct an Informal Suitability Survey by selecting a representative passage of 200 words, writing a motivation statement, and preparing five appropriate comprehension questions.
3. You will administer and score an Informal Suitability Survey following the procedures described in this module.
4. After scoring an Informal Suitability Survey, you will state the specific implications of the findings for planning differentiated reading assignments.

RESOURCES AND TIME REQUIRED

You will need textbooks or other reading materials used in your subject area to complete this module and paper for developing an Informal Suitability Survey. If you have completed Module 1 on readability, you may want to refer to it to determine the reading difficulty level of the subject area material; however, it is not essential that you complete Module 1 on readability before this module. The estimated time to complete the core Enabling Activities* is four to five hours.

PRETEST

Directions: For each question, determine the word that indicates your belief regarding your competency. If you are in doubt, choose NO.

1. Before you can develop an Informal Suitability   YES NO
   Survey, you must realize what it contains and why you might use it. Can you describe an Informal Suitability Survey and state the reasons for using one in subject area classes?
2. The materials needed to construct an Informal   YES NO
   Suitability Survey are commonly available. Do you have a collection of selections and accompanying motivation statements and comprehension questions? Have you developed an Informal Suitability Survey using these materials?

---

*Core Enabling Activities are marked with an asterisk.

3. If you want to implement the concept of an Infor-   YES   NO
    mal Suitability Survey in your classes, you must
    learn how to administer and score one. Can you
    administer and score an Informal Suitability Sur-
    vey to determine the suitability of required read-
    ing material?

4. The results of any evaluative procedure are use-   YES   NO
    less if they are not interpreted. Do you know how
    to interpret and use the results from an Informal
    Suitability Survey to plan differentiated reading
    assignments?

BRANCHING PROGRAM ALTERNATIVES FOR PRETEST RESPONSES

1. If you cannot describe an Informal Suitability Survey and
    state the purpose for applying the concept in your classroom,
    Enabling Element 1 will help you acquire this information. If
    you can describe an Informal Suitability Survey and state its
    major purpose, you are ready for Enabling Element 2.

2. You are well prepared if you have a selection with accompany-
    ing motivation statement and comprehension questions to use
    in determining the suitability of your textbooks. Enabling Ele-
    ment 2 will help you develop these materials into an Informal
    Suitability Survey if you have not done so.

3. If you have already administered and scored an Informal Suit-
    ability Survey to determine the suitability of materials for
    your students, you need not do Enabling Element 3. This ele-
    ment is designed for those who have never administered and
    scored such a device, and presents procedures for both indi-
    vidual and group administration.

4. Your answer to this question is very important. The implica-
    tions from an Informal Suitability Survey are essential for
    increasing your effectiveness as a teacher. Do Enabling Ele-
    ment 4 if you have any doubts. If you already know the
    implications, you are ready for the Posttest.

ENABLING ELEMENT 1
THE INFORMAL SUITABILITY SURVEY

SPECIFIC OBJECTIVE 1

You will describe an Informal Suitability Survey and state the
major purpose for using one with your class.

ENABLING ACTIVITIES

*1. Read Study Guide 1. Determine what an Informal Suitability Survey is and the value of using such surveys.

2. Teaching is both satisfying and frustrating. Think of those things that frustrate you most. Does the fact that some students cannot read the textbook or other required material frustrate you? If so, are you committed to doing something about it?

3. Consider the students who cannot read the textbook or other required reading materials. How do they feel when you make an assignment? How do they feel when others are sharing information gleaned from the reading assignments? How do they respond?

4. Discuss why there is such a wide range of reading achievement among secondary students. Make a list of possible reasons. Module 10, "Identifying and Helping Problem Readers," can help you verify your ideas.

5. Look at the students in your classes to notice the range of their heights. If a standard size of clothing were required, it would be inappropriate for many students. Is there any reason to believe that mental abilities and achievement will not vary as do physical characteristics?

6. Collect the written materials you commonly use in teaching. You will use these reading resources as you complete the other enabling activities in this module.

STUDY GUIDE 1

The first task in bowling is to find a ball that fits. Bowlers move from one rack of balls to another to find a suitable ball. Others go to the expense of having the holes drilled to fit their own fingers, thumb, and span. One bowling ball is simply not suitable for all bowlers.

So it is with textbooks or other reading materials used in content area classes. Materials that are too difficult for some students are suitable for others, because one-third of the students in a classroom commonly read below their current grade level, one-third read at grade level, and one-third read above grade level. The range of reading levels in a typical seventh-grade class is between third and eleventh grade, and the range increases as students advance in grade level.

The wide range in reading achievement is to be expected because of the heterogeneous nature of school populations. Students vary in height, weight, attitudes, and mental ability, to mention just a few factors. Textbooks, on the other hand, vary in readability less than the group of students served in any subject area classroom. The difference between the students' reading levels and the book's reading level produces an instructional problem for subject area teachers. One text is simply not suitable for every student.

Description of an Informal Suitability Survey

For each student in their classes, content teachers must determine the suitability of textbooks or other required material. A useful technique to identify the suitability of a textbook and/or other written material is the Informal Suitability Survey. An Informal Suitability Survey is an informal device to determine if students can handle selected content area printed material.

An Informal Suitability Survey consists of a representative selection from content area material. A motivation statement and comprehension questions accompany the selection. To develop the Informal Suitability Survey, the teacher (1) selects a representative selection from required reading materials, (2) writes the motivation statement to provide a purpose for reading the selection, and (3) prepares comprehension questions covering vocabulary, facts, and inferences to check the students' understanding of the selection. The teacher then administers the Informal Suitability Survey to determine if the textbook is appropriate in terms of the students' reading capabilities. For example, the speech or language arts teacher might use the following Informal Suitability Survey, constructed from a language arts textbook.

Sample Informal Suitability Survey

Name _____ Date _____

Source _____

Circle One: Suitable Unsuitable

Motivation Statement: Many students like to find jobs, and of course, all of you will probably be employed some day. Read the following selection to answer the question, "How do I prepare for a job interview?"

Selection:

Preparing for the Job Interview

An interview is a meeting between two or more parties to exchange information. The purpose of a job interview is to provide opportunities for the employer and prospective employee to exchange information. The employer desires to know if the applicant possesses the necessary capabilities and qualities to handle certain responsibilities. The candidate wants to know if the responsibilities, working conditions, and salary are suitable for his or her needs.

There are two different ways employers interview prospective candidates. In the *open-ended* interview the employer generally begins by saying, "Tell me a little bit about yourself." The prospective employee then has the responsibility of informing the employer of his or her strengths and capabilities as a person. The *closed* interview technique is different in that the employer asks many specific questions. For example, the employer may ask questions about your grades in school, family background, previous responsibilities and interests.

In preparing for a job interview, you should try to learn about the job so you have questions to ask. You may want to discuss the type and responsibilities of the work with your family, friends, or people who have similar jobs. Make a list of the important questions you have.

Another step in preparing for an interview is simply "know yourself." Be prepared to give the interviewer a concise picture of your interests and capabilities. Evaluate yourself to determine those things you do well and the characteristics you have that others seem to like.

Make the appointment for the interview and then plan to arrive a few minutes early. Promptness is generally considered very important by most employers. Evaluate your personal appearance to see if you are creating the image you desire. Usually, simple, conservative clothing is just right for an interview. Be ready to greet the employer with a smile and simply be yourself!

Comprehension Questions:

(*V* = Vocabulary; *F* = Factual; *I* = Inference)
1. *(V)* What does *prospective* mean?
2. *(F)* What is the main purpose of a job interview?
3. *(F)* What three things should you do in preparing for a job interview?
4. *(F)* What information does an employer usually like to have about an applicant?
5. *(I)* Why do you suppose some employers like to use the open-ended interview technique?

As you can see, an Informal Suitability Survey is a sampling technique to determine if the materials you are considering are appropriate. The preceding selection consists of a 300-word passage; however, you may want to use 200-, 400-, or even 500-word selections. If you have many materials available, you can construct a series of Informal Suitability Surveys, then match the materials to the students. If only one textbook is available, you may need to determine which students are capable of reading the text and then make adaptations for other students. Suggestions for adapting materials appear at the end of this module.

You may wonder how many Informal Suitability Surveys you will need. The answer to this question depends upon the availability of textbooks and other commonly used printed materials related to your content area. If you plan to use one textbook with all the students, you need to develop only one Informal Suitability Survey. Of course, you must be aware that the book will be unsuitable for some students. You may want to give each student a copy of the textbook and adapt the reading assignments to the capabilities of the students. For example, if only one textbook is available, you know that some students will be able to read the textual materials to obtain ideas and information. Other students may be able to gain information and ideas from the pictures, diagrams, or other illustrations in the text. Because of the nature of the concepts, some parts of a textbook are easier to read than other parts. If the textbook was written by several different authors, some parts may be easier to read. If you use only one textbook, you must realize from the outset that some students will be unable to complete the reading assignments. Please do not blame the students for not doing their assignments; you are promoting failure by expecting the impossible.

We recommend that you try to find many different reading resources for your content area classes. If you are able to obtain books related to your objectives that are written at different readability levels, you will more effectively help students accomplish the content objectives. Of course, using more reading sources requires making more than one Informal Suitability Survey. The general guideline is to identify the reading resources you *commonly* use and develop one Informal Suitability Survey for each of the materials.

As mentioned in Module 1, you can also match materials to students by comparing the readability levels of the materials to the students' reading levels. To do so, you must have reading scores for all your students, although scores may be either unavailable or invalid. Students exhibit many different reading levels depending upon their interests and the background information they have on a specific topic. For example, a student who is interested in math may be able to read higher level books because he knows the specialized vocabulary and symbols and is highly motivated. This same student may read social studies books at a level two or three years lower because of lack of interest and/or a good background in social studies. Using the Informal Suitability Survey, then, is a more valid technique than using readability formulas for matching specific materials to your students. Enabling Element 2 will help you construct an Informal Suitability Survey.

ENABLING ELEMENT 2
CONSTRUCTING AN INFORMAL
SUITABILITY SURVEY

SPECIFIC OBJECTIVE 2

You will construct an Informal Suitability Survey by selecting a representative passage of 200 words, writing a motivation statement, and preparing five appropriate comprehension questions.

ENABLING ACTIVITIES

*1. Read Study Guide 2. This Study Guide provides directions for making your own Informal Suitability Surveys.
*2. Do Practicum Exercise 1 to practice constructing an Informal Suitability Survey. Compare your efforts to the answers to Practicum Exercise 1 at the end of this Enabling Element.

*3. Select a 200-word passage representative of the textbook most often used in one of your classes, and write a motivation statement and five comprehension questions as directed in Practicum Exercise 2.

*4. Evaluate your questions. When writing the factual questions, did you select significant facts? What about your question concerning vocabulary? Is the vocabulary word essential to the meaning of the selection? Does your inference question require knowledge from the selection as well as information from the reader's experiences?

5. What are the advantages of having ten questions as compared to five? Try checking comprehension with ten questions. Are there differences in your findings?

*6. Discuss why it is important to provide a statement to motivate the reader. What are the advantages of presenting questions before asking students to read the selection? Are there implications for introducing all reading assignments?

STUDY GUIDE 2

When developing an Informal Suitability Survey, remember that the final product consists of (1) a representative reading selection from any textual material commonly used in the class, (2) a motivation statement giving the student a purpose for reading the selection, and (3) comprehension questions to determine if the students understand the selection. Specific instructions for constructing an Informal Suitability Survey follow.

Step 1: Select a Representative Passage

Select a representative passage from your textbook or other reading materials. The length of the passage will vary with the grade level and nature of the materials. A 200-word passage is generally preferred; however, if it is difficult to find 200 consecutive words (as in some math books), you can use a 100-word selection. For longer textbooks, you may want to use a 300- or 400-word selection, or two 200-word passages. The selections need not contain exactly 200, 300, or 400 words, but it is necessary to mark the 200th, 300th, or 400th word for scoring purposes. The important fact is that it is essential to choose a selection that is a *representative,* self-contained sample of the material under consideration.

Select two or three passages of 200 words if you are surveying the suitability of a major textbook. The extra passages can be used as alternate forms of the Informal Suitability Survey for students whose scores you doubt.

Skip all proper nouns (capitalized name of a particular person, place, or thing) and numerals when counting words for your passages. Proper nouns are not counted because they are usually introduced to students when regular reading assignments are made. Numerals are not counted because they are not words. Mark the 200th, 300th, or 400th word by making a slash after it.

To illustrate Step 1, suppose as a social studies teacher you chose the following selection. This selection is representative of materials in the major text you would like to use with your students. Your word count (skipping proper nouns and numerals) reveals approximately 200 words.

Sample Selection from a Social Studies Textbook: Becoming a Naturalized Citizen

People who desire to become naturalized citizens of the United States must be at least eighteen years old. The applicant must be able to sign a petition in his or her own handwriting. They must demonstrate skill in reading, writing, and speaking the English language unless physically unable to do so. Those applicants who have been residing in the United States for 20 years are exempted from the English proficiency examination.

A person who desires to become a naturalized citizen must be of good moral character and well-disposed to the good order and prosperity of the United States. There are residence requirements that must be met before filing a petition to become a citizen. The petition must have two credible citizen witnesses who have personal knowledge of the applicant's character, residence, and loyalty. The applicant must demonstrate knowledge and understanding of the fundamentals of United States history and form of government.

Naturalization is denied to any person who within 10 years has been subversive, including Communists or others who favor totalitarian government and who were members of a proscribed organization (unless the petitioner was under 16 or forced under duress).

As with other federal statutes, there are exceptions to the guidelines stated above. Of course, the guidelines are subject to change by the Congress of the United States.

Step 2: Write a Motivation Statement

Write a motivation statement for each passage to provide the students with a purpose for reading. The motivation statement usually consists of two sentences. The first sentence is the topic of the passage. This sentence provides the reader with a frame of reference for reading the selection. The second statement is a question or command stating what the reader should try to learn from the passage. For example, a motivation statement for the preceding passage on becoming a naturalized citizen might read as follows:

People who desire to become United States citizens, but were not born in the United States, can become naturalized citizens. Read this selection to find the requirements for becoming a naturalized citizen.

Step 3: Prepare Five Comprehension Questions

After you have selected the passage and prepared your motivation statement, you will need to write five questions for checking comprehension. Specifically, you should write one vocabulary question, three factual questions, and one inferential question. If you have long selections of 400 words or more, you may want to write ten comprehension questions (two vocabulary, six factual, and two inferential).

Factual Questions. The factual questions require answers that are *directly stated* in the passage. These questions should concern the most important facts in the selection, rather than interesting but picayune details that are not important to remember. The easiest way to prepare factual questions is to read the selection and then list its three most important facts. After identifying the significant facts, you can write questions for each of them.

Vocabulary Questions. Vocabulary questions test the student's understanding of words used in the selection whose meanings are not necessarily obvious in the selection. When writing vocabulary questions, do not choose words that have been set off in italics and precisely defined for the reader; rather, select words that are essential to understanding the selection but are not italicized. Vocabulary questions should relate to the most important concepts in the selection.

Inferential Questions. Inferential questions require some knowledge from the selection as well as some thinking as the reader relates the selection to her experiences. A good inferential question requires the reader to combine information presented in the passage with her experiences to answer the question. The answer to an inference question cannot be stated directly in the selection. Because each student's experiences are different, there may be more than one correct answer to any inference question.

You can determine the format for your questions. Essay and short-answer questions usually require more memory; however, multiple choice items may be more appropriate when you need to administer and grade the selections for large groups of students. Samples of the three types of questions are given below. The questions are over a 200-word selection typical of selections found in social studies textbooks. Notice the different types of questions and the possible formats (essay or multiple choice).

Sample Questions

Essay or Short Answer
(F = Factual; V = Vocabulary; I = Inference.)
1. (F) How old must a person be before he can apply to become a naturalized citizen? (18)
2. (F) Name two proficiencies a person must have to become a naturalized citizen. (Skill in using the English language and knowledge of United States history and government)

3. *(F)* Which applicants do *not* have to take a test to demonstrate proficiency in reading, writing, and speaking English? (Those who have been residing in the United States for 20 years and those who are physically unable to do so)
4. *(V)* What does *subversive* mean? (Tendency to destroy or overthrow)
5. *(I)* Why is it necessary for the applicant to have certain proficiencies? (The applicant must know the form of government because he or she will be under its rules and regulations. The applicant must know English so he or she can communicate with others in the country.)

Sample Multiple-Choice Questions
(F = Factual; *V* = Vocabulary; *I* = Inference.)

1. *(F)* Circle the letter that indicates how old a person must be to be eligible to become a naturalized citizen.
   a. Seventeen   **c.** Twenty
   b. Eighteen   **d.** Twenty-one
2. *(F)* Circle the letter that indicates the two proficiencies a person must have to become a naturalized citizen
   a. Knowledge of English and science
   b. Knowledge of the government of the United States and communistic government
   c. Knowledge of English and the history and government of the United States
   d. Knowledge of English and mental health
3. *(F)* Applicants who want to become naturalized citizens do not have to demonstrate proficiency in using English if
   a. They are proficient in using some other language.
   b. They are physically unable to do so.
   c. They have resided in the U.S. for 20 years.
   d. Both *b* and *c.*
   e. All of the above.
4. *(V)* Circle the letter that indicates the meaning of *subversive.*
   a. communist   **c.** tendency to disagree
   b. tendency to overthrow   **d.** tendency not to believe
5. *(I)* An applicant must have certain proficiencies in order to become a naturalized citizen because
   a. The applicant should know the forms of government under which he or she will be living. The applicant needs to know the language to communicate most effectively so that he or she can be a productive citizen.
   b. United States citizens are at a higher intellectual level than citizens in other countries; therefore, all citizens must have certain proficiencies to maintain the high standards found in the United States.
   c. Knowledge of English and history is important so that the person will not feel like a foreigner in his or her own country.
   d. Good moral character and knowledge of English and government are important because the United States already has a high rate of crime and illiteracy.

Now that you know how to develop an Informal Suitability Survey for the major material you hope to use with your students, go on to the Practicum Exercises, which give you an opportunity to apply this knowledge.

PRACTICUM EXERCISE 1

Suppose as a science teacher you want to determine the suitability of a textbook you really like and want to use with your students. You have looked through the textbook and selected a passage representative of the textual materials. You have counted the number of words and indicated the 300th word, skipping all proper nouns and numerals in your word count.

Now it is time to write a motivation statement and five comprehension questions. Read the following selection; then write a motivation statement and five short-answer or essay comprehension questions consisting of three factual questions, one vocabulary question, and one inference question. Then check your response with ours at the end of this Enabling Element.

Sample Science Selection

A cloud is a mass of small water droplets or tiny ice crystals that float in the air. Some clouds have rounded bumps and appear to be piled up. Other clouds appear in layers or sheets.

Seeing clouds does not always mean it is going to rain. Rain clouds only form when so much water vapor gathers that the water droplets become large and heavy. When the water droplets become too heavy, precipitation will occur, usually in the form of rain or snow.

You may wonder where this water vapor comes from. Water vapor comes from water that has evaporated from lakes, oceans, rivers, or from moist soil and plants. When this water evaporates it is called water vapor. Of course, the air can only hold a certain amount of water vapor at any given temperature; when the temperature drops, some of the water vapor begins to condense. *Condense* means to change into a liquid form, or in our case, to change into tiny droplets of water.

Water vapor can rise to form clouds in many different ways. First, some clouds are formed by *evaporation*. When the sun warms the ground, the air next to the ground is heated. Since the warm air is lighter than the same volume of cooler air, the warm air rises. As the air rises, it expands and becomes cooler. If enough water vapor is in the expanding air, the vapor will condense and form clouds.

Second, some clouds are formed by *lifting*. When warm, moist air moves up the side of a hill or over a range of mountains, it is lifted and cooled by expansion. This cooling causes the water vapor to condense and form clouds that seem to hang over the mountains.

Finally, weather fronts where masses of warm and cool air meet each other produce clouds by what is called *frontal activity*. The water vapor in the rising air becomes cooler and condenses, thus creating the water droplets that form clouds.

Determining Suitability of Materials

Motivation Statement:

Essay or Short-Answer Questions to Check Comprehension
1. *(F)*

2. *(F)*

3. *(F)*

4. *(V)*

5. *(I)*

ANSWERS TO PRACTICUM EXERCISE 1

When you check your responses with ours, you may find that they do not exactly match our motivation statement and/or questions. There is more than one purpose for reading this selection and many different questions for determining if the student comprehended the selection. As you compare your responses to ours, keep in mind that the motivation statement should consist of two sentences. The first sentence indicates what the selection is about; the second provides a command or question directing the student to read the selection. When evaluating your questions, see if

1. The factual questions ask for details important to the comprehension of the selection.
2. The vocabulary question asks for a definition for a word that is not defined in the selection but is important for understanding the selection.
3. The inferential question requires the student to combine knowledge from the selection with information from her background of experience.

Sample Answers to Practicum Exercise

Motivation Statement: Did you ever wonder how clouds are formed? Read this selection to find out what clouds are and how they are formed.

Sample Essay Questions
1. *(F)* What are clouds made of? (Small water droplets or ice crystals.)
2. *(F)* When do rain clouds form? (When enough water droplets become large and heavy.)

Determining Suitability of Materials

3. *(F)* Name two ways that clouds are formed. (When moist air moves up the side of a hill, it is lifted and cooled. This cooling causes the water vapor to condense and form clouds. Second, sometimes weather fronts are formed because warm and cool air meet each other. Thus, the water vapor in the warm air rises and becomes cooler and condenses.)
4. *(V)* What is precipitation? (Rain or snow, which is made up of water droplets or ice crystals.)
5. *(I)* Why do some areas get more rain than other areas? (It all depends upon the direction of the wind, temperature, and closeness to bodies of water and mountain ranges.)

PRACTICUM EXERCISE 2

Are you ready to prepare an Informal Suitability Survey for your students? You can do so by following these steps:

1. Select a representative 200-word passage. Make sure the passage is self-contained, that is, does not refer to pictures or illustrations. Skip all proper nouns and numerals when you count the 200 words. If the selection does not end with the 200th word, mark the 200th word by putting a slash after it.
2. Write a motivation statement to provide a specific purpose for reading.
3. Prepare five questions to check comprehension: one vocabulary, one inferential, and three factual.

After you have developed an Informal Suitability Survey, go to Enabling Element 3, which explains how to administer and score this device.

ENABLING ELEMENT 3
ADMINISTERING AND SCORING AN
INFORMAL SUITABILITY SURVEY

SPECIFIC OBJECTIVE 3

You will administer and score an Informal Suitability Survey following the procedures described in this module.

ENABLING ACTIVITIES

*1. Read Study Guide 3. It provides directions for administering and scoring an Informal Suitability Survey. Do the Practicum Exercise to apply your new knowledge.
*2. Administer an Informal Suitability Survey to an individual and to a small group of students. Which procedure seems better suited to your purpose? What are the advantages and limitations of administering the Informal Suitability Survey to an individual? Group?

3. Give examples of the ways comprehension is affected by (a) insertions, (b) substitutions, and (3) omissions.

4. If your instructor has a tape of a student reading a selection, practice recording the word recognition errors.

*5. If a student reads a 300-word selection, makes fourteen word recognition errors, and misses one of the five comprehension questions, is the material suitable? Check your response with the Summary Scoring Guide in Table 3–1.

*6. If you administer a selection individually and find that the student recognizes the words perfectly but fails to answer three of the five comprehension questions, can you consider the material suitable? Check your response with the Summary Scoring Guide.

7. Make a chart to record the results of the Informal Suitability Survey.

STUDY GUIDE 3

An Informal Suitability Survey can be administered to individuals or groups of students. Content area teachers are advised to administer the survey initially to the entire class, and later, to individual students who exhibit doubtful results.

Before administering an Informal Suitability Survey to a group of students, you must prepare enough copies of the selection so each student will have one. The motivation statement should appear above the selection and the questions after the selection. As an alternative, you can give each student a copy of the text and write on the chalkboard the location of the selection to be read along with the motivation statement and questions. When all the materials are available, you can administer the survey. To administer the Informal Suitability Survey to an individual student, you do not need to duplicate the passage; simply use the actual textual material along with the motivation statement and questions.

Group Administration

1. Be sure to allow at least fifteen to thirty minutes for the test. Suggest work for those who finish early, so they do not disturb others.

2. Explain to the students that you want to determine how well they can read the textual material for the course. Tell them grades will not be given for the survey, but that you will use the results to help determine useful material for teaching the course.

3. Distribute the selection and questions to the students, and ask them to keep the materials face down on their desks. When all the students have a copy of the selection, read the motivation

Determining Suitability of Materials

statement to them and tell them they can have as much time as they need to read the selection. When they finish reading the selection, tell them to answer the comprehension questions. If you do not want them to refer to the selection when answering the questions, collect their copies before you distribute the questions. Since students will be able to refer to a text when studying, they should probably be permitted to refer to the selection when answering the questions. The decision is yours.

4. Your main responsibility for step 4 is observing the students to make sure they are taking the test seriously and not simply marking the answers randomly without reading the selection. You can also observe (a) the rate at which different students finish, (b) attitudes toward the task, and (c) reading habits, such as head movements and finger pointing.

5. Check the papers to see how many questions are answered correctly, and refer to the scoring guide to determine for whom the selection is suitable or unsuitable.

Individual Administration

The individually administered Informal Suitability Survey requires more time than group administration, but is also more informative because, in addition to silent reading, the students read orally.

1. Make sure you can spend seven to ten minutes with the student in a quiet place.

2. Tell the student you want to determine how well she can read the course textbook and/or other required reading material.

3. Read the motivation statement to the student, and ask the student to read the selection silently. Tell the student you are going to ask questions after she reads the selection.

4. When the student finishes reading the selection silently, ask the five comprehension questions you have prepared. Put a check mark after the question if the student's response is incorrect, and leave it blank if the response is correct. If there is more than one part to the answer, you may give partial credit.

5. After checking comprehension, tell the student to read the selection aloud. As the student reads the selection, follow along on your copy. Look for four major types of word recognition errors: substitution, omission, pronunciation, and insertion.

   a. *Substitution*—If the student says, or substitutes, one word for another word, cross out the word the student should have said, and write in the word she did say. Do not mark errors on proper nouns or numerals, because they are not counted in the passage. For example:

Determining Suitability of Materials

A subpoena is a legal notice to appear as a witness in court.

b. *Omission*—If a student omits a word or an entire sentence, circle the omitted word or sentence. Again, do not count errors in proper nouns or numerals; if the student omits proper nouns or numerals, simply pronounce them. Count single or multiword omissions (entire sentence) as one error.

A subpoena is a legal notice to appear as a witness in court.

c. *Pronunciation*—If the student hesitates when attempting to pronounce a word (other than a proper noun or numeral), ask her to try, allowing at least five seconds. If the student does not say the word, pronounce it and write a capital *P* above the word. Also write a capital *P* above a word if the student asks you to pronounce it.

A subpoena is a legal notice to appear as a witness in court.

d. *Insertion*—If a student inserts a word, write in a caret where the word was inserted and write the word above the caret.

A subpoena is a legal notice to appear as a witness in court.

6. As you administer the Informal Suitability Survey, observe the student's reading habits and obtain a feeling for her attitude toward reading. Specifically, consider the following questions:
   a. Is the student relaxed and comfortable when reading? Some students display many signs of anxiety or even refuse to read out loud because they are so far behind in reading.
   b. Is it necessary for the student to point or use some marker to keep her place?
   c. Does the student read word by word, or in phrases?
   d. How much confidence and enthusiasm are displayed?
7. Refer to the scoring guide to determine the suitability of the selection.

Criteria for Scoring an Informal Suitability Survey
One criterion for classifying materials as suitable is the student's comprehension of at least 75 percent of the information. We do not want students to comprehend *only* 75 percent of what they read, but if they are able to comprehend 75 percent, you can increase their comprehension with these techniques: introduce specialized vocabulary words

(Module 4); help with comprehension (Module 5); teach a study strategy (Module 6); and provide specific purposes for reading (Module 9). The other criterion for classifying materials is that students recognize 95 percent of the words. Again, you want the student to recognize all the words, but if he is able to read 95 percent independently, you can help by applying the word pronunciation strategy introduced in Module 7.

Scoring Surveys Administered to Groups

Informal Suitability Surveys usually have five questions; thus, a student who misses one question scores 80 percent for comprehension. Two questions would be 60 percent, and so forth. A selection can be considered unsuitable if the student misses two or more of the five questions. If he misses only one, or one and a half, the material can be considered suitable. Although missing one and a half questions out of five is equal to 70 percent, we have found no significant difference between 70 percent and 75 percent when determining suitability, especially when using only five questions.

If ten questions are used to check comprehension, the selection can be considered unsuitable if a student misses *more than* three of the ten questions. If the student misses three questions or fewer, the material can be considered suitable.

Scoring Surveys Administered Individually

When an Informal Suitability Survey is administered individually, each student receives a score for comprehension and a score for word recognition. Word recognition errors (omissions, insertions, substitutions, and words the teacher must pronounce) are recorded. The general guideline for scoring word recognition errors is that students should be able to recognize 95 percent of the words for the selection to be considered suitable. If students recognize fewer than 95 percent of the words, the teacher can introduce vocabulary (Module 4) and help the students pronounce multisyllable words (Module 7) before asking them to read the selection.

You probably realize by now why we do not mark proper nouns and numerals as word recognition errors. In selecting the passage for the Informal Suitability Survey, you did not count proper nouns because they are usually introduced by the teacher in making reading assignments. Numerals are not counted because they are not words. Since the criterion for word recognition is that the student recognize 95 percent of the words, we can consider only errors on words included in the word count. You should now also understand why you were directed to mark the 200th, 300th, or 400th word in the selection. When marking word recognition errors, you only mark errors up to these lengths. If the selection is longer, do not mark errors past these word limits.

Determining Suitability of Materials

In a 200-word selection, students can make as many as ten word recognition errors and the material is still classified as suitable. In a 100-word selection, the student can make only five word recognition errors for the material to be classified as suitable. A student may make as many as fifteen word recognition errors on a 300-word selection, twenty on a 400-word selection, and so forth. The criterion for comprehension described earlier is used to determine the suitability of an individually administered Informal Suitability Survey.

If the survey is administered individually, both scores will probably indicate either that the selection is suitable or that it is unsuitable. However, a word recognition score may indicate suitability while the comprehension score indicates unsuitability, or vice versa. If the student scores below the suggested criteria (75 percent comprehension and 95 percent word recognition) for *either* word recognition or comprehension, the selection should be considered unsuitable. The Summary Scoring Guide in Table 3-1 can be used to determine suitability of materials.

A student may be on the borderline of the scoring guide in Table 3–1. For example, if a student makes six errors in 100 words, he is on

Table 3–1 Summary Scoring Guides for Informal Suitability Surveys

Group Administration (Comprehension Only)

Suitable	Unsuitable
5 Questions: 3½–5 correct *10 Questions:* 7–10 correct	*5 Questions:* 0–3 correct *10 Questions:* 0–6 correct

Individual Administration
(Word Recognition and Comprehension)

Suitable	Unsuitable
Comprehension *5 Questions:* 3½–5 correct *10 Questions:* 7–10 correct	Comprehension *5 Questions:* 0–3 correct *10 Questions:* 0–6 correct

Word Recognition		Word Recognition	
Number of words	Errors	Number of words	Errors
100	0– 5	100	6 or more
200	0–10	200	11 or more
300	0–15	300	16 or more
400	0–20	400	21 or more
500	0–25	500	26 or more

Reminder: Errors made when pronouncing proper nouns and numerals are not counted as word recognition errors. If the survey was administered individually, the scores for *both* comprehension and word recognition must meet the criteria for suitability for the material to be classified as suitable.

the border. (The limit is five word recognition errors for 100 words.) You need to analyze the types of errors the student made in word recognition, because some errors are more important than others. For example, if the student reads the sentence, "A subpoena is a legal notice to appear as a witness in court," and substitutes the word *subject* for *subpoena,* the meaning of the sentence is lost. But if the student simply substitutes the word *an* for *a,* the word recognition error is not as important. Likewise, if the student inserts the word *the* in front of the word *court,* the meaning is not drastically changed. On the other hand, if the reader inserts the word *supreme* before the word *court,* the meaning does change drastically. If a student is on the borderline of the number of allowable errors, analyze the errors to determine whether or not meaning has drastically changed. You can decide suitability or unsuitability based upon your analysis.

PRACTICUM EXERCISE

Suppose you have administered a group Informal Suitability Survey constructed from the major textbook you desire to use in the course. Of five comprehension questions, Alfredo missed four. You now decide to individually administer an Informal Suitability Survey from a book with a lower readability level.

You call Alfredo aside during your planning period and tell him you want to find materials he will be able to read. You mention that you have a sample selection from another textbook and would like him to read it. You read the motivation statement to him and observe as he reads silently. After the silent reading, you check his comprehension. (Alfredo's responses are presented after the selection). You then ask him to read the selection aloud and he makes the errors marked. Is the selection suitable?

Venezuela

Venezuela is located on the north coast of South America. Venezuela's neighbors are Brazil, Colombia, and Guyana. Venezuela was originally a part of the Spanish vice royalty of New Granada. It was freed from Spanish rule by Simon Bolivar in 1818. It is now an independent republic.

The population of Venezuela is approximately twelve million five hundred thousand people. All citizens over eighteen are allowed to vote in the elections that take place every five years.

Many of the big oil companies—Exxon, Shell, and Gulf—have operations in Venezuela. As a result, the per capita income conceals many disparities in the actual income among the different groups in the population. Some people live in beautiful castles on the hillsides, whereas others live in shanty huts. About 3 percent of the population own 90 percent of the land.

The comprehension questions you asked, along with Alfredo's answers, are as follows:

1. *(F)* In what continent is Venezuela located? (South America)
2. *(F)* What country originally ruled Venezuela? (Spain)
3. *(F)* Do the people in Venezuela get to elect their own rulers? (Yes. You must be eighteen years old to vote.)
4. *(V)* What does the term *per capita income* mean? (I don't know.)
5. *(I)* Would you like to live in Venezuela? Why or why not? (Yes. If I worked for the oil companies and owned lots of land I would like to live there.)

ANSWERS TO THE PRACTICUM EXERCISE

Yes, this material is suitable for Alfredo. He answered four of the five questions correctly and made only three word-recognition errors in 100 words.

Keeping Records of Results from Informal Suitability Surveys

You may want to keep a record of the results from your Informal Suitability Survey. You can use the chart in Figure 3–1, or make a chart that includes the names of your students and a list of the materials you surveyed. You can mark a *U* on the same line as the student's name under each type of material you found unsuitable and an *S* under the material you found suitable. A chart like this is especially helpful if you administer a series of Informal Suitability Surveys to determine the appropriateness of different materials. As we mentioned, it is unlikely you will find one type of material suitable for all students. Your chart will guide you as you select suitable materials for different students.

Another Way to Use the Informal Suitability Survey

You already know that the Informal Suitability Survey can be used to match your students with textual material, as described earlier. There are also situations where a less structured approach can be used, such as when you need to immediately determine suitability of material. For example, you may be working with your students in the library while they locate supplementary material to expand upon the content in their textbooks. You move around the library, helping students find material appropriate to the topic and suitable for them to read. If you find a book you want to suggest to Josephine, you quickly survey the book to find a representative passage. Rather than count 200 words, you simply count the words in the first two lines, divide by two for the average, and use this figure to determine approximately how many lines you will need to have approximately 200 words. You then give Josephine a purpose for reading and have her read the

Determining Suitability of Materials

Figure 3–1 Material suitability chart

Names of Students	Names of Materials			
1.				
2.				
3.				
4.				
5.				
6.				
7.				
8.				
9.				
10.				
11.				
12.				
13.				
14.				
15.				
16.				
17.				
18.				
19.				
20.				
21.				
22.				
23.				
24.				
Total				

Code: U = Unsuitable
       S = Suitable

200-word selection silently. As she reads the selection, you quickly read it over her shoulder to formulate your five questions. When Josephine finishes, you ask her the five questions. If she answers three or more correctly, you ask her to read the 200-word passage aloud. As she does so, you count her pronunciation errors. You now have all the information you need to determine if the material is suitable for Josephine. If it is, you encourage her to read the material; if not, to find another. This procedure probably takes less than three minutes.

ENABLING ELEMENT 4
PLANNING DIFFERENTIATED READING ASSIGNMENTS

SPECIFIC OBJECTIVE 4

After scoring the Informal Suitability Survey, you will state the specific implications of the findings for planning differentiated reading assignments.

ENABLING ACTIVITIES

*1. Read Study Guide 4. Determine specific classroom practices as you use the results of suitability surveys.

*2. Do Practicum Exercise 1, which calls for you to develop a differentiated reading assignment. Share your plan with colleagues to give them ideas for providing for individual differences. Perhaps they will like the idea and work with you and the media specialist to develop differentiated reading assignments.

*3. Talk with your students about their different achievement levels in reading. You can begin by pointing out differences in height, talents, interests, and/or color of hair. Lead your students to realize that these differences make life interesting and exciting. Help them understand that you are happy about their differences and hope to help each one become better in your content area.

4. The next time you visit a materials display or talk with sales representatives from publishing companies, ask what low-level reading materials they have for your content area. Publishers generally try to market the kinds of materials teachers demand. If many teachers begin to request materials at different reading levels, publishers will make more materials available.

5. Are you beginning to see how the modules in this textbook interrelate? You can review Module 1 on determining readability levels as you evaluate textbooks and materials for potential use. Module 2 suggests preparing teacher-made materials appropriate for your classes. This module helps you determine the suitability of selected materials. As you progress through the modules, correlate the competencies you are developing.

STUDY GUIDE 4

As a teacher, you will need to use the Informal Suitability Survey to locate reading materials for your students. Because of the expected range in reading achievement among your students, you will need a variety of reading and other materials to achieve content objectives. This Study Guide will help you organize information sources and make assignments.

Planning Differentiated Reading Assignments

As mentioned earlier, it is impossible to find one textbook suitable for all students. Therefore, content area teachers need to plan differentiated reading assignments. A differentiated reading assignment is a teaching plan for individualizing reading assignments in science, social studies, and other content areas. It is a common procedure with content area teachers who have students reading from different sources but for the same purpose. The differentiated reading assignment permits the classroom teacher to have common objectives while varying (differentiating) reading assignments according to each student's capabilities.

The first part of a differentiated reading assignment is the *unit theme*, a brief statement about the focus of the unit. In the following sample differentiated reading assignment, the unit focuses on the skin; thus, the theme might be "Caring for Your Skin."

The second part of a differentiated reading assignment contains the *directions* for the students. Directions tell the students what they are to do to complete their assignment. Directions usually tell students to read the recommended resources and answer specific questions or indicate projects or other activities in which the students might want to become involved.

The *reading questions* make up the third part of the differentiated reading assignment. These questions usually develop through teacher-student discussions. The teacher might begin the unit by sharing background information, then ask students what questions they would like to explore. Some teachers like to list major questions and have the students add others.

The fourth part of a differentiated reading assignment lists *reading sources* to be used by the students to gather the information they need to answer the questions. Teachers generally use their knowledge of the difficulty of the materials and reading capabilities to assign specific sources to specific students, or they may have students select sources they would like to use and with which they feel comfortable.

The last part of the differentiated reading plan contains the actual *reading assignments.* This section can include the students' names and the appropriate references for each student to read. Although the assignments are differentiated according to the teacher's knowledge of the students' reading achievements, the materials are not designated as "more difficult" or "easy reading." Some teachers make the reading assignments informally by telling each student which resources she may want to use, rather than listing reading assignments and distributing copies. We recommend that you jot down possibilities and then suggest these orally to individual students or groups of students.

Determining Suitability of Materials

Sample Differentiated Reading Assignment

I. *Unit Theme:* Caring for Your Skin

II. *Directions:* You will soon be discussing the following questions. These questions will help you understand more about caring for your skin. To prepare for the discussion, you will need to do some reading. Each of you will find a reading assignment and recommended resources at the end of this plan. Read them and prepare to answer the following questions.

III. *Reading Questions*
   1. What are the causes of acne?
   2. What is the best way to treat acne?
   3. What is the easiest and safest way to get a tan?
   4. What causes warts and moles?
   5. How are face-lifts done?
   6. What are some of the best ways to treat impetigo?
   7. Why do some people have birthmarks?
   8. What causes freckles?
   9. How can you best treat athlete's foot and jungle rot?
   10. Why do some people have dry skin and other people have oily skin?
   11. What can you do about caring for oily skin or dry skin?
   12. How is skin grafted?
   13. Why are there different colors of skin?
   14. What is the function of skin?

IV. *Reading Sources*
   1. *World Book Encyclopedia*—Articles about skin, acne, athlete's foot and warts
   2. *First Aid*, by the American Red Cross
   3. Film—*Care of the Skin*, by Encyclopedia Britannica Films
   4. Film—*Healthy Skin*, by Coronet
   5. *The Skin*, by Patrick Hare
   6. *Question and Answer Book About the Human Body*, by Ann McGovern
   7. *Cosmetic Surgery*, by William Brown
   8. *Plastic Surgery: Beauty You Can Buy*, by Harriett LeBarre
   9. Filmstrip—*Caring for Acne*
   10. *Encyclopedia Britannica*
   11. Pamphlets by The American Medical Association and Dermatology Foundation
   12. Selected articles in *Glamour* and *Today's Health*
   13. *Medical and Health Encyclopedia*, edited by Morris Fishbein, M.D.
   14. *Structure and Function of the Skin*, by W. Montagna
   15. *Fungus Diseases and Their Treatment*, by Ivan Sarkang
   16. Textbook—*You and Your Body*, chapter 7, "Care of Your Hair and Skin"
   17. *You and Your Skin*, by Norman Goldsmith
   18. Filmstrip—*Acne: Cause and Care*

Determining Suitability of Materials

V. *Reading Assignments: Plan 1*

Students	Reading Sources
Group A: Nathaniel, Josephine Harvey, Lara Rocky, Alfredo	1, 6, 7, 16
Group B: Ruth, Don O.J., Susan Holly, Jorge, Billie	3, 12, 17, 18
Group C: Mary, Paul, Martha Rex, Ed, Dalia, Tina	2, 4, 9, 11
Group D: Jeff, Jackie, Sharon Nikki, Angie, David Diane, Bill	10, 13, 14
Group E: Patricia, Melita Bob, Dick, Barbara Ann, Jeff	5, 8, 15

Notice that the last part of the differentiated reading assignment—the actual assignment list—is presented as Plan 1. As you examine Plan 1, you will probably notice that the students in Group B are those who are reading far below grade level. As you peruse the list of reading sources, notice that Group B will be using filmstrips, a low readability level book, and articles from magazines to answer the questions. The best readers in the class, those in Group D, will use some of the more difficult reading sources. Regardless of reading level, however, all students will be able to find information to answer some of the questions you planned with them about care of the skin. In this way, each person can make a contribution.

Another way to differentiate reading assignments is to divide students into teams (refer to Plan 2). You will have excellent readers on each team as well as those who read far below grade level. You will then ask each team to find answers using a variety of sources. You can designate particular sources, or discuss all the available sources and ask them to choose some. If you decide to divide the reading sources among the teams, the assignments for your differentiated reading plan might look like this:

V. *Reading Assignments: Plan 2*

Students	Reading Sources
Group A: Nathaniel, Ruth Mary, Jeff Patricia, Josephine, Don	1, 3, 7, 14
Group B: Paul, Jackie, Melita Maria, O.J., Martha Sharon	2, 5, 10, 15
Group C: Bob, Harvey, Holly Rex, Nikki, Dick Lara	4, 8, 13, 17

Group D: Jorge, Ed, Angie   6, 9, 11
         Barbara, Rocky
         Billie, Dalia
Group E: Diane, Anne   12, 16, 18
         Alfredo, Tina
         Bill, Jeff

The advantage of Plan 2 is that the groups now include students with many different reading levels. Rather than compete with each other, the students compete as teams. Team A will want to find as many good answers to the questions as the other teams, and frequently, teammates help each other learn. Another advantage of this plan is that students who are poor readers are not categorized as such and given "easy" materials. When students work together as a team, the students in each group will naturally choose the reading resources provided for them. Students who have reading difficulties will prefer to watch filmstrips or read materials at a lower readability level.

We recommend using Plan 2 to allow students of many different achievement levels to work together and compete as teams. We have found that students do learn from each other and can work together well if there are many information sources. We also believe that students' self-concepts are enhanced with a team approach.

You can readily see the advantages of a differentiated reading plan. If you realize that one textbook is not suitable for all, yet want all of your students to accomplish the objectives of your content area, the advantages of a differentiated reading assignment are apparent. The method helps each student use her own capabilities to accomplish the objectives you set.

PRACTICUM EXERCISE

Now it is time to try planning a differentiated reading assignment. Choose a unit topic you are about to study with your students. Talk with the students to see what questions they have about the central theme of the unit. You may want to list additional questions. Next, talk with the media specialist or librarian to learn what available reading sources relate to the unit topic and the questions and compile a list of sources. Finally, consider the reading capabilities of your students, and suggest differentiated reading assignments using either Plan 1 or Plan 2.

After developing a differentiated reading assignment, plan how to share it with your students. As we mentioned, it is not necessary to write out your plan and provide every student with a copy; rather, explain the directions in the reading plan and specify the sources the different teams or individuals should use to answer the questions. You may want to suggest projects for the students in addition to the reading assignments.

Determining Suitability of Materials

You may believe that making a differentiated reading assignment requires too much time. Although extra hours are necessary when using more than one textbook with students, you will be more effective if you use a variety of resources. If you continue to develop a repertoire of reading resources for the various topics in your content area, you will soon have a large collection of appropriate reading materials. If you begin by simply suggesting a few sources to your students, you are on the right track!

Other Ways to Help Students Read Textual Materials

In addition to making differential reading assignments, what else can you do to help the students read the textual materials in your content area? Here are four responsibilities we hope all content teachers will accept—even when reading materials are suitable.

- If the textbook or other required material is suitable, you have a responsibility to introduce the specialized vocabulary (especially proper nouns) that may cause difficulty. Module 4 on word meanings gives specific suggestions for helping students develop the meanings of words; see Module 7 for ways to help students pronounce long words.
- When introducing assignments, be sure to provide students with purposes for reading. When you give your students a motivation statement as part of the Informal Suitability Survey, you actually provide them with a purpose for reading. Module 9, "Motivating Reluctant Readers," gives detailed examples for providing purposes when you introduce reading assignments.
- Another way you can help students get more from textual materials is to continually remind them to use appropriate study strategies. Module 6 suggests study strategies and ways to demonstrate them to your students.
- If your textbooks include material that requires new or infrequently used reading skills, such as interpreting cartoons or graphs, discuss these materials in class. Also point out special aids in the textbook: index, appendixes, or glossary.

Additional Techniques for Helping Students Who Cannot Read Available Materials

Suitable content area reading materials are not always available. For those occasions, consider these suggestions:

- If suitable reading materials are not available for all your students, talk to the department chairperson or librarian. See if new books are being ordered that cover the same concepts but are written at a lower readability level. Many publishing companies publish books that include the same information as your textbook, but are written at different reading levels. Write

Determining Suitability of Materials

to some of your favorite publishers to see what materials are available. Of course, if the textbook is unsuitable for most of your students, you will want to consider selecting new textbooks. Remember to determine the readability of textual materials you are considering purchasing.

- If you do not have suitable materials for some of the students, perhaps you can have a few of the better readers read the important parts of the text on to a tape to which other students can listen. Often, students understand better through listening than reading.
- There are many ways to gather information other than by reading. Audiovisual materials help students develop concepts by seeing and hearing. Besides audiovisual aids, you can provide more involvement activities during class. Students generally enjoy role playing and simulation activities.
- Read some of the most difficult parts of the textual materials to your students. This gives them an opportunity to listen and learn and, at the same time, to observe your model of reading. By varying your rate, volume, and pitch, you can make the textbook come alive. Remember to use the illustrations, charts, and tables in the textbook.
- You may want to create appropriate handouts for the students. The suggestions in Module 2 will help. Some teachers like to develop the handouts with their classes, then put them on a ditto, particularly when concluding a unit of study. The title of the handout might concern "big ideas" or "things to remember" about the topic.

Perhaps the most important fact to keep in mind is that students who have difficulty reading can survive in the content areas if you make these adaptations. Poor readers are often labeled as lazy, uninterested, turned off, or slow. If you read the article, "Teachers Don't Want to Be Labeled," a sample in Module 1, you will realize that everyone is slow, average, gifted, interested, and uninterested, depending on the task at hand. Students and adults generally avoid tasks that are difficult or frustrating. Students who are reluctant to read are not necessarily reluctant to learn. Module 10, "Identifying and Helping Problem Readers," has even more suggestions. Commit yourself to this challenge rather than "writing off" those who cannot read.

If you are now aware of the importance of finding materials suitable to the students' reading capabilities and have the procedures for developing, administering, and using results from an Informal Suitability Survey, you are ready for the Posttest. Remember, the final evaluation of your competency rests solely in how you conduct your classes. We have demonstrated the importance of finding suitable materials to help students accomplish your objectives; now, implement these ideas with your students.

POSTTEST

Directions: The following questions are designed to test your accomplishment of the objectives in this module. Check your responses with the answers on the following pages. Review as necessary after checking your responses.

1. Describe an Informal Suitability Survey and state the major purpose for using one.
2. Outline and explain the three major procedures in constructing such a survey.
3. What information can you get from an individually administered survey that cannot be obtained when you administer one to a group?
4. Suppose, as a math teacher, you individually administer the following 200-word Informal Suitability Survey to John, who was absent the day you administered the survey to the group. Is the selection suitable?

Solving Math Problems Stated in Paragraph Form

The first step in solving mathematical problems written in paragraph form is to read the problems carefully to determine what you are supposed to find. After knowing this, reread the problem to find the relevant or irrelevant facts. For example, sometimes problems include facts that are not necessary to find the answer to the problem. The fact that Mrs. Jones waited in line for 12 minutes may be interesting, but it does not help you determine how much change she should receive, considering her purchase.

The next step is to decide what process you must use to find the answer. Remember that sometimes it is necessary to use two or three processes in order to answer the question. For example, if the problem says that Mrs. Jones bought three cans of milk at 19 cents a can, you must multiply the cost of the milk and then add this to the other groceries. Of course it would be necessary then to subtract the total cost from the amount given to find how much change she should receive.

After you have done the computation, you should ask yourself if the answer makes sense. If it does not, check your arithmetic and question the process that you used.

Comprehension Questions
(*V* = Vocabulary; *F* = Factual; *I* = Inference.)
1. *(F)* What is the first step in doing math problems that are stated in paragraph form?
2. *(V)* What does *process* mean?
3. *(F)* What are ways of checking your answer?
4. *(F)* After you determine the question that is asked and the relevant facts, what is the next step to solve the math problem?

5. *(I)* Why do math problems stated in paragraph form sometimes include irrelevant facts?

John's Answers to the Comprehension Questions:
1. The first step in doing a math problem that appears in paragraph form
is to determine what you are supposed to find.
2. Process means add, subtract, multiply, or divide.
3. You can check your answers by questioning the process you used or
by redoing the computation.
4. Decide what process you should use to find the answer.
5. The book tries to get you mixed up. The teacher is trying to fool you.

5. With this information about John, state two ways you should
help him read textual materials.
6. Describe the components of a differentiated reading assignment and the major purpose of the plan.

POSTTEST ANSWERS

1. An Informal Suitability Survey consists of a representative
selection from textual material you plan to use, an accompanying motivation statement, and questions to check comprehension. It is designed to determine if students can handle
selected textual material.
2. The major procedures in constructing a survey are as follows:
   a. Select a 200-word passage representative of the reading
   material in a commonly used textbook or other written
   material. Skip all proper nouns and numerals when counting the 200 words, and mark the 200th word with a slash.
   (The selection may be more than 200 words.)
   b. Write a motivation statement to give the students a purpose for reading.
   c. Write three factual questions, one vocabulary question,
   and one inferential question.
3. Information concerning the student's skill in recognizing words
while reading orally is obtained when a survey is administered individually.
4. John's word recognition and comprehension errors for this
selection indicate that the selection is suitable. He made seven
word recognition errors in this 200-word selection and missed
only one of the five questions.
5. You would still have to introduce new vocabulary words and
provide John with a purpose for reading. You could also remind him of appropriate study strategies and help him read
specialized materials, such as graphs.
6. The major components of a differentiated reading assignment
are (a) unit theme, (b) directions, (c) reading questions,

6. (d) reading sources, and (e) reading assignments. The major purpose of the plan is to provide suitable reading assignments for all students.

Final Comment

Using an Informal Suitability Survey technique helps you determine the appropriateness of instructional materials for your students and lessens the likelihood of frustrated readers. The results should yield a higher number of completed reading assignments. Now that you understand the concept of an Informal Suitability Survey, you should be able to administer one without extensive preparation. For example, you can take a book from a shelf, read a selection rapidly, mentally note a motivation statement and comprehensive questions, and administer the survey. Duplication of materials may not always be necessary.

If you have accurately completed all the Posttest items, you are ready for another module. If not, refer to the appropriate Enabling Element for clarification of your difficulty. If you cannot clarify the difficulty, contact your instructor.

REFERENCES

Campbell, A. "How Readability Formulae Fall Short in Matching Student to Text in the Content Areas." *Journal of Reading* 22, no. 8 (1979): 683–89.

Cheek, E. H., and M. C. Cheek. *Reading Instruction Through Content Teaching.* Columbus, Ohio: Charles E. Merrill, 1983.

Estes, T., and J. Vaughan, Jr. *Reading and Learning in the Content Classroom.* Boston: Allyn and Bacon, 1978.

Graves, M. F., J. A. Boettcher, and R. A. Ryder. *Easy Reading: Book Series and Periodicals for Less Able Readers.* Newark, Del.: International Reading Association, 1979.

Harker, W. J. "Selecting Instructional Materials for Content Area Reading." *Journal of Reading* 21, no. 2 (1977): 126–30.

Johnson, M. S., and R. A. Kress. "Informal Reading Inventories." *Reading Aids Series.* Newark, Del.: International Reading Association, 1965.

Kealey, R. J. "Helping Students Read the Content Area Textbook." *Reading Improvement* 17, no. 1 (Spring 1980): 36–39.

Lamberg, W. J., and C. E. Lamb. *Reading Instruction in the Content Areas.* Chicago: Rand McNally, 1980.

Mavrogenes, N. A., C. K. Winkley, E. Hanson, and R. J. Vacca. "Concise Guide to Standardized Secondary and College Reading Tests." *Journal of Reading* 18 (1974): 12–22.

Rakes, T. A. "A Group Instructional Inventory." *Journal of Reading* 18 (1975): 595–98.

Shepherd, D. L. *Comprehensive High School Reading Methods.* 3rd ed. Columbus, Ohio: Charles E. Merrill, 1982.

Smith, E. D., B. M. Guice, and M. C. Cheek. "Informal Reading Inventories for the Content Areas: Science and Mathematics." *Elementary English* 49 (1972).

Stine, D. E. "Tenth Grade Content—Fourth Grade Reading Level." *Journal of Reading* 14 (1971): 559–61.

Vacca, R. T. *Content Area Reading.* Boston: Little, Brown, 1981.

Vaughan, J. L., and P. J. Gaus. "Secondary Reading Inventory: A Modest Proposal." *Journal of Reading* 21, no. 8 (1978): 716–20.

M O D U L E 4

TEACHING WORD MEANINGS

CONTENTS

PROSPECTUS

RATIONALE

No one needs to convince you that teaching word meaning is an important part of your subject area teaching responsibility. You know that without the specific technical vocabulary, students will not be able to read assignments or understand lectures.

Research (Spearitt, 1972) continually demonstrates that to understand reading material, readers must have knowledge of vocabulary. You are aware that subject area word knowledge correlates highly with overall knowledge, success, and grades in the subject. As a subject area teacher, you must systematically expand your students' vocabularies. This module will help you effectively teach word meanings.

OBJECTIVES

Terminal Objective

You will be able to introduce and expand word meanings in your subject area.

Specific Objectives

1. You will list three levels of word meaning and write a definition for a word at each of the three levels of word meaning.
2. You will list the seven major guidelines for teaching word meaning in your subject area.
3. You will categorize a list of instructional activites into three levels of word meaning, and you will select activities to develop the fullest meaning of words in your subject area.

RESOURCES AND TIME REQUIRED

All required resources are provided to complete the core Enabling Activities.* For the extension Enabling Activites, you will need a dictionary, thesaurus, textbooks, workbooks, or charts from your teaching area. The estimated time to complete core activities marked with an asterisk is three to four hours.

PRETEST

Directions: For each question, determine the word that indicates your belief regarding your competency. If you are in doubt, choose NO.

1. Words have many meanings, and each meaning has many denotations and connotations. The more one knows about a word, the more one will understand about what he or she reads. Can you list three levels of word meaning and define a word at each of the three levels?　　YES　NO

2. Teaching is both a science and an art. To be an effective teacher, you must be aware of what researchers and practitioners have learned about teaching your subject area and combine that knowledge with your creative ability to develop the best possible instruction. Can you list seven major guidelines for teaching word meanings in your subject area?　　YES　NO

3. Word meaning is one of the real stumbling blocks to understanding written material. The teacher who chooses appropriate activities to introduce and teach word meanings in the subject area can remove this stumbling block. Can you categorize a list of instructional activites into the three levels of word meaning, and select activites that best develop the fullest meaning of words in your subject area?　　YES　NO

BRANCHING PROGRAM ALTERNATIVES FOR PRETEST RESPONSES

1. Words can be defined at three different levels of meaning. If you can list three levels of word meaning and define a word at each level, you are ready for Enabling Element 2. If not, Enabling Element 1 will give you the information you need.

2. As teachers, we need to be aware of the guidelines for teaching word meanings suggested by research and experience. If you can list seven major guidelines for teaching word meaning, you are ready for Enabling Element 3. If not, Enabling Element 2 presents these guidelines.

3. The activities you choose to teach word meanings will dictate the level of understanding your students acquire. If you are aware of many activities for introducing new words at each of the three levels of word meaning and can select activities to develop the fullest meaning of words in your subject area, you are ready for the Posttest. If not, Enabling Element 3 will help you accomplish this task.

ENABLING ELEMENT 1
LEVELS OF WORD MEANING

SPECIFIC OBJECTIVE 1

You will list three levels of word meaning and write a definition for a word at each of the three levels of word meaning.

ENABLING ACTIVITIES

*1. Read Study Guide 1 to identify four types of vocabulary. Give examples of words in your listening, speaking, and reading vocabularies that are not in your writing vocabulary.

*2. Write a statement describing each of the three levels of word meaning. Write a definition of the word *barrier* at all three levels of word meaning.

*3. Identify five words from your subject area, and define them at each of the three levels of word meaning.

4. Ask your students to define the word *democracy*. Decide at which of the three levels of word meaning they can define *democracy*.

5. Write a statement describing how a student's understanding of what he hears and reads improves as words move through the three levels of meaning in the student's vocabulary.

6. Teach the five words from Enabling Activity 3 to students at each of the three levels of word meaning. Before teaching, ask the students to define the words; then determine and expand their present levels of understanding.

---

*Core Enabling Activities are marked with an asterisk.

Teaching Word Meanings

STUDY GUIDE 1

Everyone has four vocabularies that develop from birth in approximately this order: listening, speaking, reading, and writing. The infant listens to family members and friends as they use words with him. Soon the young child begins to say these words. For example, many parents teach a child the word *ball* by saying the word *ball* as they show the child a ball and place it in the child's hand. The parents repeat this procedure many times. To their amazement, most children begin to say the word *ball* by the time they are eleven or twelve months old. Usually when a child enters school, she begins to learn to read the word *ball* when it is presented in written form, and finally learns to write the word *ball.*

Some words in your listening and speaking vocabularies may not be in your reading and writing vocabularies. For example, you may be able to listen to someone use the word *phlegm*, and can use it to describe mucus in your throat, but perhaps it looked strange to you as you just read it. Likewise, we have found that many people know the word *phlegm* as part of their listening, speaking, and reading vocabularies, but cannot correctly write the word.

A continual task for every teacher is to help students increase these four vocabularies. You will want to make sure children can listen to and understand many words, use them in conversation, recognize them in print, and (if the words are used frequently when writing) learn to spell them. Our concern in this module is helping students develop a *reading* vocabulary, which will in turn help them comprehend.

There is no precise agreement on vocabulary size at various age levels. Research findings for twelfth graders vary on estimates of vocabulary size from 15,000 to 45,000 words. Lack of agreement appears to stem from how "word" is defined. Some educators consider *walk, walking,* and *walked* as one word; others consider them three words. Other educators count each definition of a word as a new instance of the word; thus *run*, which has at least 130 definitions, would count as 130 separate words.

High school students, like all of us, constantly add new words to their vocabularies. Although the period of vocabulary growth is most rapid between 2½ and 7 years, growth remains considerable as long as schooling continues. When schooling is discontinued, most adults add only about twenty-five new words a year to their vocabularies. In the middle to later years of life, there is evidence of an overall decline in vocabulary size.

As a word comes into our vocabulary, it generally passes through at least three distinct stages of understanding. At first we have only a specific understanding or association with the word. The learner associates only a single definition, instance, event, or object with the word. For example, the word *sofa* at this level is perceived as a specific object of a precise size, shape, or color, probably located in the living room of the learner's home. The learner is not aware that there are other sofas in other homes, stores, and offices.

At the second stage, the learner has more than a specific understanding of the word; he begins to develop a functional understanding. Now the learner can answer the question, "What is the function of a *sofa*?" At this level, *sofa* becomes something we sit or recline upon, and *sofa* can be used in a sentence to demonstrate understanding.

At the third and most abstract level of understanding, the learner develops a concept of *sofa*. For our purposes, a concept can be thought of as a cluster of impressions or perceptions for which words are used as labels. At the third level, the learner understands that *sofas* come in a variety of shapes, sizes, and colors, to mention a few things, and are part of a larger category called *furniture*. Sofas are not the only type of furniture; many other things, such as tables and chairs, are also classified as furniture. At this level of understanding, the learner has a more complete understanding of the word *sofa*. Since word meanings are constantly changing, it is probably safe to say that we never acquire complete understanding of a word.

Words, as they come into our vocabularies, do not automatically or naturally rise through the three stages of this hierarchy. Many words become fixed at the specific or functional levels and never reach the general or conceptual level. Students whose vocabularies contain words principally at the specific or functional levels will have serious problems understanding reading assignments, since writers communicate at the general or conceptual level.

It is our responsibility as teachers to encourage and foster vocabulary growth in number of words as well as depth of meaning. Students need to know many words and to understand the fullest meaning possible.

Today's secondary school students take a variety of courses that contain many new words they must learn to master the subject areas. While most subject area teachers are aware of the importance of vocabulary to the understanding of their subject area, many fail to teach for conceptual understanding. Instead, their strategy is to cover as many words as possible, briefly defining each as they go along. Research does not demonstrate that incidental exposure to large numbers of words expands vocabulary or develops conceptual understandings of words. For the most part, teachers who rush through vocabulary lessons, briefly and only verbally defining words, waste both their time and that of the students.

A word becomes fixed in the hierarchy of understanding at the specific, functional, or general level depending on how it is experienced or learned. Asking students to look up a list of words in a dictionary generally fixes those words at the specific level. Asking students to define words as used in sentences, to obtain suitable synonyms, and to write a sentence for each word generally fixes words at the functional level of understanding. Providing direct experiences with new words and asking students to incorporate the new words into their written and oral assignments and daily discussions generally fixes the new words at the conceptual level.

As a general rule, the more direct experiences a student has with a word, the more likely the word will become fixed at the conceptual level of understanding. The more vicarious and incidental the experience, the more likely the word will become fixed at the specific or functional level.

As a content area teacher, it is imperative for you to listen to students to learn the levels at which they understand words that belong to your specialized area. When you ask students if they have ever heard a particular word, many will nod their heads. If you take a few minutes to ask for students' definitions of a particular word, you will be able to determine the level at which they understand the word and then plan activities to expand their meanings of the word. For example, if a music teacher asks students if they have heard the word *rhythm*, most will readily say yes. When asked to define it, however, one student may only be able to say, "She has rhythm." After hearing this specific definition, the teacher can expand the students' level of understanding by explaining the functions of rhythm in music. Listen to your students, then clarify and expand their definitions of words.

Defining Words

To be sure you understand the various levels of word meaning, we will take you through the process of defining three words. We all know these common words: *telephone, jump, vote*. Before we define them, let us review each of the three levels of word meaning. At each level we will give you an explanation as well as a sample sentence using the word *book*.

Specific Level of Word Meaning. At the specific level, the student associates a word with a single idea, event, definition, or object. Asked to define the word *book*, a student might respond, "A book is something found in schools."

Functional Level of Word Meaning. At the functional level, the student understands one of a word's major uses or functions. Asked to define the word *book*, a student may respond, "A book is something you read," or may demonstrate understanding by using the word in a sentence, "I like to read books."

Conceptual Level of Word Meaning. At the conceptual level, the student recognizes that a word has more than one meaning or function. The student recognizes that there are many ideas associated with the word and clusters the ideas by some common element. Asked to define the word *book*, he or she responds, "Since books can be used for storing, obtaining, or transmitting information, they are a way of sharing information or a means of communication."

You now should have the levels of meaning in mind and a fair understanding of their distinctions. A detailed look at the words *telephone, jump,* and *vote* will clarify these distinctions.

Telephone. At the specific level of word meaning, a student recognizes that a telephone is a colored object that hangs on a wall, sits on a desk, or the like. At the specific level, the student would define *telephone* as, "It hangs on the wall," or "There is one in the office," or a similar statement. At the functional level of word meaning, the student recognizes a major use of a telephone. Asked to define *telephone*, this student responds with something like "I use it to call my friends," or "You talk on it." At the conceptual level of word meaning, the student recognizes that a telephone is one of many different means for communicating with people and that telephones are located in many places throughout the community, nation, or world.

Jump. At the specific level of word meaning, *jump* is what a student does when he moves his or her body up and down. It is not uncommon at this level of understanding for a student to actually demonstrate by jumping. At the functional level of word meaning, a student defines *jump* as what she does when jumping rope or making high jumps, pole vaults, and other similar things. At the functional level, the student defines *jump* in terms of some accomplishment, "I like to jump up and down." At the conceptual level, *jump* is defined as a method of exercise or of moving quickly. The student will give examples of prices *jumping, jumping* an opponent in checkers, or even *jumping* a dead battery, as in starting a car.

Vote. At the specific level of word meaning, the most common association with the word *vote* is "something done during elections." Remember, at this level a student has only a single association with the word. That association may be an event, a definition, or an instance, to mention just three possibilities. At the functional level of word meaning, probably the most common usage is "a way of getting someone elected." In any event, at this level the student describes the word in terms of its major function or use. At the conceptual level, the student realizes that *vote* is just one part of a complex government process called *democracy* in which decisions or choices are made by the people.

Thus, a student has only a single association with a word at the specific level of word meaning. At the functional level of word meaning, the student can describe a major use of a word or use the word in a sentence that demonstrates understanding. At the conceptual level, the student has many facts and ideas associated with the word and recognizes and uses the word in many different sentences and contexts.

PRACTICUM EXERCISE

Now let us see if you can define a word at the three levels of word meaning, using a word everyone knows—the word *noun.* For each level of word meaning, define the word *noun.* Write your definitions here:

Specific Level of Word Meaning—

Functional Level of Word Meaning—

Conceptual Level of Word Meaning—

ANSWERS TO PRACTICUM EXERCISE

Compare your explanations with ours.

Specific Level of Word Meaning. At this level, the word *noun* can be defined as a word, or some specific noun such as *John* or *dog.* Only a single observation or definition is associated with the word.

Functional Level of Word Meaning. At this level, the word can be defined in terms of a major use or function, or used in a sentence that demonstrates understanding, that is, "a word used in talking or writing about some person, place, or thing."

Conceptual Level of Word Meaning. At this level, you have many facts and ideas associated with the word. You may see the noun as one of the major form classes or parts of speech denoting person, place, or thing. You can use and recognize the word *noun* in different sentences, and can identify nouns in written and oral language. At this level, you demonstrate a more complete understanding of the word as you differentiate proper nouns and common nouns and contrast nouns to pronouns.

If you think you can now define words at the three levels of word meaning, you are ready to move to Enabling Element 2. If not, you may want to use a dictionary or thesaurus to further clarify this concept of vocabulary development.

ENABLING ELEMENT 2
GUIDELINES FOR TEACHING WORD MEANING

SPECIFIC OBJECTIVE 2

You will list the seven major guidelines for teaching word meanings in your content area.

ENABLING ACTIVITIES

*1. Read Study Guide 2, and prepare a list of generalizations to guide you in teaching word meanings.

*2. From your list of generalizations, prepare a second list of key phrases. Examine your list of key phrases and create an acronym to help you recall them as you teach word meanings.

3. With students and teachers, discuss the guidelines for teaching word meaning. Determine if their experiences agree with findings from research and practice.

4. Using the guidelines in this Study Guide, evaluate popular vocabulary development books. For example, one guideline suggests that the study of Latin stems has questionable value for vocabulary development. Look at some of the popular books to see how much they stress the study of Latin stems. Which books would you recommend to your students?

*5. List five words from your content area that have both a general meaning and a technical meaning. Write the technical meanings as they are used in your content area. For example, the general meaning of *rich* is "having wealth"; however, the home economics teacher uses the word *rich* to mean "full of choice ingredients."

STUDY GUIDE 2

We once overheard two teachers discuss whether teaching was a science or an art. One maintained that teaching was a science, and therefore required only the application of basic principles and guidelines developed through research. The second teacher maintained that it was really an art, the talents for which were most likely transmitted genetically. After considerable discussion, the two teachers concluded that teaching was both a science and an art. As scientists, teachers read research on teaching and examine their own practices to arrive at generalizations and guidelines for becoming more effective and efficient. As artists, teachers use their creative talents to make the subject of their teaching interesting and relevant to their students' needs.

Manzo and Sherk, in "Some Generalizations Strategies for Guiding Vocabulary Learning," present an excellent list of guidelines for vocabulary improvement.[1] They developed their list after systematic examination of research on vocabulay acquisition. Teachers who follow the guidelines will improve the efficiency and effectiveness of vocabulary instruction.

---

[1]Adapted with permission from the *Journal of Reading Behavior* 4, no. 1 (Winter 1971–72): 81–82.

Guidelines for Teaching Word Meaning

1. Students learn new words best when they are taught as labels for direct experiences.
2. All classroom teachers must give continued and systematic attention to vocabulary development.
3. Students must encounter a word in many similar and differing contexts before they can learn it.
4. The teacher's attitude toward vocabulary improvement and the superiority of his or her own vocabulary are contagious and vital factors in improving student vocabulary.
5. Study of a limited number of words in depth is more productive than superficial acquaintance with lists of words.
6. It is possible, but may be practically foolish, to teach words that are not part of the students' verbal community. Lack of opportunity for use will result in eventual atrophy.
7. Introducing vocabulary consistently with only one or two activities does not encourage word learning. Teachers who employ a variety of activities help students increase their vocabularies.
8. The wide-reading method of acquiring vocabulary, which stresses little more than wide, free reading with no other attention paid to words, is usually not very effective for influencing rapid and marked improvement.
9. The study of Latin positively influences knowledge of morphemes, but does not seem to influence knowledge of vocabulary.

A review of these guidelines suggests that word meaning instruction must be intensive, systematic, and regular, provided enthusiastically by every subject area teacher. Preferably, words should be introduced with direct and real experiences in a variety of contexts and gamelike situations. The teacher should select words for daily assignments based upon students' needs, and stress continued use of these words in all assignments. Keeping these guidelines in mind as you teach will improve the effectiveness of your vocabulary instruction.

Reread Guidelines 1 through 9, and decide which are the key words in each statement. Make notes to help you remember the guidelines. When you are through, continue with the next paragraph.

In Guideline 1, did you choose *direct experiences?* Students develop the fullest understanding of words when they learn them from real rather than vicarious experiences. A teacher can create situations for teaching words through direct experiences, forcing students to use new words to communicate with each other and with the teacher.

In Guideline 2, the key words are "*continued* and *systematic* attention of all classroom teachers." Vocabulary development cannot be left up to a few teachers—it is every teacher's responsibility. Content area teachers who have specialized knowledge are the most effective in helping students understand technical words in particular subject areas; the language arts teacher is less effective. Vocabulary instruction is most effective if it occurs daily in all classes and is systematic.

The key words in Guideline 3 are *many encounters . . . in like and differing contexts.* Students need numerous encounters with words in varying types of oral discussions, reading materials, and writing assignments to develop the fullest understanding of the words you want them to learn. Many encounters are also needed to provide the *mass* and *distributed* practice necessary for taking a word and its definition from immediate to long-term memory. Keep in mind that typical beginning readers need at least thirty-eight repetitions to learn one basic sight word. Likewise, middle- and secondary-school students must hear and see a word frequently to make it a part of their listening, speaking, reading, and writing vocabularies.

In Guideline 4, the most important words are *teacher's attitude.* Most research on teaching demonstrates that the teacher is the most important school-related variable in students' success or failure. When teachers approach vocabulary instruction with enthusiasm and positive attitudes, vocabulary growth is considerable; when they approach vocabulary instruction with a casual or negative attitude, vocabulary growth is minimal.

A limited number of words in depth is the heart of Guideline 5. Many teachers believe they have too much content to cover and too little time to cover it. These teachers do not develop in-depth word meanings. Often, they assign many words for study at one time, and the burden falls on the students to develop in-depth understanding. The best vocabulary instruction focuses on a few words, their varied meanings, uses, and application in reading, writing, listening, and speaking. A major responsibility as a content area teacher is to decide which words are most important for all students to understand. It is better to select 10 words for in-depth study than to select 100 words the students will define and forget.

Guideline 6 contains two separate but related important ideas. The first idea deals with teaching words that . . . *are not part of the verbal community in which the student lives*; the second is *the lack of opportunity for use must result in eventual atrophy.* This guideline does not suggest that teachers teach *only* those words and meanings common to the students' verbal community, but that they select words for vocabulary instruction that will help students in daily communication of information. Lack of opportunity to use words will cause them to be forgotten.

Some teachers use the same technique for teaching vocabulary words over and over again. A common practice is to list new words for a chapter or unit on the chalkboard or refer to a list of words at the end of a chapter, then ask students to look up the definition of each word and study it for a vocabulary quiz. According to Guideline 7, this is an inefficient way to encourage vocabulary development. It is better to use a variety of activities to introduce words, because some words need more explanation than a simple glossary or dictionary definition.

Some people believe that if students read about a variety of topics from many materials, they will automatically increase their vocabularies. Although it is true that people who read more have larger vocabularies, the point of Guideline 8 is that we must give attention to words so that students learn meanings. We must encourage students to note unfamiliar words and use a variety of techniques to learn their meanings. If the reader does not try to learn the meanings of new words, wide reading does not effectively increase vocabulary.

For years, Latin was a required subject in many junior high and high schools, and students who took Latin enlarged their vocabularies as a result. We now know, however, that unless one is studying a field related to science or mathematics, knowledge of Latin does not necessarily increase vocabulary. Children should probably know some of the common morphemes, but Latin courses are not necessary to expand vocabulary.

The most important guidelines are probably the first seven, because they suggest ways to help students increase their vocabularies. You can remember the seven major guidelines with the help of an acronym. Acronyms are words composed from the beginning parts or beginning letters of other words. Sometimes these are real words and sometimes nonsense words. Select key words for building an acronym for the seven major guidelines to make your vocabulary instruction more effective. Here is our acronym:

Guideline	Acronym	Key Words
6	V	Verbal community; variety of activities
3	O	Opportunities for use
2	C	Classroom teacher
4	A	Attitude
1	B	Build meanings through direct experience
5	S	Study in depth

The Necessity for Applying the "VOCABS" Guidelines

The English language is difficult to master because many of our words have multiple meanings. Many have both a general and a technical meaning. According to the *Guinness Book of World Records*,[2] the word *set* has more meanings than any other word in the English language—at least 194! In a general sense, *set* means "to place," but it also has many technical meanings. Consider the definitions in Table 4-1 from different content areas.

---

[2]N. McWhirter, *Guinness Book of World Records* (New York: Bantam, 1980), p. 211.

Table 4–1 Definitions of "Set" in Different Content Areas

Content Area	Use or Definition of Set
Art	Describes the process in making a color fast, as in dying. In jewelry making, means to cover and encrust with gems.
Business Education	To put down on paper, or in a record book. Also used to describe putting a seal on a document.
Language Arts	May refer to a collection of books.
Health	The teacher refers to "setting" a broken leg or finger.
Homemaking	The students learn proper ways to "set" the table or to let the Jell-o "set."
Industrial Arts	To put a moveable part of a machine in place. For example, you are going to "set" the gears into motion.
Math	A group of things.
Music	The teacher encourages students to "set" down, or write, words to music.
Physical Education	Prepare to begin, "Get set." Also, in square dancing "sets" are formed, and in tennis you can play a "set."
Psychology	A mind "set."
Science	In botany, *set* means to develop after pollination, or to form fruit in the plant's blossom. Science teachers talk about the sun "setting" as it appears to descend below the horizon.
Social Studies	To fix a bond or fine at a certain amount of money; to appoint; or to fix limits or boundaries.
Speech and Drama	The scenery, or to make up scenery.

Content area teachers must assume responsibility for vocabulary development. You know the technical definitions of words in your content area better than other teachers in the school; thus, you are the best person to help students learn these technical definitions. If every teacher in your building has a favorable attitude toward vocabulary development, builds meanings through direct experiences, helps the students study a limited number of words in depth, provides opportunities for students to use the words, and uses a variety of activities to help students learn the meanings of words, the students will derive more meaning from their reading assignments.

As you apply the suggestions in this Study Guide, you may want to encourage students to use a strategy for building reading vocabulary, such as this one:

- Be alert for new words when you read.
- Ask me to explain the word to you and/or look it up in a

dictionary. Make sure you find the definition that goes with the way the word is used in context.
- Keep a vocabulary notebook. Make a separate entry for each word. Include the pronunciation, the general meaning, and the technical meaning as it applies to our class. For each definition, write a sample sentence using the word.
- Try to use the new word, and listen to hear how others use it.

Enabling Element 3 provides various instructional activities to help students develop technical meanings of words as they apply to the content area. If you encourage students to ask you the meanings of words, you will need a variety of activities to increase their levels of understanding. Enabling Element 3 gives you more than twenty such activities.

ENABLING ELEMENT 3
ACTIVITIES FOR TEACHING WORD MEANING

SPECIFIC OBJECTIVE 3

You will categorize a list of instructional activities into three levels of word meaning, and you will select activities to develop the fullest meaning of words in your subject area.

ENABLING ACTIVITIES

1. Prepare a list of all the activities you can think of for teaching word meanings. Place a plus (+) in front of those you feel develop the most complete understanding of a word. Place a minus (–) in front of those you feel develop the least complete understanding.

*2. Read Study Guide 3 to become familiar with a number of activities for teaching word meanings and to determine with which of the three levels of word meaning each activity is associated.

3. Compare the list of activities you prepared in Enabling Activity 1 with those in Study Guide 3. Did you learn new ways to teach word meaning?

*4. Do the Practicum Exercise. Choose a word you want all students to know. Now define the word at each of the levels of word meaning—specific, functional and conceptual. Finally, think of activities for teaching the word to your students at levels appropriate for their understanding.

5. Teachers are learners! Many teachers say they always learn more than their students. Make it a habit to continue to increase your vocabulary by looking for new words and/or ex-

panding your level of word meanings. If you can analyze how you learn word meanings, you can pass these techniques on to your students.

STUDY GUIDE 3

This Study Guide provides models for developing instructional activities for word meaning, arranged according to the three levels of word meaning. The three levels of word meaning are:

- **Specific level of understanding.** At this level the student has one object, event, instance, definition, or the like associated with a word. The student can usually only recognize and/or recall the single association. He may associate the word *democracy* with a type of government or the United States, but have no further understanding or associations with the word.
- **Functional level of understanding.** At this level the student states a major use of the word or uses the word in a sentence that demonstrates understanding. At this level the student not only understands that a democracy is a type of government, but understands that in a democracy, people vote to select representatives who pass laws and administer the government. "In a democracy, people select their representatives."
- **Conceptual level of understanding.** At this level the student has many facts and ideas associated with the word. He recognizes and can use the word in a variety of sentences or contexts. The student recognizes that a democracy is government by many people based on the belief that all people have the same rights, freedoms, and responsibilities. He may further understand that the United States has a representative democracy whereby the people elect public officials who act according to the people's wishes.

By classifying activities according to levels of word meaning, we hope to help you evaluate the activities you have been using to develop word meaning. We also hope to give you ideas for selecting future activities. One word of caution before we begin: activities at the specific level are not inherently bad. Coupled with higher level activites, they sometimes form a learning chain from the simple to the complex. They become undesirable when they are overemphasized and are the only activities used to develop word meanings.

Read each of the following sets of activities classified by level of word meaning. Determine where the activities you listed and rated are classified.

Activities at the Specific Level

The following activities develop primarily, but not exclusively, the specific level of word meaning. The activities usually lead to a single association between word and object, event, instance, or definition.

1. *Write definitions.* Locate isolated words in a glossary and write a definition.
2. *Write sentences.* Locate isolated words in a dictionary and write a definition and sentence.
3. *Play word games. Scrabble, Probe, Boggle, Spill and Spell,* and such games are generally useful for word identification, although they rarely bring about a discussion of word meaning. When they do, usually only one definition or synonym is mentioned.
4. *Use vocabulary exercise books.* Programmed vocabulary enrichment books introduce a single word at a time, define the word, and use it in a number of sentences. The programmed technique often works for words related to the student's academic or social needs. The problem with most of the programmed texts is that the words do not match the student's academic or social needs; therefore, atrophy results soon after the lesson is completed.
5. *Memorize and associate.* Memorize Latin or Greek stems, prefixes, and suffixes and associate them with single meanings. For example:
    the prefix *in* means not.
    The stem *cred* means believe.
    The suffix *ible* means can be.
    Incredible means cannot be believed, or unbelievable.
6. *Give a simple definition* when a student asks the meaning of a word. If a student asks what *picayune* means, and you respond by saying, "petty," the student will have one specific definition.
7. *Show a picture of an object*, or present the object itself, without much discussion. For example, if you show a picture of a conch shell or bring a shell to class and tell the students, "This is a conch shell. It is spiral," they will have a specific level of understanding.

Activities at the Functional Level

The following activities develop primarily, but not exclusively, functional understandings of words. Examples of directions to the students are included with each sample activity. These activities develop and expand a major use or function of a word.

1. *Suggest synonyms.* When defining a word, you can usually suggest many synonyms. You might define *ludicrous* by saying its meaning is similar to those of *comical, ridiculous, laughable*, or *funny.*
2. *Give antonyms.* Frequently, you can tell students words that mean the opposite of the word they are learning. Antonyms of *ludicrous* are *serious, sorrowful*, or *tragic.*

3. *Classify words.* Telling students the group to which a word belongs helps them understand its function. If you tell them *ludicrous* is an adjective that describes situations or ideas, they can suggest situations that are ludicrous or absurd.

4. *Make analogies.* Sometimes you can make comparisons to help students learn words. If a student wants to know what *potable* means, you might say that *potable* is to beverages as *edible* is to foods. You could carry on the explanation with examples of beverages that are potable as compared with nonpotable beverages.

5. *Explain, give examples, and discuss.* Before reading new material, the teacher selects words that need explanation and usually presents them in phrases or sentences so that *context clues* can be used. Then the teacher explains or checks the students' knowledge of the word meanings, shows illustrative material if available, and gives additional examples. Students should also give additional examples of use. Teachers and students can explain meanings by using different types of sentences or contextual clues.

   a. *Definition clues.* The unknown word is defined in the descriptive content. For example, to teach the word *peruse*, you might say, "I want you to peruse chapter 2 so you will know the material thoroughly."

   b. *Synonym clues.* A synonym clue uses a familiar word with the same meaning to define an unfamiliar word; for example, "I want you to peruse, or study, chapter 2."

   c. *Familiar expression clues.* A common expression is used to relay an idea or offer clarity. "I want you to peruse chapter 2 until you know it forward and backward."

   d. *Comparison or contrast clues.* The unknown word is compared to or contrasted with something known. "I want you to peruse, not survey, chapter 2."

6. *Pictures, graphs, charts, and other visuals.* A collection of visuals associated with an object or event a word represents is useful for developing word meaning if you allow opportunities to discuss similarities, uses, and other explanations. If you show a picture of a conch shell and then explain the uses of the shell, talk about where conch shells are found, and have students note the similarities and differences of conch shells as compared to other shells, you help students understand at the functional level.

7. *Studying functions* of prefixes, suffixes, and stems. Research suggests that this method of vocabulary study is more beneficial for the more able students. Most of this study should occur after the fourth grade.

8. *Demonstration.* At times it may be necessary for you to become an actor or actress to demonstrate a word meaning. Verbs are especially appropriate for demonstrations; you can pretend to be *perambulating* (strolling), *perusing* (examining something thoroughly), or *dartling* (to dart again and again).

Activities at the Conceptual Level

The following activities develop primarily, but not exclusively, the conceptual understandings of words. To understand a word at the conceptual level, many different activities are necessary.

1. *Provide real and direct experiences.* To help students understand what a democracy is, it would be most valuable to have them visit a capitol building to see *democracy* in action. One limitation teachers face is that it is often not possible to provide real and direct experiences. Some students get to visit places with their parents and have many experiences; others never leave their neighborhood during their childhood. If you can take students on field trips, we encourage you to do so.

2. *Use simulation.* Since it is difficult to provide real and direct experiences, teachers attempt to provide simulation experiences. For example, you can set up a mock legislature in your classroom. Although such a simulation requires many hours of work and preparation, it gives students a better understanding of a democracy. The science teacher who wants to teach about the digestive system may dissect a frog or chicken and compare the animal digestive systems to that of human beings. Use as many simulation activities as possible.

3. *Compare meaning.* Comparison of the geographical, historical, social, or psychological significance of words is a good way to develop higher level word meaning. To help the students understand the word *tree* at the conceptual level, you might teach them about the different regions of the world and the fact that different types of trees grow in different temperate regions. You might also talk about the historical significance of trees, about conservation, and how products from trees affect the economy. The more comparisons you and your students make, the higher the level of word meaning.

4. *Use audiovisual aids.* When it is not possible to provide first-hand experiences, movies, slides, filmstrips, or recordings will help students understand a word at the conceptual level. A science teacher may be able to find a filmstrip that defines *chlorophyll* better than any teacher could. A history teacher could use voice recording of historical events to help students better understand the meanings of words such as *war* and *catastrophe.*

5. *Discuss connotations.* Connotations are implied emotional meanings attached to words through stress, gesture, or past experience. Connotations can be positive or negative. Discussions of connotative word meanings should start with denotative (dictionary) meanings. For example, to define the word *yellow*, begin with the dictionary definition of color, and go on to explain the meaning of *yellow* as it is used to imply fear or cowardice. You would need to combine this activity with several others to develop understanding of the word *yellow* at the conceptual level.

6. *Study changes in word meaning.* Studying changes in word meaning over a period of time can create interest in the study of etymology. Most desk dictionaries have a code to indicate obsolete word meaning (obs), Old English meaning (OE), and the like. Study of word changes expands students' associations with a word and moves a word to the conceptual level of understanding.

7. *Use many reference materials.* After students understand a word at the functional level, they may be able to explore different reference materials to understand the word at the conceptual level. For example, students learning about the word *glass* can look in the encyclopedia and specialized books for more information about glass. Pictures and other aids in reference materials help students expand the level of understanding.

Putting It All Together to Expand Word Meanings

As mentioned in Study Guide 2, teachers should use a variety of activities to introduce new words and to help students learn meanings. The following lesson plan uses a variety of activites to teach the meaning of a word.

Demonstration Lesson Plan

Objective: The students will be able to define the word *potable* at a higher level of understanding.

Instructional Procedures:

Write the word *potable* on the chalkboard and pronounce it (po-tə-b'l). Ask students if any of them have heard the word or seen it written before. Listen to their definitions to determine their present level of understanding. Remember, your task is to help students understand the word at a higher level. For some students, this higher level will be the specific level of understanding; for others, it may be the functional; and for some it may be the conceptual level of understanding.

At the *specific* level, the word *potable* simply means drinkable. At the *functional* level, *potable* is a term used to describe beverages, especially water.

Teaching Word Meanings

A student who understands *potable* at the functional level realizes it describes the quality of water. For example, at a campground you may see the word *potable* when the water is coming from a hose rather than from a water cooler. At the *conceptual* level of understanding, *potable* is one of many words used to describe drinkable beverages in addition to water. The word *potable* is an adjective that may apply to many different types of beverages, such as chocolate, eggnog, ginger beer, punch, lemonade, as well as alcoholic drinks. At the conceptual level of understanding, students also understand why some beverages are potable and others are not potable. These students further understand the results of drinking water or some other beverage that is not potable.

As you begin to teach the word *potable*, you may want to define it with the synonym *drinkable*. After doing so, you can give the students many examples. You might say, "The water in the drinking fountains is potable, or drinkable." This means the water is good for drinking. You may give adverse examples by saying, "The water in some countries is not potable, and if you drink it, chances are you will become sick." Now you are using the word in context.

If students know the meaning of the word *edible*, you may want to compare the word *potable* to the word *edible*. You can make the following analogy: *edible* is to food as *potable* is to water. This analogy may help students who understand the word *edible* to understand the word *potable*.

You might want to ask students to recall direct experiences by having them tell where they have seen the word *potable*. Some students have seen the word in the restrooms of airplanes, others at campgrounds, and others have seen it at mineral springs or near wells. You can provide simulation experiences by having them make signs to put on the drinking fountains in the school. The signs can say, "This water is potable." Students will enjoy watching others' puzzlement at the signs!

Next you may want to have students list beverages that are potable and some that are not. In doing so, students can indicate some of their favorite beverages and contrast them to poisonous liquids such as liquid chlorine.

You may want to have the students look up the word in the dictionary to see if there is a description of the word origin. Some students who are studying foreign languages may be able to provide a foreign word that means the same as *potable* and point out similirities and/or differences.

To help students remember the word and make it part of their listening, speaking, reading, and writing vocabularies, you will have to provide many opportunities for them to use the word. Use the word frequently during the next few days; come into the classroom tomorrow and say, "I had something that was potable." Have the students try to guess what you had that was drinkable to help them review the meaning of *potable*.

Evaluation:

You can evelute students' knowledge of the meaning of *potable* by having them write a definition or by observing whether or not they use the word in their speaking vocabularies. You might also notice whether or not they use the word in writing and or in conversation with each other.

Did you notice that the lesson plan uses a variety of activities? The teacher defines the word for the students, provides opportunities for students to give definitions, uses the word in sentences, uses a synonym and an analogy, provides a simulation activity, and has students classify ideas associated with the word. Instead of just saying, "Look up the word *potable*," the teacher uses many different instructional activities to fix the word in students' minds.

PRACTICUM EXERCISE

Now it is your turn to select activities from those in this Study Guide. Choose a word in your content area that you want all students to understand and write a definition at each of the three levels of understanding. Now go through the activities for each level of understanding and select those you could use to teach the meanings of the word. Try to incorporate a variety of activities. Make sure you list activities for each level of understanding, because your students probably have different levels of definitions for the word you have chosen.

ANSWERS TO THE PRACTICUM EXERCISE

It is impossible to give an exact answer to this Practicum Exercise, since the words you have chosen are different. We will give a sample answer, to which you can compare your response to see if it meets the criterion of providing a variety of activities to help students understand words.

Suppose you are an English teacher, and have had the students read a short story written by a British author. In this short story, the author uses the word *perambulate*, as in this sentence: "After dinner they decide to *perambulate* around the garden."

In discussing the selection with the students, you ask them what *preambulate* means. As they share their definitions, you listen for understanding of the word at the specific, functional, or conceptual level. A student at the specific level of understanding defines *perambulate* as "to walk or to stroll." At the functional level, a student defines *perambulate* as "a movement that may or may not have a purpose." The student further explains that *perambulate* can be to stroll about without any particular purpose, or to move about as you take a survey of some property. At the conceptual level of understanding, a student says that *perambulate* is a verb that designates moving about, through, over, or around, especially in examining or inspecting something. The student gives examples—you can perambulate in order to fix the boundaries of a forest as well as to scour the ground or to track a course. On the other hand, *perambulate* might mean simply to go for a walk or to push a baby carriage or pram, which is sometimes called a *perambulator*. A student who understands *perambulate* at the conceptual level will be able to compare it to other words that indicate movement or travel, such as *jogging, roaming, driving, hiking,* and *meandering.*

You may want to write *perambulate* on the board and pronounce it, then say that you are going to *perambulate*. Begin to stroll around the classroom and ask the students what you are doing. As they describe what you are doing, write the descriptions on the board. For example, some may say you are walking, some may say you are strolling, others may say you are examining. Through these definitions, you can have them define *perambulate.*

You may want to have the students examine the origin of the word. You can tell them that *perambulate* comes from the root word *ambulare*, which means to walk or to move. The prefix *per* means *through*. So the word *perambulate* means "walk through," especially as in examining or inspecting something.

At this time you may want to ask what the opposite of *perambulate* is. The students may indicate "to stay put or stationary," giving you an antonym; at the same time, you can ask for synonyms for *perambulate*. When the students provide words such as "go over the ground, go for a walk, pace, or cover territory," they will be indicating their understanding of the word *perambulate.*

If you have pictures of people perambulating, you can show them to the students. Throughout the day, you can provide opportunities for students to perambulate, and ask, "Who is that *perambulating* around our class?"

Finally, you may want to have the students look up the word in the dictionary to see what definitions are given. Continue to use the word frequently throughout the day in many contexts. You can give sentences with definition clues, such as "They perambulated around the block," or synonym clues, such as "They were perambulating or walking about the school grounds." If you continue to use the word in different contexts during the next few days, the students will soon use it, too.

POSTTEST

Directions: Read the following statements and complete each Posttest item.

1. You must strive to develop the broadest meanings of words specific to your subject area. List and describe the three levels of word meaning, and write a definition of the word *barrier* at all three levels.

2. To teach new words and meanings more effectively and efficiently, you need to follow certain instructional guidelines identified through research and practice. List the seven major guidelines for teaching word meanings to ensure effective vocabulary instruction.

3. You have become familiar with a number of common activities for teaching word meanings. Recall that activites for introducing the meaning of a word can determine the level at which that word is eventually understood. Read the following list of nine instructional activities, and specify the level of word meaning developed by each activity. Use *S* to indicate specific level, *F* to indicate functional level, and *C* to indicate conceptual level of word meanings, then decide which two activities are best for developing the fullest meanings of words.

    _____**a.** Suggesting synonyms

    _____**b.** Using context clues

    _____**c.** Providing real experiences

    _____**d.** Looking up words in a glossary and writing sentences

    _____**e.** Studying relationships among prefixes, suffixes, and stems

    _____**f.** Memorizing Latin roots

    _____**g.** Playing word identification games

    _____**h.** Using vocabulary exercise books

    _____**i.** Using films

POSTTEST ANSWERS

1. The three levels of word meaning and a description of each follow:

    a. *Specific instance or association level.* At this level the student has only one object, event, observation, or definition associated with a word. Some possible ways to define the word *barrier* at the specific level are (1) "a fence"; (2) "mountains out there"; (3) "the reef in the ocean."

    b. *Functional level.* At this level the student can describe a major use of the word and/or use the word in a sentence that demonstrates understanding. These are some ways to use *barrier:* (1) "It is like when you put a fence as a barrier in front of a house to keep dogs out." (2) "The mountains were a barrier that made it difficult for the early settlers to get to California from the east coast of the United States." (3) "A barrier reef separates deep from shallow water or warm from cold water."

    c. *Conceptual level.* At this level the student has many facts and ideas associated with the word and recognizes and uses the word in many different sentences or contexts; for example: There are many types of barriers. Barriers to physical movement, barriers to developing personal relationships, and more. Almost anything can be used as a barrier if it is used to block or inhibit something else."

2. The seven major guidelines for effectively teaching word meaning are:

   a. New words are learned best when taught as labels for direct experiences.

   b. Vocabulary development requires the continued and systematic attention of all classroom teachers.

   c. Many encounters with a word in similar and different contexts are necessary before one can acquire the fullest meaning of the word.

   d. The teacher's attitude toward vocabulary improvement and her own superior vocabulary are contagious and vital factors in improving student vocabulary.

   e. Study of a limited number of words in depth is more productive than superficial acquaintance with lists of words.

   f. It is possible, but perhaps impractical, to teach words that are not part of the verbal community in which students live. Lack of opportunity for use results in eventual atrophy.

   g. Use a variety of activities to teach new words rather than only one or two activities.

3. The nine instructional activities for teaching word meaning are categorized into the three levels of word meaning. The circled letters designate the two activities that develop the fullest meaning of words. (S = specific level of word meaning; F = functional level of word meaning; C = conceptual level of word meaning.)

   F a.   Suggesting synonyms.

   F b.   Using context clues.

   C c.   Providing real experiences.

   S d.   Looking up words in a glossary and writing sentences.

   F e.   Studying relationships among prefixes, suffixes, and stems

   S f.   Memorizing Latin roots

   S g.   Playing word identification games

   S h.   Using vocabulary exercise books

   C i.   Using films

REFERENCES

Abbass, M. "The Vocabulary of Application Forms." *Reading Improvement* 16, no. 1 (Spring 1979): 28–31.

Bergman, J. R. "Reducing Frustration by An Innovative Technique for Vocabulary Growth." *Reading Improvement* 14, no. 3 (Fall 1977): 172–74.

Bloom, B. S., J. T. Hastings, and G. F. Madaus. *Handbook on Formative and Summative Evaluation of Student Learning.* New York: McGraw-Hill, 1971.

Dale, E., J. O'Rorke, and H. A. Bamman. *Techniques of Teaching Vocabulary.* Palo Alto, Calif.: Field Educational Publications, 1971.

Dupuis, M. M., and S. L. Snyder, "Develop Concepts Through Vocabulary: A Strategy for Reading Specialists to Use with Content Teachers." *Journal of Reading* 26, No. 4 (1983): 287–305.

Fry, E., J. Polk, and D. Fountoukidis. *The Reading Teacher's Book of Lists.* Englewood Cliffs, N. J.: Prentice-Hall, 1984.

Gipe, J. P. "Investigating Techniques for Teaching Word Meaning." *Reading Research Quarterly* 14, no. 4 (1978–79): 624–44.

Johnson, D. D., and P. D. Pearson, *Teaching Reading Vocabulary.* New York: Holt, Rinehart, and Winston, 1978.

Lange, J. T. "Using S2RAT to Improve Reading Skills in the Content Areas." *The Reading Teacher* 36, No. 4 (1983): 402–4.

McKenna, M. "Etymologies in the Reading Process." *Reading Improvement* 14, no. 1 (Spring 1977): 55–56.

Manzo, A. V., and J. K. Sherk, "Some Generalizations and Strategies for Guiding Vocabulary. Learning." *The Journal of Reading Behavior* 4, no. 1 (1971–72): 78–89.

Petty, W. T., C. P. Herold, and E. Stoll. *The State of Knowledge About the Teaching of Vocabulary.* Champaign, Ill.: National Council of Teachers of English, 1968.

Spearitt, D. "Identification of Subskills of Reading Comprehension by Maximum Likelihood Factor Analysis." *Reading Research Quarterly* 8 (1972): 92–111.

Templeton, S. "Using the Spelling/Meaning Connection to Develop Word Knowledge in Older Students." *Journal of Reading* 27, no. 1 (1983): 8–14.

Thomas, E. L., and H. A. Robinson, *Improving Reading in Every Class: A Sourcebook for Teachers.* Boston: Allyn and Bacon, 1972.

Thorndike, E. L., and I. Lorge. *The Teacher's Word Book of 30,000 Words.* New York: Teachers College Press, Columbia University, 1944.

M O D U L E   5

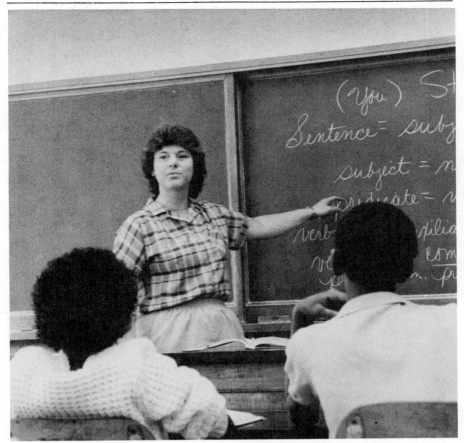

HELPING STUDENTS COMPREHEND

CONTENTS

PROSPECTUS

RATIONALE

As students progress through the educational system, the reading materials they use become increasingly more technical and put greater demands upon their comprehension skills. For many students, the demands eventually overtake their comprehension competencies. Unless these students receive help in deriving meaning from the printed material in subject areas, their performance will dwindle and they may eventually fail.

Subject area teachers are generally the most qualified persons on the school faculty to help these students with their comprehension needs in the subject areas. No other teachers are better acquainted with the nature of the reading material, style of writing, and the strategies for content analysis than subject area specialists. Subject area teachers also know the qualifications of subject area writers and the subtleties with which they communicate. Subject area teachers are the most qualified teachers in our secondary schools to teach subject area-related reading comprehension skills. *Subject area teachers are the best readers of the materials in their respective areas, and the best readers should teach students how to read in their subject areas.*

To help students improve their comprehension of subject area material, subject area teachers need to make only minor instructional changes. This module deals with four basic competencies subject area teachers need to improve the comprehension achievement of their students. First, teachers need to know the basic comprehension behaviors. Second, they need to know how to prepare questions to assess comprehension behaviors. Third, they need to know how to analyze the questions they ask to determine the thinking processes students go through to arrive at answers. In this module, we will refer to this procedure for achieving answers as a "question-answering strategy." Fourth, teachers need to plan ways to teach question-answering strategies that will improve students' comprehension. The purpose of this module is to help subject area teachers attain these four competencies.

OBJECTIVES

Terminal Objective

You will prepare a lesson plan to improve the comprehension achievement of students in your subject area.

Specific Objectives

1. You will name and describe the six major categories of questions in the Classification Scheme for Reading Questions.
2. You will write one question for each of the six categories in the Classification Scheme for Reading Questions.
3. You will write a step-by-step procedure for answering a question.
4. You will list the steps in a plan for teaching question-answering strategies, and you will prepare a lesson plan designed to teach a strategy for answering a specific type of question on a reading assignment.

RESOURCES AND TIME REQUIRED

Besides paper and a writing instrument, the participant will need a copy of a subject area textbook to complete this module. Other materials for completing the module are provided. The estimated time to complete the core Enabling Activities* is four to six hours.

PRETEST

Directions: For each question, determine the word that indicates your belief regarding your competency. If you are in doubt, choose NO.

1. It is important for teachers to have students read   YES   NO
    material and answer specific questions about the
    material. Can you name and describe six major
    categories of questions in a classification scheme
    for reading questions?
2. Students must be asked questions by their teach-   YES   NO
    ers at various levels in a hierarchy of questions.

---

*Core Enabling Activities are marked with an asterisk.

Can you write one question for each of six categories in a classification scheme of reading questions?

3. Teachers have a responsibility to help students figure out the answers to questions teachers ask. Can you list the steps you mentally go through to determine the answer to questions you ask? YES NO

4. By slightly altering present instructional approaches, subject area teachers can improve their students' comprehension of textual materials. Can you list the steps in a plan for teaching question-answering strategies and prepare a lesson plan to teach students how to answer specific types of questions? YES NO

BRANCHING PROGRAM ALTERNATIVES FOR PRETEST RESPONSES

1. If you can name and describe the six major categories of questions in the Classification Scheme for Reading Questions, you are ready for Enabling Element 2. If not, Enabling Element 1 will provide you with this information.

2. Knowing how to write questions at various levels of difficulty is an important prerequisite for teaching comprehension. If you can write questions for each of six categories in a classification scheme for reading questions, you are ready for Enabling Element 3. If not, Enabling Element 2 will help you develop this important competency.

3. If you can write in detail the procedure you follow for answering questions, you are ready for Enabling Element 4. If not, Enabling Element 3 will help you understand your question-answering strategies.

4. The reading comprehension of your students will improve when they know how to answer the questions you ask them. If you can list the steps in a plan for teaching question-answering strategies and prepare a lesson plan to teach a specific question-answering strategy, you are ready for the Posttest. If you cannot, Enabling Element 4 will be of interest to you.

ENABLING ELEMENT 1
COMPREHENDING COMPREHENSION

SPECIFIC OBJECTIVE 1

You will name and describe the six major categories of questions in the Classification Scheme for Reading Questions.

ENABLING ACTIVITIES

*1. After completing Study Guide 1, list the six major categories of questions in the Classification Scheme for Reading Questions.

*2. Share the Classification Scheme for Reading Questions with your colleagues. Together determine if there are types of questions for your subject area that are not included in this scheme. If there are, add them to the appropriate list.

*3. Randomly select questions from lesson plans in your subject area textbook. Compare them with the questions in the classification scheme. Are there types of questions proposed by the textbook authors that are not listed in the Classification Scheme for Reading Questions? If so, add them to the appropriate list.

4. As you examine the questions asked by the textbook authors, tally the number that fall into each of the six categories of the classification scheme. You may be surprised at how few questions fall into certain categories. It is not uncommon to find that most questions fall into the Recognition and Recall or Translation categories.

*5. Use the Classification Scheme for Reading Questions to prepare questions for a future reading assignment. Duplicate the questions and distribute them to your students. Direct your students to use these questions as purposes for reading. Determine if having purposes that require different levels of comprehension make the reading assignment more interesting for your students.

STUDY GUIDE 1

Students in your subject area will usually demonstrate their comprehension of printed material with some type of oral or written response, generally to a question you ask. Each day, you will ask your students many questions and received hundreds of answers.

An inventory of all the questions subject area teachers ask could be used to demonstrate the comprehension behaviors required for success in content areas. Questions could be classified into a few basic types, and the types could probably be arranged in a hierarchy from simple recognition and recall questions to difficult and complex evaluation questions. Subject area teachers could use the classification scheme for developing reading questions, and to illustrate for students the types of reading comprehension behaviors they will need in the various subject areas.

The Classification Scheme for Reading Questions included in this Study Guide is a collection of questions classified into six categories, arranged in approximate order from simplest to more difficult and complex. The scheme was developed by Nativadad Santos after a thorough examination of taxonomies prepared by Bloom and Sanders.

We include the Santos Classification Scheme for Reading Questions because it is a valuable tool for both assessment and instruction of comprehension behaviors. It has these specific advantages:

- It includes most of the questions that teachers ask.
- It is divided into six major categories of questions.
- Each category requires a different comprehension behavior.
- The categories are arranged in approximate order from simple recognition and recall to the more difficult and complex evaluation.

To become familiar with the Classification Scheme for Reading Questions, first skim the classification scheme to identify the six major categories of reading questions. Next, read the introductory statement following each category and ask yourself, "What type of thinking or comprehension behaviors are required to answer questions that fit this category?" Last, look at the specific types of questions that fit each category.

Classification Scheme for Reading Questions

A. Recognition or Recall Questions. A reading question falls in the recognition or recall category if it can be *answered verbatim* with specific information in the reading selection, and if it requires the reader to locate or repeat the information. When a teacher asks a student to answer a question by locating what the author said, she is asking a *recognition* question. When he asks a student to remember what the author said, he is asking a *recall* question. Recognition questions require a student to locate an answer; recall questions require the student to use only memory. Teachers use recognition or recall questions when asking students to do the following tasks.

1. Respond to direct factual questions when the fact appears in the selection
2. Enumerate or list information in the selection
3. Quote the author or a character in the selection
4. Recall who in a selection made a particular statement
5. Recite a stanza of a poem, an essay, or a rule from memory
6. Read aloud the part of a selection that answers a factual question or some other specified part

B. Translation Questions. A reading question falls in the translation category if it requires the reader to answer a question by *restating* in his own words what the author said. The reader must keep the author's idea and not change facts. When asking a student to give the answer to a question in his own words, a teacher is asking a translation question. Teachers use translation questions when asking students to do the following tasks.

Helping Students Comprehend

1. Explain in the reader's own words the meaning of technical terms, vocabulary words, and stated meanings
2. Restate a problem, generalization, principle, rule, or procedure the author has described
3. Paraphrase or summarize a selection
4. Retell a selection or describe or retell parts or events of a selection to prove a point
5. Explain printed directions
6. Change poetry to prose or vice versa
7. Change a statement to a question
8. Illustrate or draw information presented verbally
9. Describe a picture, poster, sketch, drawing, painting, or object
10. Present information through a graph, diagram, chart, table, or map

C. Application Questions. A reading question falls in the application category if it requires the reader to use information obtained by reading. Asking students to use information they have just acquired by reading is asking them to apply what they have read. Teachers use application questions when asking students to do the following tasks:

1. Use what they have learned from reading a selection to explain how two or more people, places, or things are alike or different
2. Use what they have learned to explain a situation or outcome or to answer a question
3. Follow directions to complete a task or project
4. Use information they have read to solve a problem
5. Prepare an outline of the information in the reading assignment
6. Group or classify the ideas in a reading assignment
7. Prepare time lines, graphs, charts, and other forms for displaying information

D. Analysis Questions. A reading question falls in the analysis category if it requires the reader to analyze what he has read to find information to explain or support a statement. Teachers use analysis questions when asking students to do the following tasks:

1. Find the supporting statements for a main idea, conclusion, or inference
2. Find the steps to follow in solving a problem
3. Locate information for solving a mystery or problem
4. Identify missing information
5. Identify clues that explain a character's actions or traits or a remark the character makes
6. Identify relationships, as in (a) cause-effect, (b) past-present, (c) main idea-details, (d) central theme-main idea
7. Identify statements that reveal an author's bias or viewpoint

8. Identify propaganda devices
9. Identify statements that make a communication false

E. Synthesis Questions. A reading question falls in the synthesis category if it requires the reader to join or combine information to form a new communication. Asking a student to generalize over the details in a paragraph to create a main idea statement is an example of synthesis. Teachers use synthesis questions when asking students to do the following tasks:

1. Generalize details to form a main idea
2. Generalize from facts to form a conclusion
3. Generalize from facts and opinions to form an inference
4. Summarize the main points
5. Substitute words or phrases to make ideas more correct or easier to understand
6. Read a selection aloud showing the author's intended expression
7. Suggest different titles for a story, chapter, side heading, or other item
8. Suggest solutions to a problem
9. Give a different beginning, ending, or title to a story or other piece

F. Evaluation Questions. A reading question falls in this category if it requires the student to determine whether a communication *meets standards* set up by that student or presented to the student. It requires the student to make decisions and to support his views in his own words. Asking a student to establish evaluation criteria, gather facts to compare with the criteria, judge how well each fact matches a given criterion, and form an evaluation is an example of an evaluation question. Teachers use evaluation questions when asking students to do the following tasks:

1. Evaluate a communication for:

accuracy	completeness
authenticity	practicability
relevance	reasonableness
adequacy	authoritativeness
value	logical consistency
imagination	truth
falsity	merit
agreement	appropriateness
suitability	objectivity, etc.

2. Evaluate pictures for accuracy, appropriateness, suitability, and richness of imagination, and justify one's views
3. Evaluate suggested endings to a story, summaries, a performance, a declamation, an oration, or a speech, and justify one's views and/or suggest improvements

4. Evaluate statements for ambiguities, overspecificity, omissions, distortions, inconsistencies, inaccuracies, or overstatements, and justify one's views

5. Evaluate to determine if a conclusion, inference, main idea, or thesis logically follows the facts; select the best conclusion, inference, etc., from a set of suggested conclusions, inferences, etc., and justify one's view

6. Evaluate to form an opinion or to take a stand on an issue

7. Judge agreement between ideas or sources of information, and justify one's views

8. Judge and prove the truth or falsity of statements by pointing out supportive statements or evidence, and justify one's views

9. Judge ideas as similar, different, contradictory, supportive, related, relevant, essential, or in proper sequence, and justify one's views

10. Judge the relative merits of information from different sources, or the sources, and justify one's views

11. Judge characters in a story, and justify one's views

The Classification Scheme in Review

As you read the Classification Scheme for Reading Questions, you noticed that each of the six major categories of questions requires its own comprehension behaviors, or "thinking strategies." You noticed that each level of the strategy tends to build on the preceding level, suggesting a true hierarchy.

Recognition or Recall questions are the first category in this classification scheme, and questions of this type require the reader to identify or recall exact statements from the passage to give verbatim answers. Since the comprehension behaviors required at this level are rather simple, the question-answering strategy is not elaborate.

Translation questions relate closely to Recognition and Recall questions; the chief difference is that translation questions require the reader to answer questions in his own words, not verbatim, and are thus a higher level question-answering strategy than Recognition or Recall.

Application questions require that the learner use the information obtained through reading in some new situation. The information can be used in any way as long as a change results. The information can be used to make comparisons, to outline, or to locate information, to mention just a few types of application.

Analysis questions require the learner to analyze a reading selection to locate specific information. Sometimes the information is used to explain, justify, or prove a point; other times, the information is used as a basis for forming generalizations, in which case analysis leads to synthesis. Analysis questions thus require a still higher level question-answering strategy.

Helping Students Comprehend

Synthesis questions require the reader to combine information to form a new statement or communication. Synthesis is often the other side of analysis; for example, a reader may first analyze a reading selection to find detail and later synthesize the details to form a main idea. The synthesis question-answering strategy builds upon but is more complex than preceding strategies because it requires the reader to combine or synthesize information into a new communication.

Evaluation questions are the final category in the classification scheme. Evaluation questions require the learner to make a decision after reading for information and judging it against evaluation criteria. The decision, information gathered, and evaluation criteria must be justified by the reader. The evaluation question-answering strategy is the most complex and difficult for students to master.

Table 5–1 summarizes factors in the Classification Scheme for Reading Questions, showing the interrelatedness and increased complexity of comprehension behaviors as questions move from Recognition and Recall to Evaluation.

Upon reflection, you will probably realize that the Classification Scheme for Reading Questions is a rather complete model of the reading comprehension requirements of your subject area. The classification scheme probably contains most of the questions you answer or ask your students to answer in your subject area. Because of its

Table 5–1 Summary Form: Classification Scheme for Reading Questions

Question Categories	Type of required response					
	Recognize or recall answer verbatim	Change verbatim answer to own words	Use information to alter some situation or product	Separate communication into parts for analysis	Combine information for various sources to form something new	Evaluate and justify the decision
Recognition or Recall	X					
Translation	X	X				
Application	X	X	X			
Analysis	X	X	X	X		
Synthesis	X	X	X	X	X	
Evaluation	X	X	X	X	X	X

comprehensiveness, the classification scheme will be invaluable for preparing questions that will stimulate your students' thinking.

If you can now name and describe the six major categories for classifying reading questions from the Classification Scheme for Reading Questions, you are ready for Enabling Element 2. If not, complete the task before moving on. If you are having difficulty, reexamine this Enabling Element or see your instructor.

ENABLING ELEMENT 2
PREPARING READING QUESTIONS

SPECIFIC OBJECTIVE 2

You will write one question for each of the six categories in the Classification Scheme for Reading Questions.

ENABLING ACTIVITIES

*1. Read Study Guide 2. Prepare one question for each of the six categories on the reading selection, "Comprehension is the Cornerstone of Education."

*2. Identify some reading selections from your subject area textbook. Prepare two or three questions for each of the six categories of reading questions. Use these questions to establish purposes for reading the assignment.

3. Make copies of the Classification Scheme for Reading Questions available to your students. Familiarize them with the various kinds of reading questions that can be constructed. Have students construct questions for each of the six categories to use in establishing purposes for reading.

4. Exchange copies of questions with other staff members who have prepared, from common reading assignments, questions in each of the six categories. You may find that some teachers are better than others at writing certain types of questions.

*5. Get together with a group of colleagues in your subject area and, using the classification scheme, identify the more important types of questions for your subject area. Arrange the questions in a hierarchy from least to most difficult. This activity will give you a classification scheme for reading questions specific to your subject area. Use this scheme for developing questions when you plan future reading assignments.

STUDY GUIDE 2

Your first step toward improving students' comprehension is to write a variety of questions. Not only is variety necessary, but the questions should range on a hierarchy from Recognition and Recall to

Evaluation. The hierarchy in the Classification Scheme for Reading Questions introduced in Enabling Element 1 will be used to prepare questions in this Enabling Element.

It is now time to begin writing questions using the Classification Scheme for Reading Questions. At this point, you should reacquaint yourself with the classification scheme, particularly the variety of questions that fall under each classification. When you have completed this task, read the following selection, "Comprehension is the Cornerstone of Education."

Comprehension Is the Cornerstone of Education

Comprehension of subject matter materials is one of the major objectives of public and private education. As a major objective of education, it becomes one of the chief responsibilities of every teacher. Many teachers, however, teach as if they believe comprehension to be an innate ability, which students have or have not. Their teaching behavior leads an observer to conclude that developing comprehension abilities is the objective of the student and not of the teacher. Teachers such as these make no attempt to explain the processes involved in obtaining information from textual material. They merely make assignments and leave it to the student to discover the intricate processes that lead to understanding. Given that human beings are our most important natural resource, we can no longer allow miseducation such as this to take place. In the future, subject area teachers will have to assume their rightful responsibility for developing the comprehension skills indigenous to their specific subject areas.

The classification scheme contains six basic categories for questions; each category describes questions that can be classified in the category. Examining each category reveals that it is highly unlikely that all the questions in the category would apply to one reading selection. The nature and the author's purpose will differ for each selection so the types of question will vary.

For the selection, "Comprehension is the Cornerstone of Education," there are questions for each category, but the number for each is not the same because some questions are appropriate for the passage and some are not. Next to each question is a code number corresponding to a category on the Classification Scheme for Reading Questions; for example, question A1 corresponds to 1 on the scheme, "respond to direct factual questions in which the fact is given in the selection read." Compare each question with its appropriate classification to see how easy it is to prepare questions using the scheme.

Also notice that we have provided code numbers for preparing additional questions under each category, so you can see which additional categories lend themselves to questions you might prepare.

Outline for Preparing Questions, Form A
"Comprehension Is the Cornerstone of Education"

A. *Recognition or Recall*
    1. According to the author of this selection, what is one of the major objectives of public and private education?
    3.

    6.

B. *Translation*
    1. In your own words, define *comprehension*.
    4.

C. *Application*
    2. Does this selection explain the observation that comprehension scores on standardized tests do not continue to improve as students go through high school? Explain.

    5.

D. *Analysis*
    1. What major facts presented by the author underlie his conclusion regarding future responsibilities of subject area teachers?

    4.

    7.

E. *Synthesis*
    2. What is the major conclusion we can reach from the facts presented by the author?

F. *Evaluation*
    1. Did the author objectively present his point of view?
    6.

PRACTICUM EXERCISE

Now it is your turn to write some questions. On the Outline for Preparing Questions, Form A, we provide code numbers for questions under each classification and questions after some of the code numbers. Your assignment is to formulate questions for the categories that do not have them. Using the selection, "Comprehension is the Cornerstone of Education," and the Classification Scheme for Reading Questions, write at least one question for each of the six categories. We are sure you will find the task easy enough to encourage you to design additional questions under the Recognition and Recall and the Analysis classifications. You may want to examine the classification scheme to determine if you could prepare still more questions. When you have finished, begin reading with the following paragraph.

ANSWERS TO THE PRACTICUM EXERCISE

Now that you have completed your task, we are sure you will agree that the classification scheme makes it easy to prepare questions. Now compare your questions with ours. Look at the six categories of questions in the following Outline for Preparing Questions, Form B. The comparison should demonstrate the adequacy of your questions as well as reinforce our point that the classification scheme makes writing questions effortless.

Outline for Preparing Questions, Form B
"Comprehension Is the Cornerstone of Education"

A. *Recognition or Recall*
   1. According to the author of this selection, what is one of the major objectives of public and private education?
   3. What did the author say the behavior of many teachers leads an observer to conclude?
   6. Read aloud the sentence in which the author states the future responsibilities of subject area teachers.
B. *Translation*
   1. In your own words, define *comprehension*.
   4. In your own words, state the author's major points.
C. *Application*
   2. Does this selection explain the observation that comprehension scores on standardized tests do not continue to improve as students matriculate through high school? Explain.
   5. How might the author have outlined the facts in the selection?
D. *Analysis*
   1. What major facts presented by the author underlie his conclusion regarding future responsibilities of subject area teachers?

4. Did the author leave any important information out of the selection?

7. Which statements reveal the author's point of view?

E. *Synthesis*

2. What is the major conclusion we can reach from the facts presented by the author?

9. What would be another appropriate title for this selection?

F. *Evaluation*

1. Did the author objectively present his point of view?

6. How would you defend the author's conclusion?

Now that you are familiar with the Classification Scheme for Reading Questions and can use it to prepare questions in each of the six categories, it is time to look at strategies for answering questions.

ENABLING ELEMENT 3
STRATEGIES FOR OBTAINING
IMPROVED ANSWERS TO QUESTIONS

SPECIFIC OBJECTIVE 3

You will write a step-by-step procedure for answering a question.

ENABLING ACTIVITIES

*1. Read Study Guide 3, and list the steps in your question-answering strategy for an analysis question.

*2. For a passage of your choosing, write six questions at the various levels of the Classification Scheme for Reading Questions. When you finish, list the step-by-step procedure you went through to answer each question.

*3. Arrange a meeting with a group of colleagues to discuss and refine strategies for answering questions. Share the sample strategies from this Study Guide to initiate the discussion. Group discussion is probably the best way to refine thinking on question-answering strategies.

4. Reproduce the sample question-answering strategies and distribute them to your students. Use the various strategies as a basis for discussing comprehension improvement in your subject area.

5. Discuss with colleagues in your subject area the various strategies students use to answer questions. How well students answer certain types of questions will provide insight into which types of questions you should stress in future reading assignments.

STUDY GUIDE 3

Each question you prepared for the reading selection in Enabling Element 2 has its unique answer; likewise, each question requires a different procedure or thinking process to obtain an answer. This procedure or thinking process is the *question-answering strategy.*

It is your responsibility as a teacher to improve question-answering strategies of students in your subject area. Because your strategies have become highly refined as a result of years of reading and studying in your specialty, you are the most appropriate teacher to improve the students' strategies.

Before you can help your students, however, you need to become more familiar with your own strategies for answering questions. This will take some time, because you probably execute your strategies automatically. The following Practicum Exercise will help you develop an awareness of your question-answering strategies.

PRACTICUM EXERCISE 1

Directions: (1) Read the question that establishes a purpose for reading the selection. (2) Read the essay. (3) Determine your answer to the question. (4) List the step-by-step procedure you followed to arrive at your answer.

Purpose for reading: What is the best title for the selection?

The American Red Cross

The American National Red Cross is part of an organization found in more than 120 countries throughout the world. The Red Cross was founded in Switzerland in 1863 for the purpose of relieving human suffering around the world. The worldwide organization has a paid professional staff, but consists mostly of volunteers. There are more than 30 million volunteer members of the Red Cross throughout the world. The services provided by this multinational organization are paid for from voluntary contributions.

Write your answer to the question here:

Write the steps in your question-answering strategy here:

ANSWERS TO PRACTICUM EXERCISE 1

Did you write your answer? Did you list the step-by-step procedure you used to arrive at your answer? If you did, compare your question-answering strategy and answer with ours.

1. We read the question and surveyed the passage to be sure neither contained unfamiliar words, expressions, or ideas. Many questions are misunderstood or answered incorrectly because the reader does not take time to clarify an unfamiliar word, expression, or idea.

2. Next, we restated the question in our own words to be sure we understood the intent. Many students answer questions incorrectly because they misunderstand them. In this case, "Is the title for the selection the best or most correct title?" can be changed to "Should the author have given this selection another title?"

3. Then we examined the passage to find the facts we needed to answer the question. Since we were looking for a title that was representative of all the ideas in the selection, we reread the selection sentence-by-sentence and found the following:

    a. Sentence 1 explains that the American National Red Cross is part of an organization that is found around the world.

    b. Sentence 2 tells where, when, and why the Red Cross was founded.

    c. Sentences 3 and 4 tell about the paid staff and volunteers who run the global organization.

    d. Sentence 5 explains how the worldwide organization is funded.

4. We believed all the information needed to answer the question was in the passage; therefore, we did not look for additional information from other sources.

5. Next, we studied each sentence to determine if it presented information represented by the title. We found that the sentences gave information about the worldwide organization called the Red Cross. The title was too narrow because it focused on only the American National Red Cross, only one of over 120 organizations that make up the global organization. After examining the facts, we answered the question. "The American Red Cross" was not the correct title for his selection. A more appropriate title would be "The Red Cross Organization," which more adequately represents or explains the information in the selection.

6. Finally, we checked our answer against the facts in the sentence to be sure it was the best answer to the question.

Does your strategy agree with this one? If not, how does it differ? Your answer may agree with ours even if you used a different strategy;

strategies can differ even if the answers do not. We do not know enough about the way people think to conclude that only one strategy exists for answering a particular type of question. If the answers agree, it makes little difference that the strategies differ. Different question-answering strategies are important if the answers differ; that is when the teacher provides the student with a new strategy to help him answer a question. You will learn more about using your own strategy to help students develop question-answering strategies in the next Enabling Element.

Occasionally, we can find equal support and arguments for two or more answers to the same question. At this impasse, both answers should be accepted as possibilities of equal merit. Remember, however, that your goal is to identify the one *best* answer; emphasizing the need to identify the best answer encourages precise thinking.

You have now had an opportunity to read our question-answering strategy and compare your strategy to ours. If you think your strategy is incomplete, now is the time to refine your strategy so it will be useful to your teaching.

PRACTICUM EXERCISE 2

Now you are familiar with the processes for writing questions and examining your step-by-step procedure for answering questions. From the following selection, formulate one question for each category in the Classification Scheme for Reading Questions, then examine the Sample Question-Answering Strategies. Using the sample strategies as guides, create a specific question-answering strategy for each of your questions. This activity will further develop insight into your question-answering strategies and enhance your effectiveness in working with your students' comprehension problems.

Fish Propulsion

Fish, like humans, do not all use the same method for propelling, or moving, through the water. Some fish move through the water with snakelike motions. These snakelike motions are caused by muscle contractions throughout the body. Other fish propel through the water using a combination of muscle contraction and the side motion of their caudal, or tail fin. The third type of swimmer uses the caudal fin almost exclusively. This swimmer keeps its body almost rigid while moving through the water. One category of fish has a unique way of propelling through the water. The flying fish emerges from the water, spreads its large pectoral fin, and glides over the water for hundreds of feet. The method used for propulsion seems to be related to the size of the fish and the speed at which the fish swims.

Directions: Using the preceding selection, create one question for each category in the Classification Scheme for Reading Questions.

Recognition or Recall question:

Translation question:

Application question:

Analysis question:

Synthesis question:

Evaluation question:

When you finish preparing questions, read the Sample Question-Answering Strategies. Follow the directions that appear after the sample strategies.

Sample Question-Answering Strategies

These sample question-answering strategies for the six categories of reading questions are *general* strategies. Question-answering strategies for specific questions within each major category will differ slightly from the sample strategies. You will need to amend the strategies slightly to fit the intent of each question.

Recognition or Recall Strategy

1. Check the question and passage to be sure they do not contain unfamiliar words, expressions, or ideas. If you detect an unfamiliarity, clarify it before proceeding.
2. Be sure the intent of the question is clear. Rephrasing the question sometimes serves as a check on understanding.
3. Read the selection and identify the precise statements that answer the question.
4. Reread the selection to verify that you have identified all the information necessary to answer the question.
5. Answer the question in precisely the same words of the passage.

Translation Strategy

1. Survey the question and passage to see if they contain unfamiliar words, expressions, or ideas. If you detect an unfamiliarity, clarify it before proceeding.

2. Be sure the intent of the question is clear. Rephrasing the question sometimes helps to ensure clarity.
3. Read the selection and identify the precise statements that answer the question.
4. Check the passage to be sure you have identified everything necessary for answering the question.
5. Answer the question in precisely the same words of the passage.
*6. Restate the answer in your own words.
*7. Compare your restated answer with the quoted answer to be sure it contains all of the facts or ideas.

Application Strategy

1. Determine whether or not the question or passage contains unfamiliar words, expressions, or ideas. If it does, clarify before going further.
2. Obtain a clear understanding of the specific problem or situation contained in the question. Be sure to understand how the information from the reading will be applied to the specific problem or situation. Identify and state the problem or situation. Restate the question so it specifies what information is necessary to solve the problem or change the situation.
3. Read and locate the precise information required by the restated question.
4. Reread the selection to be sure all available information has been extracted.
5. Examine the information to be sure it does not contain new or inaccurate information.
*6. Using the information from the selection, solve the problem or change the situation as directed by the question.
*7. Check the answer to be sure the problem or situation has been appropriately solved or changed.

Analysis Strategy

1. Examine the question and passage to identify unfamiliar words, expressions, or ideas. Clarify before proceeding.
2. Be sure the intent of the question is understood. Restate the question if necessary to clarify the intent.
*3. Read the selection to identify the information needed to answer the question.
*4. If necessary, gather additional information from other sources.
*5. When you have obtained all the necessary information, prepare an answer.
*6. Check your answer to be sure it is the best answer to the question.

---

*Indicates new step(s) not contained in preceding strategy.

Synthesis Strategy

1. Check the question and passage for unfamiliar words, expressions, or ideas. Clarify them before going further.
2. Be sure the intent of the question is clear. Restate the question if necessary.
3. Identify all relevant information available from the passage.
4. Supply information from other sources as needed.
*5. Synthesize the information and compose an answer to the question. The answer should be new, different, and broader than the sum of its parts.
*6. Test the answer to be sure it covers all the information.

Evaluation Strategy

1. Check the question and passage to be sure it does not contain unfamiliar words, expressions, or ideas. Clarify as necessary.
2. Be sure the intent of the question is understood. Rephrase the question, if necessary, to show that you understand its intent.
3. Identify important information from the passage.
*4. Establish the evaluation criteria.
*5. Evaluate each basic unit of information in terms of the appropriate criteria.
*6. Examine all evaluations and prepare a final decision.
*7. Justify the information gathered, evaluation criteria, and your final decision.

Directions: As previously directed, formulate the answer to each of your questions and list the steps in your question-answering strategy.
   Recognition or Recall answer:

   and strategy:

   Translation answer:

   and strategy:

---

*Indicates new step(s) not contained in preceding strategy.

Application answer:

and strategy:

Analysis answer:

and strategy:

Synthesis answer:

and strategy:

Evaluation answer:

and strategy:

ANSWERS TO PRACTICUM EXERCISE 2

Because we could not anticipate what questions you would write, it was impossible to provide strategies for each of your questions. By now, however, you should be able to evaluate your own strategies. Compare your strategies to the samples. Since your strategies are specific to questions within each category and ours are *general strategies* for each category, your strategies probably contain steps in addition to those we have listed. If you are having difficulty listing the steps in your strategy or feel uncomfortable with the strategy you have developed, reread appropriate components of this Study Guide, complete additional Enabling Activities, examine reference sources by Bloom or Sanders, or see your instructor.

You should now be able to prepare questions and develop question-answering strategies. You are now ready to discuss improving students' reading comprehension in your subject area. Enabling Element 4 addresses itself to this topic.

ENABLING ELEMENT 4
TEACHING QUESTION-ANSWERING STRATEGIES

SPECIFIC OBJECTIVE 4

You will list the steps in a plan for teaching question-answering strategies, and prepare a lesson plan to teach a strategy for answering a specific type of question on a reading assignment.

ENABLING ACTIVITIES

*1. Read Study Guide 4. When you finish reading it, list the steps for teaching such a strategy.

*2. After completing Study Guide 4, prepare a lesson plan to teach a strategy for answering a specific question.

*3. Using reading material you will soon assign to your students, prepare questions at each of the six levels in the classification scheme. Assign them to your students. From their answers, identify students who have difficulty answering specific types of questions and group the students according to the type of questions they could not answer. Teach the students a question-answering strategy following the suggested procedure.

*4. Organize open discussion groups so students can meet informally and discuss their reading habits and strategies.

5. Teach your aides or more capable students how to teach the question-answering strategies so they can work with students who need additional instruction.

6. Share your lessons plans and materials with your colleagues. By doing so, each of you will gather an excellent collection of lesson plans.

STUDY GUIDE 4

Now that you are familiar with the classification scheme, can prepare questions at different levels in a hierarchy, and have examined your own processes for answering questions, you are ready to teach.

---

*Includes core Enabling Activities.

Teaching your students to comprehend subject area material with strategies for answering different types of questions is not a long or involved process, nor does it detract from study of the subject area. In fact, teaching students to comprehend reading assignments for different purposes enhances their understanding and appreciation of the subject area.

This Study Guide introduces a simple plan for teaching question-answering strategies that draws heavily on the subject area teacher's background and reading style. The plan is based on the assumption that subject area specialists are the best readers of their subject's materials.

The four steps for teaching question-answering strategies are to:

1. Set the purpose for learning. This step substantiates for your students their need for instruction.
2. Assess the comprehension strategy. This step determines the precise steps in the learner's strategy for answering a specific type of question.
3. Teach the comprehension strategy. This step teaches a strategy for obtaining the best answer to a question.
4. Apply the comprehension strategy. This step determines whether or not the learner understands the strategy you taught.

The procedure for teaching question-answering strategies is the same format you would follow when teaching students how to comprehend subject area material. The instructional plan is set in motion when a student *incorrectly* answers a number of questions of the same type: Recognition and Recall, Translation, Application, Analysis, Synthesis, or Evaluation. Study of the instructional plan should begin with a survey of the four steps. Then, read the material under each step.

Plan for Teaching Question-Asnwering Strategies

A. *Set the purpose for learning.* The purpose of this step is to substantiate the need for instruction. A lesson is taught because a group of students had difficulty answering two or more questions of the same type—probably in similar material. That material would be used for this lesson. Tell the students that their difficulty in answering a type of question is the reason for the lesson; explain that after some instruction, they will be able to answer such questions and, as a result, will improve their comprehension.

B. *Assess the comprehension strategy.* The purpose of this step is to determine what procedure students followed in answering the question incorrectly.
   1. The teacher restates one or two questions and supplies the answers students gave earlier. As an alternative, the

teacher may ask students to state their own answers. Write the answers on the chalkboard for reference.

2. Ask a student to explain step-by-step how she arrived at her answer. You can repeat this procedure with another student.

3. As the students reveal their question-answering strategies, list the steps on a chalkboard.

4. Do not accept "I don't know" answers. Continue to question the students to determine the specific steps they followed.

C. *Teach the comprehension strategy.* The purpose of this step is to teach the necessary components in a strategy for identifying the best answer to a question.

1. Using the passage in which students demonstrated difficulty, direct them to observe while you read the passage aloud.

2. As you read the passage aloud, describe and demonstrate how you are determining the preferred answer to the question they answered incorrectly.

3. As you describe and demonstrate your strategy, write the steps on a chalkboard. (You learned these strategies in Enabling Element 3.)

4. When you have finished reading, describing, and demonstrating your strategy, review the steps with the students, then cover or remove the steps from their view.

5. To be sure they understand the question-answering strategy you have just taught, ask selected students to list and explain the steps in the procedure.

6. Next, have the students compare their original strategies to your strategy to identify similar and different steps and explanations.

7. Discuss with the students how they must modify their strategies to obtain the preferred answer to questions of the type they are working with.

8. Have students explain how they would apply the new strategy to similar questions.

9. The students must *understand* and be able to explain the strategy before the teachers goes to the next step.
   Note: A student may arrive at the preferred answer using an equally acceptable but different strategy than the teacher's. If this is the case, the teacher should not attempt to change the student's strategy. Cognitive styles differ, and correct answers can be reached in different ways.

D. *Apply the comprehension strategy.* The purpose of this step is to determine if students understand and can use the strategy presented by the teacher.

Helping Students Comprehend

1.   Provide students with a reading assignment similar in reading level and content to the initial assignment.
2.   Prepare questions of the same type as those with which the students experienced difficulty.
3.   Direct students to read the passage silently to find the answer to one of the questions.
4.   When they have finished reading, have the students explain how they looked for the answer to the question.
5.   Students should eventually arrive at or near the preferred answer. In some cases, students fail to provide an improved answer. If this is the case, the teacher should return to the teaching step and reteach the strategy with additional demonstrations. Reteaching is most effective when done with new material, if available.
6.   Give students opportunities to answer similar questions in everyday classroom activities and assignments. Help them apply their strategies to answer questions about information in different types of subject area materials, such as newspapers, magazines, and monographs. Remember, students will forget the strategies you teach unless you provide opportunities for continuous application.

The following Teaching Plan explains how comprehension improves through the study of an analysis question. The plan was developed from "The American Red Cross" selection, to which you can refer. Recall that students were asked to answer the question, "Is this the correct title for this selection?" This Teaching Plan demonstrates how to teach students to answer analysis questions of this type.

The American Red Cross

The American National Red Cross is part of an organization found in more than 120 countries throughout the world. The Red Cross was founded in Switzerland in 1863 for the purpose of relieving human suffering around the world. The worldwide organization has a paid professional staff but consists mostly of volunteers. There are more than 30 million volunteer members of the Red Cross throughout the world. The services provided by this multinational organization are paid for from voluntary contributions.

Teaching Plan

A.   Set the purpose for learning. Assume that a number of students, in answer to the question, "Is this the correct title for this selection?" give this response: "Yes, because the passage tells about the American Red Cross." Because this answer is not correct, the teacher points out the need for instruction and explains that instructions should improve their comprehension of the passage and help them correctly answer other questions of this type.

B. Assess the comprehension strategy. Write the student's answer on the chalkboard and ask a student to explain how he arrived at the answer. Let other students contribute to the explanation. Write each step on the chalkboard, and probe to elicit as many specific steps as possible. The strategy may resemble this:

1. "I read the passage."
2. "The first sentence is usually the topic sentence."
3. "Since the name, American Red Cross, appears in the first sentence, it must be what the selection is about."

C. Teach the comprehension strategy.

1. Give the students a copy of "The American Red Cross," and direct them to read silently as you read aloud.
2. As you read aloud, describe and demonstrate each step in your strategy for answering this question. Use the Analysis question-answering strategy in Enabling Element 3 as your guide. Here is one method:

   a. Have the students read the question and examine the passage for unfamiliar words, expressions, or ideas that will detract from their comprehension.
   b. Have the students restate the question in their own words. Explain that by restating the question they can determine if they understand its intent. If they do not understand the question, they are not likely to answer it correctly.
   c. Read the first sentence aloud. Ask the students to compare the information in the sentence to the title. Ask, "Does the title represent the ideas you find in the sentence?" Repeat this procedure for each sentence.
   d. Remind the students that a title should reflect the ideas of all the sentences in the selection. If one sentence contains ideas not reflected in the title, the title needs to be changed.
   e. Lead the students to see that the sentences tell about a worldwide Red Cross organization, not just the American Red Cross. They will thus come to see that the present title is not correct.
   f. As you explain each step, write it on the chalkboard.
   g. When you have finished, review the steps in the strategy with the students, then erase the steps from the chalkboard.
   h. Ask students to recall and explain each step in the strategy.

D. Apply the comprehension strategy.
  1. Prepare two questions of a similar type dealing with one passage from familiar reading material.
  2. Direct students to read the material silently to answer one question.
  3. Call on one student to answer the question, and ask others to explain the strategy for answering it.
  4. Repeat Steps 2 and 3 to provide additional practice.
  5. Be sure to provide daily practice opportunities to answer similar questions.

PRACTICUM EXERCISE

Now it is your turn. *First*, use the Classification Scheme for Reading Questions to prepare a number of questions on a reading assignment you will soon assign to your students. Prepare questions for each of the six major levels of the classification scheme.

Second, give students the questions and the reading assignment. After they complete the assignment, ask them to write answers to the questions. You can use a group question-answer discussion technique, but it is easier for students to mislead you with this technique. Analyze the students' answers. Students who have given fuzzy, incomplete, or incorrect answers can be placed in small groups for instruction.

Third, select one group of students who are having difficulty with a specific type of question, and prepare a lesson following the guidelines.

Fourth, provide instruction following the steps in the teaching plan.

Teaching Plan

A. Set the purpose for learning.

B. Assess the comprehension strategy.

C. Teach the comprehension strategy.

D. Apply the comprehension strategy.

Helping Students Comprehend

ANSWERS TO THE PRACTICUM EXERCISE

We hope your lesson went well. If not, refer to the discussion to determine why you had difficulty or see your instructor. Since every plan will differ, it is not possible to anticipate answers; therefore, we have not provided answers for this Practicum Exercise.

If you can prepare a plan for teaching question-answering strategies, you are ready for the Posttest. If not, refer to the appropriate Enabling Elements or see your instructor.

POSTTEST

Directions: Read each of the following statements and complete each Posttest item.

1. As part of this module, you were introduced to the Classification Scheme for Reading Questions. Name and describe the six major categories of questions in the scheme.
2. The Classification Scheme for Reading Questions is a useful tool for writing questions. Write one question for each of the six categories based on the following selection.

Sleep

Sleep is an unconscious state from which a person can quickly be aroused. During sleep the function of most vital organs is reduced. This reduction causes a person to become cool and require covers for comfortable sleeping. A sleeping person goes through periods of light and heavy sleep. The person also goes through periods when he or she does and does not dream. Dreaming seems to have an effect upon the quality of sleep. Although the necessary number of hours of sleep varies from person to person, most adults sleep approximately six to eight hours a day. Sleep cannot be stored in a body like energy in a flashlight battery, and therefore most people need to sleep sometime during each twenty-four-hour period.

3. Before you can help students understand their question-answering strategies, you must understand your own. Write the step-by-step procedure for answering the evaluation question you prepared for the preceding selection.
4. A plan for teaching question-answering strategies helps students improve their question-answering abilities. First, list the steps in the Teaching Plan; second, prepare a brief statement describing what occurs at each step of the instructional process.

POSTTEST ANSWERS

1. The six categories and their descriptions follow:
    a. Recognition and Recall questions. Questions in this category require a verbatim answer.
    b. Translation questions. Questions in this category require the learner to locate the exact answers and translate it into his own words.
    c. Application questions. Questions in this category require the learner to apply what he has read to solve a problem or change a situation.
    d. Analysis questions. Questions in this category require the learner to analyze the information he reads or find support for a statement.
    e. Synthesis questions. Questions in this category require the learner to combine parts to answer a question or create a new idea or product.
    f. Evaluation questions. Questions in this category require the learner to evaluate what has been read and make a decision using specified criteria. The learner must also justify his information, decision, and the evaluation criteria.
2. Compare each question you wrote with the Classification Scheme for Reading Questions. If you have prepared at least one question for each category, you have demonstrated the required competency.
3. Compare your question-answering strategy to the following evaluation strategy taken from the Sample Question-Answering Strategies in Enabling Element 3. If your strategy contains the same steps, you have demonstrated the required competency.
    a. Check the question and passage to be sure it does not contain unfamiliar words, expressions, or ideas. Clarify as necessary.
    b. Be sure the intent of the question is understood. Rephrase the question if necessary.
    c. Identify important information from that passage.
    d. Establish the evaluation criteria.
    e. Evaluate each basic unit of information in items of the appropriate criterion or criteria.
    f. Examine all evaluations and prepare a final decision.
    g. Justify the information gathered, evaluation criteria, and your final decision.
4. *Teaching Plan*
    a. Set the purpose for learning. At this step, the teacher establishes the need for instruction.
    b. Assess the comprehension strategy. Here the teacher asks students to explain how they answered a question, to as-

sess the adequacy of the learners' strategy for answering a specific type of question.

c. Teach the comprehension strategy. This step contains the procedures for teaching the question-answering strategy.

d. Apply the comprehension strategy. This step determines if the strategy taught is understood by the learners.

Final Comment

You have now acquired a competency that will help you substantially improve students' comprehension in your subject area. Using this competency requires only minor instructional effort by most subject area teachers. We hope you will make this minor adjustment.

If you have satisfactorily completed all Posttest items, you are ready to move to another module. If not, refer to appropriate Enabling Elements, see your instructor, or see the Reference list.

REFERENCES

Altick, R. D. *Preface to Critical Reading.* 4th ed. New York: Holt, Rinehart, and Winston, 1967.

Axelrod, J. "Some Flaws in Commercial Reading Comprehension Materials." *Journal of Reading* 17, no. 6 (1974): 474–79.

Bloom, B. S. et al. *Taxonomy of Educational Objectives: Handbook I, Cognitive Domain.* New York: David McKay, 1956.

Dale, E. "Develop Critical Reading." *Reading Improvement* 13, no. 1 (Spring 1976): 30–33.

Dixon, N. P. "A Test to Help Improve Instruction in Reading Comprehension." *Reading Improvement* 17, no. 1 (Spring 1980): 22–25.

Duffy, G. G., L. R. Roeheler, and J. Mason, eds. *Comprehensive Instruction: Perspective and Suggestions.* New York: Logman, 1983.

Durkin, D. "What Classroom Observations Reveal about Reading Comprehension Instruction." *Reading Research Quarterly* 14, no. 4 (1978–79): 481–533.

Flood, J., ed. *Understanding Reading Comprehension.* Newark, Del.: International Reading Association, 1984.

Galloway, P. "How Secondary Students and Teachers Read Textbooks." *Journal of Reading* 17, no. 3 (1973): 216–19.

Johnson, P. H. *Reading Comprehension Assessment: A Cognitive Basis.* Newark, Del.: International Reading Association, 1983.

Manzo, A. V. "Guided Reading Procedure." *Journal of Reading* 18, no. 4 (1975): 287–91.

Mize, J. M. "A Directed Reading Strategy for Teaching Critical Reading and Decision Making." *Journal of Reading,* 22, no. 2 (1978): 144–48.

Moore, W. E. *Creative and Critical Thinking.* Boston: Houghton Mifflin, 1967.

Newton, B. T. "Higher Cognitive Questioning and Critical Reading." *Reading Improvement* 15, no. 1 (Spring 1978): 26–27.

Ortiz, R. K. "Using Questioning as a Tool in Reading." *Journal of Reading* 21, no. 2 (1977): 109–14.

Pearson, P. D., and D. D. Johnson. *Teaching Reading Comprehension.* New York: Holt, Rinehart and Winston, 1978.

Sinatra, R. C. "The Cloze Technique for Reading Comprehension and Vocabulary Development." *Reading Improvement* 14, no. 2 (Summer 1977): 86–92.

Smith, C. B., S. L. Smith, and L. Mikulecky. *Teaching Reading and Subject Matter in the Secondary School.* New York: Holt, Rinehart and Winston, 1978.

M O D U L E 6

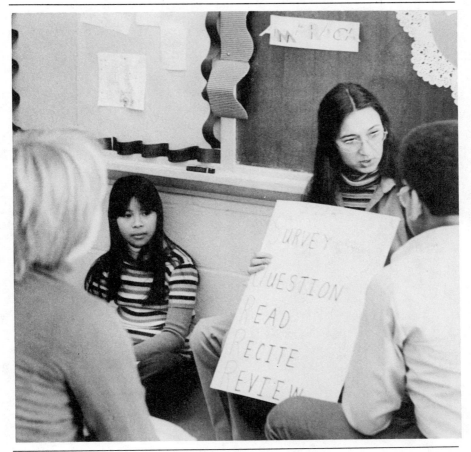

HELPING STUDENTS USE STUDY SKILLS AND STRATEGIES

CONTENTS

PROSPECTUS

RATIONALE

To read a textbook, your students need study skills and a study strategy. In fact, in a number of content area textual materials, they need *many* study skills and strategies. Study skills are necessary for locating, organizing, and interpreting information; study strategies are plans for reading textual materials that help the reader comprehend and retain more of the information while adjusting rate and style of reading according to its purposes. If you want your students to read textual materials effectively and efficiently you must teach the appropriate study skills and study strategies. In this module, you will learn the major study skills and an appropriate study strategy for your content area, and how to teach them to your students.

Terminal Objective

You will specify the major study skills from your content area, prepare a plan for teaching a study skill, and apply three study strategies.

Specific Objectives

1. You will specify the major study skills in your content area and prepare a lesson to teach a study skill.
2. You will write the associated words for each step in the SQ3R Study Strategy, write a paragraph describing each step in SQ3R, and describe a plan for teaching the strategy.
3. You will write the associated words for each step in the PQRST Study Strategy, write a paragraph describing each step in PQRST, and describe a plan for teaching the strategy.

4. You will write the associated words for each step in the SQRQCQ Study Strategy, write a paragraph describing each step in SQRQCQ, and describe a plan for teaching the strategy.

RESOURCES AND TIME REQUIRED

To complete the core Enabling Activities in this module, you will need blank paper, a writing instrument, and a subject area textbook. The estimated time for completing the core Enabling Activities* is four to five hours.

PRETEST

Directions: For each question, determine the word that indicates your belief regarding your competency. If you are in doubt, choose NO.

1. Every content area has its own reading and study demands. Can you specify the major study skills in your subject area and identify the steps in a plan for teaching a study skill?   YES   NO

2. Students who do poorly on follow-up tests based on reading assignments in social science materials can improve their performance with the SQ3R Study Strategy. Can you name the key words for the SQ3R Study Strategy and write a paragraph describing each step in the process?   YES   NO

3. Students who have difficulty with reading assignments in physical science materials can improve their performance with the PQRST Study Strategy. Can you name the key words for the PQRST Study Strategy and write a paragraph describing each?   YES   NO

4. Students who have difficulty with math problems that require reading can improve their performance with the SQRQCQ Study Strategy. Can you name the key words for the SQRQCQ Study Strategy and write a paragraph describing each step?   YES   NO

BRANCHING PROGRAM ALTERNATIVES
FOR PRETEST RESPONSES

1. You will need to teach specific study skills for effective and efficient study of required textual materials. If you know the major study skills in your content area and how to teach

---

*Core Enabling Activities are marked with an asterisk.

them, you are ready for Enabling Element 2. If not, Enabling Element 1 will be of interest.

2. Every student takes social science courses, such as social studies, government, economics, and psychology. Every student needs a study strategy for reading in the social sciences. If you can name a study strategy for the social sciences and write a paragraph describing each step in the strategy, you are ready for Enabling Element 3. If not, you will find Enabling Element 2 helpful.

3. All students receive some instruction in the physical sciences, with emphasis on physics, chemistry, physiology, and the like. When reading material from the physical sciences, all students need a reading study strategy. If you can name a study strategy for the physical sciences and write a paragraph about each step in the strategy, you are ready for Enabling Element 4. If not, Enabling Element 3 will familiarize you with such a strategy.

4. Mathematics is emphasized at every school curriculum level. Many students who do not have difficulty with straight computation problems have trouble with reasoning problems that require reading. Students can be more successful with such reasoning problems if they know and can apply a study strategy for mathematics reading. If you can name a study strategy useful for mathematics and write a paragraph about each step in the strategy, you are ready for the Posttest. If you think you need additional information, Enabling Element 4 will be helpful.

ENABLING ELEMENT 1
TEACHING STUDY SKILLS

SPECIFIC OBJECTIVE 1

You will specify the major study skills in your content area and prepare a lesson designed to teach a study skill.

ENABLING ACTIVITIES

*1. Read Study Guide 1 to identify the major skills in your content area and the steps for teaching a study skill.

*2. After reading Study Guide 1, prepare a plan for teaching a study skill from your content area. Complete Practicum Exercise 2.

3. Examine your textbook to determine all the study skills students need to understand the material in your content area. List the skills.

4. Together with colleagues, identify the study skills required for understanding and using the various textual materials in your subject area. Divide the responsibility of developing plans for teaching the study skills. Share plans with each other. After using the plans in class, meet with your colleagues to revise the plans as necessary.

5. Ask students how important it is for you to teach them the study skills necessary for locating and understanding textual materials in your subject area. Let their comments guide you in preparing future plans for teaching study skills.

STUDY GUIDE 1

In addition to being able to understand word meanings (Module 4), comprehend ideas (Module 5), and pronounce multisyllable words (Module 7), students need to understand the basic skills for locating, organizing, and interpreting information. We refer to this cluster of skills as *study skills.*

If you fan through the pages of any textbook in your area, you will notice they are full of information, pictures, graphs, charts, diagrams, work sheets, and other useful aids. The textbook also has a table of contents, and probably an index, glossary, and other front and back matter sections that are important for students to use effectively and efficiently when they study. Now consider that the textbook is only one source of information students use when they study. They also use dictionaries, encyclopedias, thesauruses, references, and guides. You can see that students need to master many study skills to study effectively and efficiently. Your students must be taught the specific study skills for reading textual materials in your content area. It is your job to teach these skills because you are most qualified. You know how to use the study skills for your content area, and through your demonstration, students will learn to study the way you do.

Study Skills

We have listed major study skills common to most textual materials; however, some study skills are unique to specific textual materials or subject areas. To make a complete list of study skills, you will need to (1) examine the following list of General Study Skills, and (2) examine textual materials in your subject area. From this examination, you should be able to compose a list of the skills students need to study textual materials in your content area and teach the study skills to your students.

General Study Skills
Locate information through:

1. Card catalog
2. *Reader's Guide to Periodical Literature*

3. Dictionary, to pronounce and define words
4. Encyclopedias
5. Thesaurus
6. Aids in the front and back of textbooks
   a. Title page
   b. Copyright page
   c. Table of contents
   d. Preface
   e. Index
   f. Glossary
   g. Bibliographies or References
   h. Appendixes
7. Government publications
8. Common references for your content area

Organize information by:

9. Preparing outlines
10. Writing summaries
11. Classifying topics
12. Associating whole to parts
13. Cause-effect relationships
14. Compare-contrast relationships
15. Problem-solution relationships
16. Time line

Interpreting information from:

17. Diagrams
18. Illustrations
19. Graphs
20. Charts
21. Time lines
22. Drawings
23. Cutaway patterns
24. Pictographs
25. Flowcharts
26. Pictures
27. Maps
28. Specific types of worksheets and/or balance sheets
29. Cartoons
30. Advertisements

PRACTICUM EXERCISE 1

Directions: List the five most important study skills for your content area. Be sure to first examine all the skills listed.

1.

2.

3.

4.

5.

ANSWERS TO PRACTICUM EXERCISE 1

If you (1) referred to the list of study skills in the Study Guide, (2) examined your textual materials for other important study skills, and then (3) listed the five major study skills, you have a good list.

Teaching Study Skills

When you introduce the textbook to your students, share with them the various study aids that are important for using the textbook. Most textbooks contain aids such as a title page, copyright page, table of contents, glossary, and index. Many also contain pictures, graphs, charts, and similar graphic aids. When you introduce the textbook, the first set of study skills you should teach students are those for understanding the purposes and uses of the title page, copyright page, table of contents, glossary, and index. As you move through the textbook, you will want to teach students how to use specific graphic aids to understand information presented in the various chapters.

When you introduce the textbook, ask students questions about the various textbook aids and identify those who do not understand how to use them. Then prepare a skills test following the suggestions in the module on diagnosis (Module 8) to determine how well students understand the aids. You will then have identified a group that needs instruction in using basic textbook aids. You can use the following lesson plan outline to prepare. Finally, with a lesson plan and a textbook and copies of the textbook for the students, you can teach them how to use the textual aids.

The basic lesson plan for teaching study skills contains four steps. (1) objective, (2) instruction, (3) evaluation, and (4) extension activities. A sample lesson plan shows you how to teach a study skill. Read the plan to see how instruction occurs. This plan can be used with a whole class or with only those students who cannot demonstrate the skill.

Demonstration Lesson Plan

Objective—The first step in any lesson plan is to state the purpose or objective. To do so, you need to determine what you want students to do after a lesson that they could not do before the lesson. Suppose students were not able to answer questions about the various sections of the textbook, perhaps because they have not seen a textbook of this type, or because they have never been taught to use the study aids in similar textbooks. The object of the lesson becomes. "Given a textbook, students will identify the major study aids and state the purpose of each."

Instruction—Here are steps to help students accomplish the stated objective:

1. Ask students to survey the textbook to identify its various sections or parts. As they identify them, list them on the chalkboard. They should identify front cover, title page, copyright page, preface, table of contents, chapters, glossary, index, and possibly other parts specific to your textbook.

2. Ask students to share what they know about each of the sections of the textbook. As they mention key points for each section, write them after the section title on the chalkboard. For example:

   a. Front cover—tells the name of the book and the author
   b. Title page—tells the name of the book, name of the authors, location of the authors, and publishing company and its location
   c. Copyright page—tells when the book was copyrighted, which is assumed to be the date the book was first available, and whether the book was previously copyrighted, which shows that this is a newer version of an older book
   d. Preface—the author explains the purpose for writing the book; may identify the audience for which the book was written and acknowledge those who helped with it
   e. Table of contents—outline of the various chapters or topics, showing how the book is organized
   f. Glossary—author defines generic and/or technical words he considers important for understanding the book
   g. Index—alphabetical listing of the various topics in the book, a finer breakdown of the topics than found in the table of contents; names of people, places, or things mentioned in the book are also included in the index

3. Now lead students through an examination of each section of the book. As you examine each section, discuss the information found there and how they can use it effectively and efficiently; as time permits, continue this way until you move through the whole textbook.

4. As you work through the textbook sections, it will be obvious that some students do not know how to use some of the more technical sections, such as a glossary and index; you will need to group them for additional study skills lessons.

Evaluation—You can determine how effective instruction was by calling on students and asking them to explain the various sections of the textbook.

Extension Activities

1. To reinforce what students have learned about the various sections of the textbook, you will want to give assignments requiring them to use the textual aids; you may want to give a list of questions that refers them to the table of contents or index to find sections where they can read to answer the questions. Some questions may ask them to define words in the glossaries. Also ask them questions that require them to read the copyright or title page.
2. Have students look through other content area textbooks to determine if they contain the same textual aids. Ask students how the textual aids will be useful, and allow them to support their statements by examining the textual aids.

PRACTICUM EXERCISE 2

One lesson usually leads to another, and it is likely that you will have a number of students who now understand the various sections of a textbook but do not understand how to use the more technical aids such as a glossary or an index. Suppose the students do not know how to use the index. On the sample lesson plan, write an objective for a lesson to teach how to use the index. Write the objective now.

Lesson Plan

Objective:

Instruction:

Evaluation:

Extension Activities:

Next, decide how you are going to demonstrate and what you are going to have students do to acquire understanding of an index. Outline what you will do, say, and require of students to accomplish your objective under the *Instruction* section.

When you have finished teaching, you need to evaluate the effectiveness of instruction. Write what you will do to evaluate how well your students have learned the purpose and use of an index. This will be not only an evaluation of how well the students learn, but also of the effectiveness of your instruction. Write your ideas under *Evaluation*.

Finally, you will need to provide students with activities for reinforcing and extending what they have learned about an index. Under *Extension Activities*, specify your ideas for helping students solidify their understanding and become more skillful at using an index.

ANSWERS TO PRACTICUM EXERCISE 2

The following lesson plan is one example for teaching students what an index is and how to use it. Compare it to your responses to see if you have provided a clear objective, appropriate instructional activities, useful evaluation techniques, and extension activities that truly reinforce and develop skill in index use.

Lesson Plan

Objective—Given a textbook index, students will state its purpose and demonstrate how to use the index to locate specific material in the textbook.

Instruction

1. Have students refer to the table of contents to locate the page on which the index begins, then have them turn to the index. Point out that each page of the index has two or more columns of information.
2. Have students use their index fingers to skim down each column on each page of the index, and point out that the index is organized in alphabetical order.

3. Next have students read the columns of information on the first page of the index, while you explain that major topics and subtopics are included in an index. Major topics are capitalized, and aligned on the far left of every column; subtopics are usually not capitalized, and are indented under major topics. Also point out the page references for topics and subtopics.

4. Direct students to a topic that has a number of subtopics. They should first read the topic and subtopics, then refer to the pages on which the subtopics appear. Lead the students to understand that a major topic may be dealt with in a number of places in a textbook, and the various page numbers after the major topic show which pages have information about it. The various subtopics are ideas that relate to the major topic; they too may be discussed on various pages, and the numbers after the subtopics in the index indicate the text pages on which they are mentioned.

5. Have students skim the major topics to see what kinds of information are included in the index. Point out that the index may mention names, places, and topics.

6. Point out any other features the index has.

7. Ask students to tell where they would locate information on various topics in their textbooks. Such an exercise gives students practice in rapidly locating topics and subtopics in the textbook.

Evaluation—Question the students to determine if they understand the purpose of an index, then give each student a topic and watch as she uses the index to locate the pages on which that topic is discussed. Watch as the students use the index to evaluate them for effectiveness and efficiency.

Extension Activities

1. At another time, ask students to locate information using the indexes in their textual materials.

2. Incorporate into your assignments activities that require your students use the index to locate information in their textbooks.

3. Hold time drills in which students compete with each other to locate information in their textbooks.

Now you should understand the basic skills that students need for independent study in your content area. You should also know how to prepare a lesson plan to teach these study skills. Some of the study skills should be taught when a textual source is introduced; others, when the need arises. The best time to teach study skills is *when students need them.*

Now that you are familiar with the basic study skills in your content area and know how to teach them, you are ready to learn about study strategies. You will learn about a different study strategy in each of the following three Enabling Elements.

ENABLING ELEMENT 2
THE SQ3R STUDY STRATEGY

SPECIFIC OBJECTIVE 2

You will write the associated words for each step in the SQ3R Study Strategy, write a paragraph describing each step in the process of using SQ3R, and describe a plan for teaching the strategy.

ENABLING ACTIVITIES

*1. Read Study Guide 2 to identify the five key words associated with this strategy and to learn how to use each step in SQ3R with a reading assignment in social science and humanities materials.

*2. Select a reading passage from a student textbook in social science or humanities. The reading passage should be approximately six to ten pages, *or* require approximately twenty to thirty minutes of sustained silent reading by the students. Follow the recommended procedures in "Using the SQ3R Study Strategy," and study the selection.

*3. Practice using the SQ3R Study Strategy with reading assignments containing few or no side headings. Prepare a plan for teaching students to use this strategy with reading assignments that have few or no side headings.

*4. Use the recommended procedure in "Teaching SQ3R" to prepare a plan. Following your plan, teach SQ3R to a group of students.

5. Reproduce the section entitled "Components of SQ3R," and distribute it to your colleagues. Discuss the possibilities for teaching this study strategy in all social science and humanities courses.

6. Compare reading rate and comprehension scores after students read two similar assignments, one using SQ3R and the other using your present reading strategy. What do your findings suggest?

STUDY GUIDE 2

Francis Robinson, concerned about the reading comprehension level of his students, found that the typical reader remembers only about half of what she is asked for on a quiz immediately following a reading assignment. This was the case for both average and superior high-school students. To deal with the problem, Robinson devised the SQ3R Study Strategy as a technique to increase immediate understanding and prolong retention. The strategy is well supported by results of studies investigating the learning process.

SQ3R is a five-step strategy: *Survey, Question, Read, Recite,* and *Review.* The first three steps evolved from research that demonstrated (1) the value of skimming over and summarizing headings before reading and (2) the value of knowing the comprehension questions before reading an assignment. Skimming to obtain an overview of the textual material orients one to the material and provides clues to what information will be presented. Questions provide specific purposes for reading and directions on how to read. Furthermore, the questions are generally connected by a thread of logic that makes them easier to remember. Because questions tell us the specific information we are looking for, they help us remember the information.

When Robinson's students applied the first three steps, Survey, Question, and Read, to assignments, the result was a higher level of immediate understanding. This result did not satisfy Robinson, because he knew that approximately 80 percent of what was read would be forgotten within two weeks. He also knew that retention could be improved by test-type reviews after the reading assignment. When test-type review sessions were held after reading, forgetting was reduced from 80 to 20 percent after a two-week period. Because of this substantial change in retention, Robinson added the last two components to his study strategy: Recite and Review.

The SQ3R Study Strategy that Robinson introduced many years ago has withstood the test of time. It has been widely accepted because the strategy serves as an advance organizer, provides specific purposes for reading, provides self-comprehension checks, and fixes information in memory. The SQ3R Study Strategy does not require additional reading time; in fact, after the technique is mastered, it generally requires less time.

Components of SQ3R

The student follows the five steps in the order they occur in the formula statement SQ3R: Survey, Question, Read, Recite, and Review. Here is an overview of the five components:

- **Survey.** When reading material includes side headings, the Survey consists of reading all side headings and the final or summary paragraph. If the material does not have side headings, the Survey consists of skimming paragraphs for topic sentences until a transition point is located. When the reader locates a transition point, he is to stop and reflect on the ideas in the last set of paragraphs and formulate a question about those ideas. This process continues until the end of the assignment.

- **Question.** Now the headings or major points are changed into questions. A question is used because, of all sentence forms, it probably provides the reader with the most specific direction. Questions serve as advance organizers for the total assignment, and each specific question provides immediate and specific direction for reading.
- **Read.** Taking each question in turn, one reads to locate the answer. The reader may skim, skip, or reread material as she chooses. The style of reading should vary with the purpose for reading.
- **Recite.** Recitation checks on clarity of ideas and fixes ideas in memory. After an answer to a question has been located or reasoned out, the reader should pause and recite the answer. Most students should recite their answers aloud. Students, like most of us, are more critical of their ideas when they are spoken aloud.
- **Review.** A review fixes in memory the overall organization as well as the specific ideas. Generally, one review should occur immediately after completing the reading assignment; second review within the next twenty-four hours, and a third, twenty-four hours later. Students with memory difficulties should periodically review throughout the reading assignment as well as continue the daily reviews.

Using the SQ3R Strategy

Before you can teach SQ3R to others, you must understand how to use it. So that you will have no difficulty teaching this strategy, follow our suggestions for using it on a reading assignment in one of the student textbooks in your subject area.

PRACTICUM EXERCISE

Identify a six- to ten-page selection in the textbook. The reading assignment should take approximately twenty to thirty minutes for your average reader to complete. Choose a selection you would like your students to read, because we will later ask you to use this passage with your students.

- *Survey.* Begin by surveying headings, charts, graphs, and pictures, then read the introductory and final paragraphs or summary. Surveying consists of a rapid reading of side headings or topic sentences to give the reader an overview of the content and the thread of organization. Stop reading and complete this step, then go to step 2.
- *Question.* After completing the survey, use the information you have obtained from headings and topic sentences to formulate questions. For most of us, questions provide a clearer focus

than other types of sentence constructions. A well-formulated question cuts down considerably on the amount of time it takes to locate information. Stop reading and complete this step, then go to step 3.

- *Read.* Now read to locate the answers to your questions. Reading here is not defined as looking at every word on every line of every page. It is legitimate to skim material, skip material, and reread material. The objective is to obtain the information necessary to answer your questions. Your style of reading should vary dramatically as the nature of the questions changes. Just as there is more than one type of question, there is also more than one style of reading. Stop reading and complete this step, then go to step 4.

- *Recite.* After you locate the answer to each question, look away from the textbook and recite the answer in your own words. It is important to recite the answer in your own words to be sure you understand what you have read and to avoid parroting. Depending on how important the information is, you may want to write a brief phrase to help you later recall the information. Stop reading and complete this step, then go to step 5.

- *Review.* When you finish the assignment, review the ideas you derived from the reading. Remember, immediate recitation followed by periodic reviews reduces memory loss from 80 to 20 percent at the end of a two-week period. Stop reading and complete this step.

ANSWERS TO THE PRACTICUM EXERCISE

How was it? If you are like most teachers, you found it very easy to apply this study strategy. You also found that you remembered more of what you read. If you timed yourself, you probably found it took you less time than you expected to complete this assignment. You surely noticed that your reading style varied with the nature of the question you asked—and it should! Remember, effective and efficient readers vary their reading style with their purpose for reading.

You are now familiar with the SQ3R Study Strategy and have applied it to a textbook in your teaching area. Now we will prepare to teach the SQ3R Study Strategy.

Teaching SQ3R

The instructional procedures for the SQ3R Study Strategy are divided into five steps.

Select Materials

1. Select a reading assignment six to ten pages in length or one requiring twenty to thirty minutes of sustained silent

reading by your students. Select reading assignments from suitable textbooks. For your first lesson, you can use the material you identified for the practice lesson from the Practicum Exercise in Study Guide 2 if it is suitable.

2. Prepare and duplicate copies of "Components of SQ3R" for each student.

3. Collect copies of nontextbook materials without side headings. You will need one copy for each student in your group. All students should have a copy of the same material.

Apply SQ3R

1. Read the six- to ten-page textbook selection using the SQ3R Study Strategy.
   a. *Survey* the selection.
   b. *Question* the material.
   c. *Read* and answer the questions.
   d. *Recite* answers.
   e. *Review* questions and answers.
2. Be sure to apply SQ3R with the same care and completeness you expect from your students.

Schedule Instruction. Schedule three fifty-minute periods for teaching the study strategy to your students. If possible, teach the three lessons within the same week.

Provide Instruction.

1. During the first fifty-minute period
   a. Explain to your students that you are going to introduce them to the SQ3R study strategy that they are to use when reading assignments in your class. Tell them the SQ3R strategy will raise their level of understanding, extend retention, and save study time. You may want to share other facts about how Francis Robinson developed the strategy.
   b. Distribute copies of "Components of SQ3R" to each student. Discuss each component so your students understand its function.
   c. Demonstrate the application of SQ3R with the selection you prepared. Answer any questions.
   d. Assign the same selection to the students, and direct them to apply SQ3R as they read it.
   e. When students finish reading the assignment, record their reading time and check their comprehension. Use this information in the following discussion.
   f. Begin a group discussion comparing SQ3R to prior reading strategies. Point out the advantages of study strategies such as SQ3R.

2. During the second fifty-minute period
   a. Review the SQ3R components.
   b. Demonstrate application of SQ3R with another textbook selection.
   c. Assign a different selection than you used for demonstration purposes and direct students to apply SQ3R as they read.
   d. When the assignment is completed, record reading times and check comprehension. Review the advantages of SQ3R.
   e. Assign another, shorter selection for additional practice using SQ3R.
3. During the third fifty-minute period
   a. Discuss application of SQ3R to materials without side headings.
   b. Demonstrate application of SQ3R to materials without side headings.
   c. Help students use SQ3R with material that does not contain side headings.
   d. When the assignment is completed, record reading times and check comprehension. Discuss advantages of SQ3R with this type of material.

Practice. Schedule ten- to fifteen-minute class periods for additional demonstrations and student practice sessions. You will need at least twenty teacher-directed practice sessions to raise this study strategy to the automatic performance level. It is just as easy on this level to apply SQ3R as it is to use any other strategy.

In stress situations, students have a tendency to resort to their most secure and automatic behavior patterns, so students may apply SQ3R in practice activities but not in actual assignments unless you provide sufficient practice to raise the skill to the automatic level of behavior. Encourage the use of SQ3R Study Strategy in every assignment by providing time for surveying and suggesting questions that can be used to guide reading. Whenever you use a new type of instructional reading material, demonstrate how to apply the strategy to the new material. Always stress and reward improved comprehension and extended memory as a result of using SQ3R.

Review the five steps of the SQ3R Study Strategy by listing them:

1.

2.

3.

4.

5.

We hope you now know how to use and teach the SQ3R Study Strategy. Take the next step and teach the strategy to someone.

ENABLING ELEMENT 3
THE PQRST STUDY STRATEGY FOR THE PHYSICAL SCIENCES

SPECIFIC OBJECTIVE 3

You will write the associated words for each step in the PQRST Study Strategy, write a paragraph describing each step in the process of using PQRST, and describe a plan for teaching the strategy.

ENABLING ACTIVITIES

*1. Read Study Guide 3 to identify the five key words associated with the strategy and write a paragraph describing each step in using PQRST with a reading assignment.

*2. In textual materials from various physical science subject areas, locate selections appropriate for your students. Identify selections that are approximately six to ten pages in length or require approximately twenty to thirty minutes of sustained silent reading by your students. Follow the recommended procedures in "Using the PQRST Study Strategy" to study the selection.

*3. Identify some reading selections in physical science materials that do not contain side headings. Practice the PQRST Study Strategy with these selections.

4. The plan for teaching SQ3R can be adopted for teaching PQRST. Write a paragraph that explains each of the basic steps for teaching PQRST and follow the plan to teach PQRST to a group of students.

5. Share with your colleagues the section "Components of PQRST." Show them how you used the strategy to improve comprehension and retention of information.

6. Contrast SQ3R and PQRST as study strategies to clarify how the strategies are applied differently to social science and physical science textual materials.

STUDY GUIDE 3

Physical science materials are written in a style that may require a unique study strategy. Although SQ3R may be useful for studying physical science materials, George Spache and Leo Fay recommend the PQRST Study Strategy. The difference between the SQ3R and PQRST Study Strategies is more than semantic; and we concur with Spache and Fay that PQRST be taught for studying physical science materials.

Scientific textual materials are written in a different style than most of the textual materials students are accustomed to reading. Science textbooks, for the most part, are not designed with the express purpose of imparting information. Their emphasis is on developing a way of thinking referred to as the *inquiry* or *scientific method.* The reader is generally required to follow a presentation of details that the author formulates into a generalization, theory, or concept. Once the generalization, theory, or concept has been formed, the student is shown how to test it through a series of experiments. Keep these points in mind as you read to understand the components of the PQRST Study Strategy, and as you see how the PQRST Study Strategy is applied to science textual reading materials. The science selections in this module are typical of, but shorter than, most selections in science textbooks.

Components of PQRST

Five steps form the PQRST Study Strategy. The reader applies the steps in the same order as they occur in the formula statement PQRST: Preview, Question, Read, Summarize, and Test.

- *Preview.* The student begins by skimming the title, side headings, and all pictures and other graphics to identify the generalization or theory the writer is presenting and supporting. The student cannot move to the next step and form questions until he identifies the writer's generalization or theory.
- *Question.* Next, the student seeks out the questions the writer is going to answer to supply information to support the generalization or theory. The student uses these questions as purposes for reading.
- *Read.* Then the student reads the selection to obtain answers to the purpose-setting questions. When there are more questions and facts than the student can trust to memory, he should write them down. Sometimes it is necessary to complete experiments before the student can obtain and understand answers to questions.
- *Summarize.* Now the student summarizes the information, preferably in written form. The facts related to each question

are grouped together, and a summary statement is prepared for each question.

- *Test.* Finally, the student tests the generalization against the supporting information. He must determine if the author answered the appropriate questions with sufficient information to support the generalization or theory. As students grow in age and scientific understanding, the criteria they use for testing generalizations will and should change.

You should now be familiar with the basis and components of the PQRST Study Strategy. Read on to see how the strategy is applied when reading scientific textual materials. First read the selection, "Your Nervous System," and then the explanation of how you should apply the strategy.

Your Nervous System

In your body the nervous system regulates all other systems. The nervous system can be divided into three separate but related systems. First is the *central nervous system*, which includes the brain and the spinal cord. Second is the *peripheral nervous system*, which includes the outward extension of nerves from the spinal cord to the base of the brain. Third is the *autonomic nervous system*, which controls both the central and peripheral systems through conscious activity and sensations. When we think of these three systems, it is best not to think of them as separate systems, but as interrelated systems, the interrelationship of which is necessary to sustain good health and life.

Here is how you should use PQRST to study-read this passage:

Preview. Skim the title and selection to gain an overall impression. You notice that the selection deals with the *nervous system*. The generalization the author is making is that the nervous system regulates all other systems in the body. The author has highlighted some important points for your attention. Anything that appears in capital letters or italics should be given special attention during previewing.

Question. There are at least one major and three minor questions to ask that are relevant to the author's basic generalization. What is a nervous system? How does the central nervous system relate to the nervous system? How does the peripheral nervous system relate to the nervous system? How does the autonomic nervous system relate to the nervous system?

Read. Using the questions as guides, slowly read the selection. Carefully attend to the facts that relate to your questions. Remember that facts are very important in scientific writing. Although many facts are needed to substantiate a theory, only a single fact is needed to refute it.

Summarize. Take the facts you have gathered and organize them into clusters around the four questions. First, summarize the facts around the three questions concerning the central nervous system, peripheral nervous system, and autonomic nervous system. Second, summarize all the facts related to the major questions on the nervous system.

Test. Examine the questions and answers to determine if the appropriate questions were asked and sufficient information was supplied to support the author's basic generalization. If the generalization passes the test, it can cautiously be accepted. If it fails, then additional information may be needed, or perhaps the generalization should be rejected. Remember, as students grow in age and scientific sophistication, their criteria for testing generalizations or theories will and should change.

PRACTICUM EXERCISE

Now it is your turn to apply the PQRST study strategy. Read the following selection using PQRST. The key words in the PQRST study strategy follow the selection; for each, describe the procedure you used to read "Weather Symbols."

Weather Symbols

The weather map used by meteorologists contains a variety of information. The quantity of information and ease of reading require that the information be codified. Three major classes of weather symbols are codified under (1) precipitation, (2) cloud cover, and (3) barometric change.

The precipitation code includes an asterisk for snow, a dot for rain, and an inverted triangle for showers. The symbols may be combined. For example, a dot over an inverted triangle means rain showers. An asterisk over an inverted triangle means snow showers.

The cloud cover code is a simple one. It uses only a circle. A clear circle indicates clearness or no clouds. A half-shaded circle indicates partly cloudy weather. A fully shaded circle means cloudy.

The barometric code is also simple. A horizontal line means steady. A line rising to the right indicates rising barometric pressure. A line falling to the right indicates falling barometric pressure.

Your knowledge of these signs will enhance your understanding of weather reporting. It will also improve your map-reading ability.

Preview:

Question:

Read:

Summarize:

Test:

ANSWERS TO THE PRACTICUM EXERCISE

The PQRST formula is a helpful mnemonic device for remembering the key words that will help you understand scientific writing. You should have found these key words helpful as you read "Weather Symbols." This is how you should have applied the PQRST study strategy to this passage:

1. *Preview.* You skimmed the title and the selection to gain an overall impression. As you were skimming, you noticed a sequence of three numbers used in the selection. The numbers should have alerted you to something important. If you stopped to read the sentence containing those numbers, you learned a great deal about the selection. You learned that the selection discussed three different types of codes. A quick glance at each of the succeeding paragraphs should have verified that observation. The generalization you searched for is in the last paragraph, where the author proposed that your understanding of weather reporting will be enhanced by an understanding of weather symbols or signs.

2. *Question.* At least two major and three minor questions should have come to mind. Although your questions may not have

been exactly like ours, they were probably similar. What are weather symbols? What are weather symbols used for? What are the weather symbols for precipitation? For cloud cover? For barometric change?

3. *Read.* Using the questions as guides, you read the selection slowly, and carefully clustered the facts around the questions.

4. *Summarize.* You took the facts you gathered and organized them into clusters around the questions you raised. You summarized the minor questions, then the major questions.

5. *Test.* You examined the questions and facts supporting each question to determine if they supported the writer's generalization. If the questions and their answers passed your test of reasonable support for the generalization, you cautiously accepted that generalization. If they did not pass the test, you reread the selection for additional questions and answers, or sought additional information from other sources, or rejected the writer's generalization.

If your answers and explanations agreed basically with those presented here, you are ready to try PQRST on scientific material of your own choosing. We hope that after you try the strategy, you will share it with your students.

Teaching PQRST

The instructional procedures outlined at the end of Enabling Element 2 for teaching SQ3R are also appropriate for teaching the PQRST Study Strategy. To teach the strategy, you first need to *select an appropriate reading assignment.* The assignment probably should be no more than six to ten pages in length or require no more than twenty to thirty minutes of reading time. Prepare and duplicate copies of "The Components of PQRST" from this study guide so that each student has a copy.

Second, apply the PQRST Study Strategy to the reading assignment you plan to use for teaching students how to use the strategy. Apply all the steps as you did in the preceding practicum activities.

Third, schedule instruction. Instruction probably should occur over three fifty-minute periods, preferably within the same week.

Fourth, provide the instruction by following the guidelines suggested for teaching SQ3R. Be sure your explanations and demonstrations are clear to your students.

Finally, provide opportunities for students to practice the PQRST Strategy both in school and home reading assignments. Remember, at least twenty teacher-directed practice sessions will be necessary before students become comfortable with the strategy. When they achieve a comfortable and automatic level, students will probably use the strategy without your reminding or prodding them. To encourage them to

continue using PQRST, always stress and reward improved comprehension and memory that results from applying PQRST.

You now know how to use and teach the PQRST study strategy in
physical science textual reading materials. Now teach it to someone to
help him become a more effective and efficient reader.

ENABLING ELEMENT 4
THE SQRQCQ STUDY STRATEGY
FOR MATHEMATICS

SPECIFIC OBJECTIVE 4

You will write the associated words for each step in the SQRQCQ
Study Strategy, write a paragraph describing each step in the process
of SQRQCQ, and describe a plan for teaching the strategy.

*1. Read Study Guide 4 to identify the six key words associated
   with this strategy and to write a brief description of each step
   in the strategy.

*2. Locate a number of math reasoning problems that require
   reading and following the procedures in "Using the SQRQCQ
   Study Strategy." Read and solve the problems. Did you find
   the study strategy helpful for solving the problems?

*3. Demonstrate the use of the SQRQCQ Study Strategy to a small
   group of students. This will give you an opportunity to practice teaching the SQRQCQ Study Strategy in a controlled
   environment.

4. Have students who successfully use the SQRQCQ Study Strategy explain and demonstrate it to students who are still mas-
   tering the study technique.

5. Select two mathematical reasoning problems that require reading and are of equivalent difficulty. Assign students to read the
   first problem using their traditional reading approach and to
   read the second problem using the SQRQCQ Study Strategy.
   After students have completed both, discuss the merits of a
   study strategy and when it might or might not be appropriate
   to use one.

6. Place your explanation of the SQRQCQ Study Strategy and an
   example of how it is applied to solve a math reasoning problem on an audiotape. Let students who are having difficulty
   answering reasoning problems and not consistently using the
   study strategy listen to the audiotape. Also, use the audiotape
   to introduce the strategy to new students who arrived after
   your initial explanation.

STUDY GUIDE 4

Students who have no difficulty with straight mathematical computations often have considerable difficulty solving problems that require reasoning and reading. This difficulty begins to appear in the intermediate and middle-school grades and continues throughout the school years. For the most part, students have difficulty with math reasoning problems because they do not know how to systematically approach and solve these problems. Leo Fay proposed a strategy for helping students solve mathematics problems requiring reasoning and reading, the SQRQCQ.

Components of SQRQCQ

The six steps in the SQRQCQ Study Strategy are *Survey, Question, Read, Question, Compute*, and *Question*.

- *Survey.* Begin by rapidly reading through the entire mathematics reasoning problem to determine what you are to do. Ask yourself a question or two about the problem to determine its intent.
- *Question.* Once you identify the intent of the problem, put the intent into question form. In addition, restate the problem, and attempt to further your understanding by visualizing, drawing, or speaking aloud.
- *Read.* Next, read to find the facts and relationships necessary for solving the problem.
- *Question.* With the facts and relationships clearly in mind, decide upon the processes for reasoning through or solving the problem by asking yourself, "What mathematical processes must I follow to obtain the correct answer to this problem?"
- *Compute.* At this point, you are ready to do the actual computation, but you must first set up the problem or problems on paper.
- *Question.* Finally, look at the answer to the problem and ask, "Does the answer appear correct? Did I answer the original question?" To answer the first question, check the computation. To answer the second question, examine the answer to verify its relationship to the intent of the problem.

Apply the SQRQCQ Study Strategy to this word problem:

John has been earning $55 a week working for Mr. Tomilson. With the money he earns, John wants to purchase a new motorcycle, which costs $330. How many weeks will John have to work to earn enough money to purchase the motorcycle on a cash sale?

1. *Survey.* Read the problem rapidly but carefully to determine the intent or outcome. From a survey of this problem, we

Helping Students Use Study Skills and Strategies

learn that (a) John wishes to purchase a motorcycle with his weekly earnings and (b) he would like to know how long it will take to buy the motorcycle if he applies the full $55 each week to the sale price.

2. *Question.* Now that the intent or outcome is clear, put it into question form. Remember, a question provides the most specific direction to the reader and serves as an advance organizer for sifting and locating key information. The question raised by this problem is, "With John's present weekly earnings, how long will it take him to buy the motorcycle?"

3. *Read.* Now it is time to look through the problem to identify the pertinent facts, which are that (a) John earns $55 a week, and (b) the motorcycle John wants to buy costs $330. Although no other substantiated facts are needed, there are some implied facts: first, that there will be no weekly deductions from John's $55 salary; second, that his weekly earnings will continue at $55 a week as long as it takes him to accumulate enough money to purchase the motorcycle. Third, it is assumed that the motorcycle cannot be purchased for a discount, nor will it increase in cost during the time John is acquiring his money.

4. *Question.* Now it is time to ask, "What mathematical process must I follow to obtain the correct answer to the question?" If the total cost of the motorcycle ($330) is divided by the weekly earnings ($55), we will obtain the number of weeks John has to work to accomplish his goal.

5. *Compute.* The computation is now carried out, resulting in an answer of six weeks.

$$55 \overline{\smash)330} \quad \overset{\text{6 weeks}}{}$$
$$\underline{330}$$

6. *Question.* At this point, one should ask, "Does the answer appear to be correct?" A simple check can determine correctness. Realizing that division is verified through multiplication, the participant multiplies six weeks times a weekly earning of $55 and obtains total earnings for the six weeks of $330.

PRACTICUM EXERCISE

Now apply the SQRQCQ Study Strategy to a mathematics problem.

Peter borrowed $95 from his father at an 8-percent annual interest rate. He agreed to repay the loan along with the interest at the end of three months. How much must he repay?

Describe the procedures you followed to solve this problem.

Survey.

Question.

Read.

Question.

Compute.

Question.

ANSWERS TO THE PRACTICUM EXERCISE

- *Survey.* Your quick but careful survey of the problem revealed that Peter borrowed money, which he would have to pay back at a specific time, along with a certain amount of interest for its use.
- *Question.* The question raised in this problem is, "What is the total principal and interest to be paid at the end of three months on a $95 loan at an 8-percent annual interest?"

- *Read.* The facts are: (1) the total amount borrowed was $95; (2) the loan is to be repaid in three months; (3) the 8 percent interest is a yearly rate, and Peter only has to pay interest on his loan for the three-month period of time he used his father's money. An assumed fact is that all the conditions of the loan will remain constant.
- *Question.* Next, ask "What mathematical processes must I carry out to solve this problem?" First, what is the yearly interest at 8 percent? This is a multiplication task. Second, what fraction of one year is three months? This is a process of reducing fractions. Third, how much is the interest for three months? This is a division process. Fourth, how much is the total principal and interest for three months? This is an addition process.
- *Compute.* The yearly interest at 8 percent is $7.60. Three months equals one quarter of a year. ($\frac{1}{4}$ of $7.60 = $1.90) ($95 + $1.90 = $96.90)
- *Question.* At this step, ask yourself "Is the answer reasonable?" Next, check each step of your answer to see if it is correct. Your verification revealed that the total principal plus interest payment of $96.90 is correct.

Teaching SQRQCQ

Now is the time to learn how to teach SQRQCQ to students who are having difficulty solving mathematics reasoning problems that require reading. An adaptation of the outline for teaching SQ3R and PQRST can be used to teach SQRQCQ Study Strategy. The instructional procedures are divided into five steps.

Select Problems.

1. Select a mathematics reasoning problem that requires reading and is typical of those with which your students are having difficulty. The best way to demonstrate the value of the SQRQCQ Study Strategy is to show students how it makes it easier to solve problems.
2. Prepare and duplicate copies of "Components of SQRQCQ" for each student.

Apply SQRQCQ. Apply the study strategy to the reading problems with the same care you expect from your students. Be sure to:

1. *Survey* the problem to determine what is to be accomplished.
2. Ask yourself a *question* that captures the intent of the problem.
3. *Read* to find the facts and relationships necessary for solving the problem.
4. Ask yourself a *question* regarding the mathematical processes necessary for solving the problem.
5. *Compute* as necessary.

6. *Question* the accuracy of your answer and its appropriateness for your original question.

Schedule Instruction. Schedule three fifty-minute periods for teaching the study strategy to your students. They will not master the strategy after a single lesson, so you will need to prepare additional lessons with other problems to help them develop mastery.

Provide Instruction.

1. During the first fifty-minute period
    a. Begin by explaining that you are going to teach the students how to use the SQRQCQ Study Strategy, which is designed for studying mathematics reasoning problems. Tell them the SQRQCQ Study Strategy will give them a structure for answering mathematics reasoning problems effectively and efficiently.
    b. Distribute a copy of "Components of SQRQCQ" to each student. Discuss each component so that students understand its function.
    c. Demonstrate how SQRQCQ is used to solve a mathematics reasoning problem. Answer any questions.
    d. Now have students work independently through the same problem, applying the SQRQCQ Study Strategy as they read to solve the reasoning problem.
    e. Have students write a statement describing how they use each step in the SQRQCQ Strategy to solve the problem.
    f. Hold a group discussion comparing SQRQCQ to prior reading strategies. Bring out the advantages of this study strategy.
2. During the second fifty-minute period
    a. Review the SQRQCQ components.
    b. Demonstrate application of SQRQCQ with another mathematics reasoning problem.
    c. Assign a different mathematics reasoning problem for students to read using the SQRQCQ Study Strategy.
    d. When the assignment is completed, call on students to explain how they applied the various steps in the strategy. Discuss their feelings about how they have grown in effectiveness and efficiency by using SQRQCQ.
3. During the third fifty-minute period.
    a. Again, discuss the components of SQRQCQ.
    b. Assign a number of reasoning problems to different individuals in the group. Tell the students to solve the problems with the SQRQCQ Study Strategy.
    c. As students work, circulate among them to answer questions and ensure that they are applying the steps in the strategy as you have taught them.

d. When the assignment is completed, allow students to share with each other how they applied the study strategy to solve the problems.

Practice. Continue to provide students with opportunities to practice SQRQCQ under your supervision. As with the previous study strategies, it will take at least twenty teacher-directed practice sessions before students reach the automatic performance level. You will know they have reached the automatic performance level when they begin to apply the strategy without your reminder. Always stress and reward the improved mathematics reasoning that results from using SQRQCQ.

Now it is your turn to identify a mathematics reasoning problem that requires reading and prepare a lesson for teaching SQRQCQ to a group of students. After you do this, you will have a good feeling about the new study strategy you have learned to teach. If you now understand and can apply SQ3R, PQRST, and SQRQCQ, you are ready for the Posttest. If you cannot, you should reexamine the appropriate Enabling Elements or talk with your instructor.

Important Cautions
A few words of caution are necessary before we leave the discussion of study strategies. SQ3R, PQRST, and SQRQCQ Study Strategies are all effective study tools; however, to be successful, students must (1) be familiar with the vocabulary, (2) be able to comprehend ideas, and (3) be able to pronounce the words. For the strategies to succeed, the material must be generally suitable for the students. The strategies should not be used to force students through material that is basically unsuitable for them. If textual materials are unsuitable, all the teacher can do is select new materials or rewrite the old; the first is the better solution.

Of course, to apply PQRST, a student must also be familiar with the scientific method as applied to the various areas of the physical sciences. Similarly, to use SQRQCQ successfully, the student must have mastered the basic mathematical operations.

POSTTEST

Directions: Read each of the following statements and complete each Posttest item as directed.

1. Study skills are techniques students use when they read textual assignments. List the five major study skills in your content area, then identify the components of a lesson plan to teach study skills.

2. The SQ3R Study Strategy was introduced by Francis Robinson to help students study social science reading assignments. We propose teaching this strategy to students for studying reading in social science and humanities materials. Write the key words associated with each letter in the SQ3R formula statement and write a brief description of each step.
3. PQRST was introduced by George Spache to help students read physical science textual materials. Write the key words associated with each letter in the PQRST formula statement, then briefly describe each step.
4. *SQRQCQ* was proposed by Leo Fay to help students solve mathematical reading/reasoning problems. Write the key words associated with each letter in the SQRQCQ formula statement, then describe each step.
5. Identify and briefly describe the steps in the instructional procedure for teaching any one of the three study strategies.

POSTTEST ANSWERS

1. Check your list of study skills against what you wrote for the Practicum Exercise in Study Guide 2. The four lesson plan components are *objective, instruction, evaluation*, and *extension activities*.
2. The key words associated with the SQ3R formula statement are:

    Survey
    Question
    Read
    Recite
    Review

    These are the procedures for applying SQ3R to reading assignments:

Survey	Begin by making a quick survey of the reading assignment to get a general idea of the selection. Refer to side headings and/or topic sentences as appropriate.
Question	Turn each heading into a question. If there are no headings, key topics should be turned into questions.
Read	Read to answer each question. Answer questions in the order they occur.
Recite	Recite the answer to the question with eyes averted from the passage. It is often beneficial to write key phrases in outline form.
Review	Review your questions and answers immediately after reading the assignment. Periodic reviews enhance retention.

3. The key words associated with the PQRST formula statement are:

    *P*review
    *Q*uestion
    *R*ead
    *S*ummarize
    *T*est

    These are the procedures for applying PQRST to reading assignments:

Preview	Skim the selection for an overall impression and to identify the writer's generalization or theory.
Question	Form questions to use as purposes for reading.
Read	Using the questions as guides, read the selection.
Summarize	Organize information and summarize, preferably in writing.
Test	Test the generalization or theory against the supporting information.

4. The key words associated with the SQRQCQ formula statement are:

    *S*urvey
    *Q*uestion
    *R*ead
    *Q*uestion
    *C*ompute
    *Q*uestion

    These are the procedures for applying SQRQCQ to math problems that require reading:

Survey	Read rapidly to determine the problem's intent.
Question	Determine what question the problem is asking or what problem needs to be solved.
Read	Read for facts necessary to answer the question to solve the problem.
Question	Decide what process to use.
Compute	Do computation.
Question	Ask yourself, "Does the answer appear correct?" Check the answer against the problem and facts.

5. The five steps for teaching any of the three strategies are:
    a. *Select* materials or math problems.
    b. *Apply* the strategy to the materials or problem.
    c. *Schedule* instruction for appropriate number of periods or length of time.
    d. *Provide instruction* following the suggestions provided.
    e. *Hold practice sessions* after instruction to help students apply the study strategy automatically.

REFERENCES

Askov, E. N., and K. Kamm. *Study Skills in the Content Area.* Boston: Allyn and Bacon, 1982.

Cheek, E. H., and M. C. Cheek. *Reading Instruction Through Content Teaching.* Columbus, Ohio: Charles E. Merrill, 1983.

Fay, L. "Reading Study Skills: Math and Science." In *Reading and Inquiry,* ed. J. A. Figurel, Newark, Del.: International Reading Association, 1965.

Harris, A. J. "Research on Some Aspects of Comprehension: Rate, Flexibility, and Study Skills." *Journal of Reading* 12, no. 3 (1968): 205–10, 258–60.

Herber, H. L., ed. "Developing Study Skills in Secondary School." *Perspectives in Reading*, vol. 2. Newark, Del.: International Reading Association, 1965.

Lamberg, W. J., and C. E. Lamb. *Reading Instruction in the Content Areas.* Chicago: Rand McNally, 1980.

McClain, L. J. "Study Guides: Potential Assets in Content Classrooms." *Journal of Reading*, 24, no. 4 (1981) 321–25.

Pyrczak, F. "Knowledge of Abbreviations Used in Classified Advertisements on Employment Opportunities." *Journal of Reading* 21, no. 6 (1978): 493–97.

Riley, J. D., and A. B. Pachtman. "Reading Mathematical Word Problems: Telling Them What to Do Is Not Telling Them How to Do It." *Journal of Reading* 21, no. 6 (1978): 531–33.

Robinson, F. P. "Study Skills for Superior Students in Secondary School." In *Improving Reading in Middle and Secondary Schools*, 2d ed., Ed. L. E. Hafner, New York: Macmillan, 1974.

Robinson, H. A. *Teaching Reading and Study Strategies: The Content Areas*, 2nd ed. Boston: Allyn and Bacon, 1978.

———, and E. L. Thomas, eds. *Fusing Reading Skills and Content.* Newark, Del.: International Reading Association, 1969.

Roe, B. D., B. D. Stoodt, and P. C. Burns. *Reading Instruction in the Secondary School*, rev. ed. Chicago: Rand McNally, 1978.

Singer, H., and D. Donlan. *Reading and Learning from Text.* Boston: Little, Brown, 1980.

Smith, C. B., S. L. Smith, and L. Mikulecky. *Teaching Reading and Subject Matter in the Secondary School.* New York: Holt, Rinehart and Winston, 1978.

Smith, C. F. "Read a Book in an Hour: Variations to Develop Composition and Comprehension Skills." *Journal of Reading* 23, no. 1 (1979) 25–29.

Spache, G. D. *Toward Better Reading.* Champaign, Ill.: Garrard, 1963.

Tadlock, D. F. "SQ3R—Why it Works, Based on an Information Processing Theory of Reading." *Journal of Reading* 22, no. 2 (1978) 110–12.

Viox, R. G. "Evaluating Reading and Study Skills in Secondary Classroom." *Reading Aids Series.* Newark, Del.: International Reading Association, 1968.

M O D U L E 7

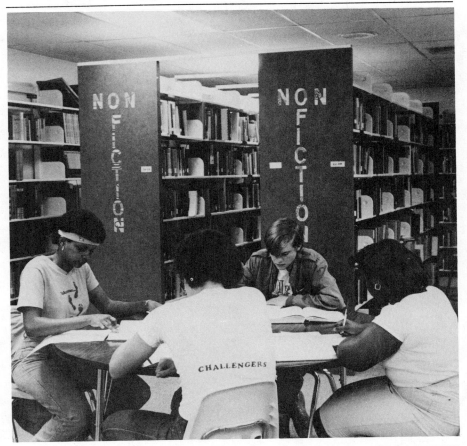

HELPING STUDENTS PRONOUNCE MULTISYLLABLE WORDS

CONTENTS

PROSPECTUS

RATIONALE

One characteristic of subject area textual material is its unique vocabulary. Generally, this vocabulary will consist of hundreds, if not thousands, of multisyllable words, such as *dispensation, tambourine,* and *horticulture.* Your students must learn to pronounce these words as well as acquire their meanings. Module 4 explained how to develop word meanings for technical words in your subject area; this module addresses pronunciation of technical words.

Most middle-school and secondary-school students will have acquired the necessary skills for pronouncing multisyllable words, but there will be some who have not. These students will rely on you to provide them with the necessary word-pronunciation strategy to read the textual material in your subject area.

This module will not acquaint you with the word-pronunciation skills taught in the primary grades; if you have students who need primary-grade reading skills, Module 10 offers suggestions for helping problem readers. For the most part, this group of students needs the help of trained reading specialists.

The purpose of this module is to provide subject area teachers with a brief but useful strategy for helping students pronounce multisyllable words. You will teach this strategy to students who did not acquire this strategy in the upper-elementary grades. Soon they will be able to handle reading materials that would previously have been difficult.

Helping Students Pronounce Multisyllable Words

OBJECTIVES

Terminal Objective

You will determine the word-pronunciation strategies students use and help them use a strategy for pronouncing multisyllable words.

Specific Objectives

1. You will prepare a written list of steps that make up the word-pronunciation strategy in this module.
2. You will prepare and use the Quick Test of Word Pronunciation, Word-Pronunciation Strategy Test, and Class Record Form.
3. You will list the major organizational steps and their purposes in lesson plans for teaching word-pronunciation skills and strategy.

RESOURCES AND TIME REQUIRED

Most of the materials required for the core Enabling Activities* are provided. You will also need eleven three-by-five inch, white index cards, a single sheet of two-by-three foot newsprint, and a few sheets of white paper. The estimated time to complete the core Enabling Activities is three to five hours.

PRETEST

Directions: For each question, determine the word that indicates your belief regarding your competency. If you are in doubt, choose NO.

1. During reading assignments, many students are confronted with multisyllable words they cannot pronounce, even when the words are in their listening vocabulary. Can you list the steps in a word-pronunciation strategy that can help students pronounce subject area words they have heard but not seen?   YES   NO

2. It is not always easy to identify students who are having difficulty pronouncing multisyllable words. Do you know how to construct, administer, record, and use the results of tests for assessing word-pronunciation skills and strategies?   YES   NO

3. To enable students with word-pronunciation difficulties to achieve in your subject area, you may need to teach them certain word-pronunciation   YES   NO

---

*Core Enabling Activities are marked with an asterisk.

skills and a strategy. Can you list each major organizational step and its purpose in lesson plans for teaching word-pronunciation skills and strategies?

BRANCHING PROGRAM ALTERNATIVES FOR PRETEST RESPONSES

1. Some students will confront multisyllable words they cannot pronounce in your subject's textual material. If you can list the steps in a word-pronunciation strategy, you are ready for Enabling Element 2. If you cannot, Enabling Element 1 presents a word-pronunciation strategy to use.

2. Since all students will not need to learn word-pronunciation skills or word-pronunciation strategy, you must identify those who need instruction. If you know how to construct, administer, record, and use the results of tests for assessing these skills and strategy, you are ready for Enabling Element 3. If you do not, Enabling Element 2 will help you achieve the objective.

3. After you identify students who need to acquire word-pronunciation skills and strategy, you must plan for their instruction. Can you list each major organizational step and its purpose in lesson plans for teaching a skill and strategy? If you can, you are ready for the Posttest. If not, Enabling Element 3 will give you this information.

ENABLING ELEMENT 1 A WORD-PRONUNCIATION STRATEGY

SPECIFIC OBJECTIVE 1

You will prepare a written list of steps that make up the word-pronunciation strategy in this module.

ENABLING ACTIVITIES

*1. Read Study Guide 1 and list the seven steps in the strategy.

*2. On a sheet of two-by-three foot newsprint or similar material, record the word-pronunciation strategy. Display the strategy permanently in the classroom. When students have difficulty pronouncing words, refer them to the strategy. Students will find the chart a valuable aid. Look at the "Strategy Chart" at the end of this Study Guide for suggestions.

3. Students who struggle to pronounce longer words may benefit from a discussion and examination of the more common

3. prefixes and suffixes. You can use the lists of common prefixes and suffixes in this module.

4. You may wish to do a content analysis of your subject area material to identify its many prefixes and suffixes. A form, the Subject Area Inventory, at the end of this Study Guide will help you with the analysis. Also, Appendix C of Burmeister's book (1978, pp. 364–88) includes an extensive list of prefixes and suffixes in specific content fields. Exposure to the isolated prefixes and suffixes will help students identify them in unrecognized words.

5. Provide small-group practice sessions for pronouncing multisyllable words from textual material. Spend one or two minutes daily in such groups to increase students' pronunciation effectiveness and efficiency.

6. Duplicate the word-pronunciation strategy on bookmarks and distribute them to every student. Give the extras to the librarian or other teachers.

7. Use the word-pronunciation strategy to practice pronouncing these words: *temperature, legislature, dramatic, stationary, exercise, inclination, bilingual, urbanize.*

STUDY GUIDE 1

By the end of sixth grade, some students will not have acquired all the necessary skills to identify some of the longer, technical words in the various content areas. If you wish to assign content area reading material to these students, you will need to provide word-pronunciation instruction. After you provide this instruction, you will find that students complete more reading assignments.

Characteristics of Problem Words

Some students struggle with reading assignments because they cannot pronounce all the words. Analyzing words the students have difficulty pronouncing will reveal that:

1. Many words begin with a prefix and/or end with a suffix.
2. Many words contain stems composed of two or more syllables. A stem is a base word or unit to which a prefix and/or suffix is affixed, such as *pay* in re*pay*ment.
3. Students who have difficulty pronouncing words approach unrecognized words in a haphazard way rather than with a definite strategy.
4. Many of the struggling students have the elementary phonics skills to pronounce the common one- and two-syllable words.

Word-Pronunciation Strategy

Using what we know about the kinds of difficulties students have pronouncing words, we can develop a strategy that will help many of them pronounce longer and more complex words. Teach students to:

Helping Students Pronounce Multisyllable Words

1. Look for a prefix.
2. Look for a suffix.
3. Locate the stem.
4. Divide the stem into syllables.
5. Try the word in context.
6. Look in a glossary or dictionary.
7. Ask someone how to pronounce the word.

Prefixes are language units that occur *before* a stem to change its meaning. Examples are *un-* in *uncertain* and *pre-* in *preview.* Many of the longer words that perplex struggling readers contain prefixes. Since prefixes are easy to spot, occur frequently in words that present pronunciation problems, and have highly reliable pronunciations, teaching prefixes is a likely place to begin a strategy.

Suffixes are language units that occur *after* the stem to change the function of a word. Examples are: *able* in *portable, -ly* in *miserly,* and *-tion* in *education.* Many of the longer and more perplexing words also contain suffixes. Since suffixes are also easy to spot, occur frequently, and have highly reliable pronunciations, they appear second in the strategy.

When the prefix and suffix are removed from a word, the *stem* remains. The stem is the next component of the word that must be identified. It is a base word to which a prefix and/or suffix may be added; it is the underlying language unit. Examples are *dance* in *dancer, fair* in *unfairly,* and *skill* in *unskillful.* A stem may not always be recognized as a word, however, as with *trac* in *subtraction* or *cep* in *perception.*

After isolating the stem, the reader must determine whether it has more than one syllable. If the stem is only a single syllable, chances are the student can pronounce the syllable, and can skip this step. Stems containing more than one syllable have more than one vowel, usually separated by one or more consonants; for example, mis-*cal-cu-late*, re-*fur-bish*, and uni-*lat-er-al*. When the stem is two or more syllables, it is necessary to divide it into separate syllables before pronouncing it. These are helpful guidelines for dividing stems:

- Stems following the consonant-vowel-consonant/consonant-vowel-consonant (CVC/CVC) pattern usually divide between the double consonants; examples are *but/ton, can/cel,* and *nor/mal.* This rule works well as long as the middle two consonants are not consonant clusters (*ch, ph, th, bl, st, cr*); natural clusters are usually not divided.
- Stems following the consonant-vowel/consonant-vowel (CV/CV) pattern usually divide after the first vowel; examples are *la/bor, fla/grant,* and *fi/nite.* After dividing the stem into syllables, the student can pronounce each syllable using reading skills acquired in earlier grades.

- Sometimes stems that follow the consonant-vowel/consonant-vowel (CV/CV) pattern do not divide after the first vowel, but rather after the consonant that follows the vowel; examples are *cab/in, pun/ish, trag/ic, plan/et,* and *man/age.* When CV/CV does not work, the students should be encouraged to try CVC/V.

When prefix, suffix, and stem have been identified and pronounced, the student should again read the word in the sentence. *Sentence sense,* or *context clues,* can be the most useful and reliable word-pronunciation clues if the word is in the student's listening vocabulary.

If these steps in the word-pronunciation strategy do not help, the student should be directed to use a textbook glossary or a dictionary to look up the pronunciation. If this fails, he should be directed to ask someone for the correct pronunciation.

Now you have the components of a word-pronunciation strategy. These instructional aids will help you teach the strategy.

1. *The Strategy Chart.* This is an abbreviated list of key components of pronunciation strategy. You can duplicate the strategy and distribute it to students, or construct a larger chart for display in the classroom.
   Key Terms to Remember
   1. Prefix
   2. Suffix
   3. Stem
   4. Syllables
      a. CVC/CVC
      b. CV/CV or CVC/V
   5. Context
   6. Glossary or Dictionary
   7. Ask

2. *List of Most Common Prefixes.* Bring this list to the attention of your students to ensure that none of these prefixes is causing word-pronunciation difficulties (Stauffer, 1942).

ab	dis
ad	en
be	ex
com	in
de	pre
pro	sub
re	un

3. *List of Most Common Suffixes.* This list can also be introduced to ensure that none are causing word-pronunciation difficulties. Pronunciation difficulties occur more often with suffixes than with prefixes (Thorndike, 1941).

ness	ant	ing	ed (d)
er	ment	ful	ly
tion	est	able	ed (ed)
ily	al	ed (t)	ent
y	ive	ance	ous

4. *Subject Area Inventory.* This form can be used to inventory prefixes and suffixes in subject area materials. Once identified, the prefixes and suffixes familiarize students with additional causes of word-pronunciation difficulties.

Subject Area Inventory

Source:		Source:	
Prefixes	Suffixes	Prefixes	Suffixes

The technical words you want students to pronounce in textual materials must be in their listening vocabularies before they can successfully use the word attack strategy, so you must first introduce the words orally in sentences. Second, write the words on the chalkboard for the students to see and study. Third, have the students say the words aloud to hear how they sound when they say them. Finally, for words that are likely to be most troublesome, have students write the words for further reinforcement.

PRACTICUM EXERCISE

Look through textual materials in your content area to identify 20 words that are potentially difficult to pronounce. Write the words, then use the seven-step word-pronunciation strategy to see how it would help students pronounce the words. To use the context-clues step in the strategy, read the sentences in which the words appear.

ANSWERS TO THE PRACTICUM EXERCISE

Answers will vary according to the words you chose, so check them over with a colleague and, as necessary, with your instructor.

If you know the steps in the word-pronunciation strategy, you are ready for Enabling Element 2, to help you identify students who need to develop their strategy. If not, review the elements as necessary or talk with your instructor.

ENABLING ELEMENT 2
ASSESSING WORD PRONUNCIATION

SPECIFIC OBJECTIVE 2

You will prepare and use the Quick Test of Word Pronunciation, Word-Pronunciation Strategy Test, and Class Record Form.

ENABLING ACTIVITIES

*1. Read Study Guide 2, then prepare the Quick Test of Word Pronunciation, Form A; Word-Pronunciation Strategy Test; and Class Record Form.

*2. Prepare the Quick Test of Word Pronunciation, Form B. Follow the same guidelines as for Form A.

*3. Administer the Quick Test of Word Pronunciation and the Word-Pronunciation Strategy Test to two students. Fill out the Class Record Form for these students.

4. After providing instruction following the suggestions in Enabling Element 3, administer Form B of the Quick Test of Word Pronunciation to see how students have grown in word pronunciation achievement. Readminister the Word-Pronunciation Strategy Test to see how they have grown in awareness of the strategy.

5. Construct and use tests of word pronunciation with different prefixes, suffixes, and syllabication generalizations.

6. You may discover that some students lack the basic pronunciation skills taught in the primary grades. You can refer to *Phonics in Proper Perspective* by Arthur Heilman for suggestions in teaching these skills.

STUDY GUIDE 2

A characteristic of subject area material is the introduction of specialized vocabulary—words used to label concepts in the subject. Specialized vocabulary is one element that differentiates one subject area from another.

Generally, specialized vocabularies consist of multisyllable words formed with prefixes, suffixes, and compound stems. Prefixes alter the meaning of words, suffixes change the function of words, and compound stems form new words.

Students often learn to pronounce new subject area words by looking at a word while listening to the teacher pronounce it. If there are only a few new words to learn, the student can memorize them. When there are many new words, memorization is inappropriate for most students; they must have another method or strategy to help them pronounce words.

During elementary school, many students acquire adequate methods or strategies for pronouncing unfamiliar words. These students will probably not need additional instruction. Others will need assistance to acquire a workable word-pronunciation strategy. If you take the time to identify these students and teach them the strategy in this module, they will be better able to accomplish the course objectives.

This Study Guide will familiarize you with simple tests to iden-

Helping Students Pronounce Multisyllable Words

tify students who need word-pronunciation skills and strategy. Enabling Element 3 contains detailed lesson plans for teaching skills and strategy.

Preparing Tests and Record-Keeping Materials

1. *Quick Test of Word Pronunciation, Form A*
   Print or type each of these nonsense words on the unlined side of a three-by-five inch index card. Print or type the "dictionary" spelling on the back of each card.

Front of Card	Back of Card
pronabment	pro/năb/ment
abstraimance	ab/strāīm/ance
comteationly	com/tēa/tion/ly
subsumptarant	sub/sŭmp/tär/ant
demomenence	de/mō/měn/ence or de/mŏm/ĕn/ence

   You can use Form B of the *Quick Test of Word Pronunciation* at the end of this Study Guide for students who were absent or to evaluate achievement after instruction.

2. *Word-Pronunciation Strategy Test*
   Take one three-by-five index card and print or type the following question on one side.

   > When you come to a word in a sentence that you do not immediately recognize, how do you go about pronouncing that word? (What do you do first, second, third, etc., may be asked if further elaboration is necessary.)

3. *Class Record Form*
   Prepare a Class Record Form as in Table 7-1 for recording students' word-pronunciation difficulties. You will need one record form for each class.

Table 7-1 Quick Test of Word Pronunciation Class Record Form

Names of Students	Skills Unknown						Strategy Not Known
	Prefix	Suffix	Single Syllable Stems	Multiple CVC/CVC Stems	Multiple CV/CV CVC/V Stems	Context Clues	

Test Administration, Interpretation, and Record Keeping

1. On a Class Record form, record the name of every student in the class you have decided to test.
2. Arrange your class schedule to allow about three minutes for testing each student.
3. Each student must be tested separately, where other students cannot hear what is said. It is not necessary to be out of sight.
4. When the student arrives at the testing center, explain that you want to determine whether he has the necessary word-pronunciation skills and a strategy for pronouncing longer words in the textual material.
5. Begin by exposing, one at a time, the cards containing the multisyllable nonsense words. Explain that these are nonsense words and you want the student to pronounce them as if they were real words.
6. As the student pronounces each nonsense word, look for the following difficulties. As a difficulty is identified, place a check mark after the student's name under the appropriate category on the Class Record Form.

Nonsense Word	Sources of Difficulty
pronabment	pro—prefix
	nab—stem
	ment—suffix
abstraimance	ab—prefix
	straim—stem
	ance—suffix
comteationly	com—prefix
	tea—stem
	tion—suffix
	ly—suffix
subsumptarant	sub—prefix
	sump/tar—stem (CVC/CVC)
	ant—suffix
demomenence	de—prefix
	mo/men—stem (CV/CV or CVC/V)
	ence—suffix

These are how the nonsense words were pronounced by a student. Look at the errors, then see how they are classified on the Class Record Form.

Nonsense Word	Pronounced by Student	Errors
pronabment	pro/nab/ent	1 suffix
abstraimance	ab/strum/ent	1 stem; 1 suffix
comteationly	com/tea/tal/ty	2 suffixes
subsumptarant	sub/sumpt/ent	1 CVC/CVC; 1 suffix
demomenence	de/mome/nence	1 CV/CV; 1 suffix

Helping Students Pronounce Multisyllable Words

The errors are recorded on the Class Record Form in Table 7-2.

Table 7-2 Quick Test of Word Pronunciation Class Record Form

Names of Students	Skills Unknown						Strategy Not Known
	Prefix	Suffix	Single Syllable Stems	Multiple CVC/CVC Stems	Multiple CV/CV CVC/V Stems	Context Clues	
Jack		√√√ √√√	√	√	√		√

7. To determine whether students are using context clues to pronounce words, you can observe them as they read, as well as ask them if they use the clues. Students who use context clues should be able to demonstrate how they use them.

8. Next, place the single three-by-five card containing the Word-Pronunciation Strategy Test in front of the students. Ask the student to read aloud and answer the question on this card. It is acceptable to read the question to the student. (It may be necessary to probe for a student's most complete answer.) Compare the student's answer with the strategy in this module:
   a. Look for a prefix.
   b. Look for a suffix.
   c. Locate the stem.
   d. Divide the stem into syllables.
   e. Try the word in context.
   f. Look in a glossary or dictionary.
   g. Ask someone who knows.

It is not necessary for the student's answers to contain precisely the same words, or the same number of steps, or give the steps in the same order. There are other acceptable ways to state the strategy, and you will have to use your professional judgment as to whether the strategy is expressed adequately. You will become better at this with practice. If a student omits a step, place a check mark after his name in the column "Strategy Not Known." For example, we asked Jack, "When you come to a word in a sentence that you do not immediately recognize, how do you go about pronouncing that word?" He responded, "Look for a beginning and ending that I know and divide the word into syllables." When Jack was asked to tell more about how he pronounced words, he said "That's all I know." Jack appeared to be aware of prefixes, suffixes, and syllabication, but did not demonstrate awareness of context clues, glossary or dictionary, nor his responsibility to ask for the pronunciation of an unknown word.

Now it is time to identify word-pronunciation skill and strategy errors and classify them appropriately in the Class Record Form, Table 7-3.

Table 7-3 Quick Test of Word Pronunciation Class Record Form

Names of Students	Skills Unknown						Strategy Not Known
	Prefix	Suffix	Single Syllable Stems	Multiple CVC/CVC Stems	Multiple CV/CV CVC/V Stems	Context Clues	
Jack		√√√ √√√	√	√	√		√
Mary							

PRACTICUM EXERCISE

Mary pronounced the following words as indicated. Classify her errors in the Class Record Form in Table 7-3.

Nonsense Words	Pronounced by Student	Summary of Errors
pronabment	pro/na/bent	_____
abstraimance	ab/strum/any	_____
comteationly	com/tea/ton/ty	_____
subsumptarant	sub/sumt/ance	_____
demomenence	de/mon/en/ed	_____

Mary said her strategy is "I look for a beginning that I know and guess." Record your assessment.

Mary did not appear to use context clues to pronounce unrecognized words. When asked, she agreed with the observation.

ANSWERS TO THE PRACTICUM EXERCISE

Examination of Mary's errors revealed the following conclusions. Check marks should appear in the appropriate columns on the Class Record.

Nonsense Word	Pronounced by Student	Summary of Errors
pronabment	pro/na/bant	1 stem; 1 suffix
abstaimance	ab/strum/any	1 stem; 1 suffix
comteationly	com/tea/ton/ty	2 suffixes
subsumptarant	sub/sumt/ance	1 CVC/CVC; 1 suffix
demomenence	de/mon/en/ed	1 CV/CV; 1 suffix

Mary's strategy is inadequate. It is limited to looking for prefixes and guessing. A check mark should be placed in the Class Record Form in Table 7-4 under Strategy Not Known.

Table 7-4 Quick Test of Word Pronunciation Class Record Form

Names of Students	Skills Unknown							Strategy Not Known
	Prefix	Suffix	Single Syllable Stems	Multiple CVC/CVC Stems	Multiple CV/CV CVC/V Stems	Context Clues		
Jack		√√√ √√√		√	√			√
Mary		√√√√ √√	√√	√	√			√

Retesting

You will want to retest students from time to time to determine if they have improved in word-pronunciation skills and strategy. Since students may become familiar with the nonsense words used for the Quick Test of Word Pronunciation, Form A, we have given an equivalent list for retesting. Prepare the Quick Test of Word Pronunciation, Form B, in the same manner and format as Form A. It is not necessary to prepare another Word-Pronunciation Test or Class Record Form.

1. *Quick Test of Word Pronunciation, Form B*
   Print or type each of the nonsense words on the unlined side of a three-by-five index card. Print or type the "dictionary" spelling on the back of each card.

Front of Card	Back of Card
premeply	pre/mĕp/ly
exscreemest	ex/scrēḗm/est
subpeedtionous	sub/pēḗd/tion/ous
unpetsuming	un/pĕt/sum/ing
besimenable	be/sī/mĕn/able or be/sĭm/ĕn/able

Nonsense Word	Sources of Difficulty
premeply	pre—prefix
	mep—stem
	ly—suffix
exscreemest	ex—prefix
	screem—stem
	est—suffix
subpeedtionous	sub—prefix
	peed-stem
	tion—suffix
	ous—suffix
unpetsuming	un—prefix
	petsum—stem (CVC/CVC)
	ing—suffix
besimenable	be—prefix
	simen—stem (CV/CV or CVC/V)
	able—suffix

2. *Word-Pronunciation Strategy Test*
   Use the three-by-five index cards you prepared for this test to go along with Form A. Since the test is basically a question the student answers, it can be used with both Form A and Form B.
3. *Class Record Form*
   Use the same Class Record Form you used with Form A to record the results on Form B. You can thus rapidly identify the growth areas for each student you test.

If you have prepared the Quick Test of Word Pronunciation, Forms A and B, Word-Pronunciation Strategy Test, and Class Record Form, and have classified errors correctly in the Practicum Exercises, you are ready for Enabling Element 3. Enabling Element 3 provides directions and lesson plans for teaching word-pronunciation skills and strategy. If you had difficulty with any of the Enabling Elements, reexamine them, or see your instructor.

ENABLING ELEMENT 3
TEACHING WORD-PRONUNCIATION SKILLS

SPECIFIC OBJECTIVE 3

You will list the major organizational steps and their purposes in lesson plans for teaching word-pronunciation skills and strategy.

ENABLING ACTIVITIES

*1. Read Study Guide 3 to learn the major organizational steps in seven lesson plans for developing a strategy for pronouncing multisyllable words.

*2. Teach the seven plans to one or two students who need this instruction.

*3. Look through textual material to locate prefixes and suffixes not included in the lesson plans in this Study Guide. Modify the plans to include these prefixes and suffixes.

4. If you have an aide or school volunteer, familiarize her with the instructional procedure in this Enabling Element. Have the aide teach students who need a word-pronunciation strategy.

5. Peer teaching has been found effective in many situations, so you may want to use some of your better students as tutors.

STUDY GUIDE 3

Word-Pronunciation Strategy

The lessons in this Study Guide are designed to develop a precise word-pronunciation strategy. The strategy applies to longer, multi-syllable words that often perplex subject area students when the words are in students' listening vocabularies but *not* in their reading vocabularies. If the word is not in their listening vocabularies, the problem is word meaning, not pronunciation, and you should refer to Module 4, "Teaching Word Meanings." If the problem is pronunciation, the lesson plans in this Study Guide will help students improve pronunciation. The lesson plans are designed to develop an understanding of specific word-pronunciation skills, which make up a word-pronunciation strategy.

1. Look for prefix.
2. Look for suffix.
3. Locate the stem.
4. Divide the stem into syllables.
5. Try it in context.
6. Refer to glossary or dictionary.
7. Ask someone.

There are seven lessons in the instructional set, and each lesson requires twenty to thirty minutes to teach, according to the amount of teacher direction and discussion. The lessons should be taught in the sequence in which they appear in this instructional set.

There are three major organizational steps in each lesson plan: purpose, instruction, and generalization. The information in the purpose section substantiates the need for this skill. The instruction step contains directions and information for developing word-pronunciation skills and strategy. At the generalization step, the student is led to conclude that the pronunciation skill he has just acquired is one of several skills that form the strategy. The student soon learns that with each succeeding lesson, the generalization gets longer, until it consists of all seven steps in the strategy.

Helping Students Pronounce Multisyllable Words

Choosing Your Lessons

Not every student needs every lesson in the set. For example, the Class Record in Study Guide 2 reveals that Mary needs instruction in identifying suffixes, identifying single syllables, and with all syllabication generalizations. She also needs to become familiar with the steps in the word-pronunciation strategy. She appears to recognize prefixes and use context clues, so she does not need instruction in these skills. Since Mary does not know the word-pronunciation strategy, her first lesson should give an overview of the strategy. She should be shown how to use the seven steps in the strategy to recognize a written word that is in her listening vocabulary. Then Mary should receive instruction in suffix recognition (lesson 2), single syllable stems (lesson 3), and syllabication generalizations (lessons 4 and 5). Begin with the suffix lesson plan and proceed in order.

When students are familiar with the pronunciation strategy and have only specific skill difficulties, you need to teach only the specific skill lessons that correspond to their difficulty. They should be taught in the order they occur in the lesson plans that follow. When students know all the pronunciation skills but are unfamiliar with the strategy, you need to show them only the strategy. Now complete Practicum Exercise 1 to demonstrate that you understand these last guidelines for planning instruction.

PRACTICUM EXERCISE 1

If Marty demonstrates the needs shown in Table 7-5, where and how should you begin instruction?

Table 7-5 Quick Test of Word Pronunciation Class Record Form

Names of Students	Skills Unknown							Strategy Not Known
	Prefix	Suffix	Single Syllable Stems	Multiple CVC/CVC Stems	Multiple CV/CV CVC/V Stems	Context Clues		
Jack		√√√ √√√	√	√	√			√
Mary		√√√√ √√	√√	√	√			√
Marty		√√√	√√	√	√			√
Bob					√			

ANSWERS TO PRACTICUM EXERCISE 1

Since Marty does not know the word-recognition strategy, you must review it with him. Then begin teaching, using lesson 2 for suffixes, lesson 3 for single syllable stems, and lessons 4 and 5 to teach the basic syllabication generalizations.

PRACTICUM EXERCISE 2

Now look at the information in the Class Record Form for Bob. How would you provide instruction?

ANSWER TO PRACTICUM EXERCISE 2

Bob is aware of all the steps in the word-pronunciation strategy, but has difficulty with one word-pronunciation skill. He needs instruction in the generalization of CV/CV and CVC/V for syllabication.

Now you know how to use the Class Record Form to differentiate instruction. You are also aware that some students will need to be taught only the word-recognition strategy, and others will need both the strategy and specific word-pronunciation skills. Still others will need to be taught only specific skills. You are ready to read the seven lesson plans in the instructional set. Read each lesson, giving your full attention to the three organizational steps and to the directions and information under each step.

Word-Pronunciation Lesson 1—Prefix

A. *Purpose:*
   Being able to detect a common prefix can enable a student to unlock an unknown word. This lesson (1) acquaints students with common prefixes and (2) builds recognition of prefixes as pronunciation units.
B. *Instruction:*
   1. Write the following stems on the chalkboard. Have students read them, then discuss the meaning of *stem* as a base word to which a prefix is added. You may wish to have students find additional examples in the dictionary.

sent	come	verb	press	grace
fine	done	side	forest	fix
noun	ability	act	camp	

   2. Here are some common prefixes. Write each one on the chalkboard. Direct students' attention to each prefix as you pronounce it. You may wish to discuss the meaning of the prefix, but this is not necessary, since the primary purpose of the lesson is prefix identification and pronunciation.

ab	ad	be	com	de	pro	re
dis	en	ex	in	pre	sub	un

3. Attach the common prefixes to the known root words presented in step 1 and have students pronounce the new words.

absent	become	adverb	compress	disgrace
define	undone	subside	reforest	prefix
pronoun	inability	exact	encamp	

4. Now that the students are familiar with the common prefixes and have had an opportunity to see them in words, a practice activity will be useful. Place the following words on the chalkboard; as you do so, direct students to (a) identify and pronounce the prefix, (b) identify and pronounce the stem, and (c) blend the two to pronounce the affixed word.

abnormal	defame	prorate	adjoin	degrade
adjust	prewar	export	beside	bespeak
commit	unwed	disarm	input	submit

5. Tell students that many words begin with patterns that look exactly like these prefixes. In some cases, the beginning patterns are not prefixes, but some of the words can nevertheless be pronounced in the same way as the prefixed words. (Example: *preach, perk, deal, dean.*)

6. Locate words in subject area materials that contain other prefixes and teach the prefixes as you did in this lesson.

C. *Generalization:*
Through discussion, lead students to conclude that looking for prefixes is the first step in a word-pronunciation strategy. You may wish to record this step on a chart or chalkboard for reference before introducing the second lesson, or have students record it on a sheet of notebook paper reserved for the word-pronunciation strategy, as follows:

1. Look for a prefix.

Word-Pronunciation Lesson 2—Suffix

A. *Purpose:*
Being able to detect a common suffix can enable a student to decipher an unknown word. This lesson (1) acquaints students with common suffixes and (2) builds recognition of suffixes as pronunciation units.

B. *Instruction:*
1. Write the following stems on the chalkboard. Have students read them. If some students are still unclear about the meaning of *stem*, clarify its meaning. It may be necessary to have students locate examples in a dictionary.

hope	happy	move	educate	walk
mail	high	skill	arm	act
love	talk	nerve	want	

2. Here are some common suffixes. Write each suffix on the chalkboard. Direct students' attention to each suffix as you pronounce it. You may wish to discuss the meaning of the suffix, but this is not necessary, since the primary purpose of the lesson is suffix identification and pronunciation.

ness	ily	est	y	tion
ly	ous	er	ant	ent
able	ance	ed (ed)	ed (d)	ive
al	ing	ed (t)	ful	ment

3. Attach the common suffixes to the known stems presented in step 1 and ask students to pronounce the new words.

hopeful	higher	active	happily
mailable	talked (t)	nervous	happiness
lovely	movement	education	wanted (ed)
walking	army	happiest	skilled (d)

4. Now that the students are familiar with the common prefixes and suffixes and have used them to build words, they need a practice activity to help build their recognition of prefixes and suffixes to the automatic recognition level. Write the following words on the chalkboard and ask students to (a) identify and pronounce the prefix, (b) identify and pronounce the suffix, (c) identify and pronounce the stem, and (d) blend and pronounce the affixed word.

reloading	prepayment	inactive	department
refreshment	enjoyment	preheated	unfairly
preschooler	abnormally	unskillful	prolonged

5. Locate words in subject area materials that contain other suffixes. Teach the suffixes as you did in this lesson.

C. *Generalization:*

Through discussion, lead students to conclude that looking for suffixes is the second step in a word-pronunciation strategy. You may wish to record this step on a chart or chalkboard before introducing the third lesson, so students can refer to it during the lesson, or have them record it on a sheet of notebook paper reserved for the strategy. Show students that they have now developed a two-step strategy, and have them record it:

1. Look for a prefix.
2. Look for a suffix.

Word-Pronunciation Lesson 3—Stems

A. *Purpose:*

   Identification of stems precedes their pronunciation. This lessons (1) acquaints students with one- and two-syllable stems and (2) builds recognition of stems as pronunciation units.

B. *Instruction:*

   1. Write the following words on the chalkboard, pointing out that they contain prefixes and/or suffixes. Identify the stems through analysis of each word, first for the prefix and then for the suffix. Point out that once these elements have been identified, the remaining word or syllable is the stem.

camping	mainly	installment	entrenchment
discovering	enrichment	predisposition	undesirable
reboarding	unsinkable	removed	unknowingly

   2. Show students the procedure for pronouncing the words. First pronounce the prefix, then pronounce the suffix, then pronounce the stem; next, blend and pronounce the word. Now direct the students to pronounce the words using this strategy.

   3. Either teacher or students can locate words in subject area materials that contain other prefixes and/or suffixes. The words can be analyzed with the strategy in this lesson.

C. *Generalization:*

   Through discussion, lead students to conclude that they should use the following strategy when they encounter an unknown word in their reading. You may wish to record this third step on the strategy chart or chalkboard before introducing the fourth lesson, so students can refer to it during the lesson, or have students record it on a sheet of notebook paper reserved for the strategy. Their strategy should now contain these three steps:

   1. Look for a prefix.
   2. Look for a suffix.
   3. Look for a stem.

Word-Pronunciation Lesson 4—Syllabication CVC/CVC

A. *Purpose:*

   After identifying a prefix and/or suffix, students often must pronounce a multisyllable stem. A few general guidelines for dividing stems into syllables will help. This lesson (1) acquaints students with one of two common techniques for dividing stems into syllables and (2) provides practice in using this technique to pronounce words.

B. *Instruction:*

1. Ask students to listen closely as you pronounce some words. Tell them you will be pronouncing two-syllable words and want them to identify the separate syllables after you pronounce each word. Elongate each syllable as you pronounce these words:

   cargo   cattle   pencil
   person   summer   circus

2. After you pronounce the words and students identify the separate syllables in each, write the words on the chalkboard. Then review pronunciation and re-identify the separate syllables. Draw a slash mark (/) between the two syllables in each word.

   car/go   cat/tle   pen/cil
   per/son   sum/mer cir/cus

3. Show students' that each word divides between two consonants, and that each word follows the consonant-vowel-consonant/consonant-vowel-consonant pattern (CVC/CVC). Have students draw from this observation a generalization they can apply to similar words.

4. They should draw a generalization such as this: In multisyllable stems of the CVC/CVC pattern, the separate syllables usually divide between the two consonants. (The exact words need not be used.)

5. Now that students are familiar with the first syllabication technique, a practice activity is necessary to improve their skill in applying it. These words are useful for practicing this technique.

   carrot   center   donkey   picnic   valley
   corner   settle   barrel   follow   grammar
   napkin   silver   garden   suggest bottle

6. Have students skim the pages in their most recent reading assignment to locate multisyllable words that follow the CVC/CVC pattern. You can locate words in subject area materials that contain this pattern for additional practice for the students.

C. *Generalization:*

Through discussion, lead students to conclude that the CVC/CVC pattern is useful for dividing multisyllable stems into their separate syllables. Record this step on a chart or a chalkboard, or have students record it in their notebooks. Show students that the strategy is now one step longer.

1. Locate the prefix.
2. Locate the suffix.
3. Identify the stem.
4. Divide into syllables using CVC/CVC pattern.

Word-Pronunciation Lesson 5—Syllabication CV/CV or CVC/V

A. *Purpose:*

Even when a prefix and/or suffix has been identified, the stem can still be difficult for a student to pronounce, particularly if it has two or more syllables. Three-syllable stems are unusual, but two-syllable stems are quite common. One syllabication technique has already been introduced; the purpose of this lesson is to (1) familiarize students with a second syllabication technique and (2) provide them with practice in applying the technique.

B. *Instruction:*

1. Tell students to listen while you pronounce the following words, elongating and stressing each syllable as you do so. After you pronounce each word, have a student pronounce each syllable separately and indicate where the syllable division takes place.

CV/CV		CVC/V	
famous	station	river	habit
hotel	direct	damage	rigid

2. Now write the list of words on the chalkboard, and pronounce each word as you would in normal speech. Next, have a student pronounce the word and divide it into separate syllables on the basis of auditory experience. Draw a slash mark between the separate syllables:

CV/CV		CVC/V	
fa/mous	sta/tion	riv/er	hab/it
ho/tel	di/rect	dam/age	rig/id

3. Show students how multisyllable words that follow the CVCV pattern can be divided according to either the CV/CV or CVC/V generalizations. Explain that one must often apply both generalizations to achieve the correct pronunciation. Have students draw a generalization from this observation that they can apply to similar words.

4. A generalization containing the following information is appropriate: Multisyllable words following the CVCV pattern usually divide CV/CV or CVC/V. Try CV/CV first and then CVC/V.

5. Now that your students are familiar with the CV/CV and CVC/V patterns for syllable division, they need practice to improve their skill. The following words lend themselves to these division techniques.

pupil	locate	image	devil	blatant
spider	cement	pirate	dozen	timid
petal	seven	comic	final	novel

6. You may wish to locate other words that follow these patterns in your subject area material.

C. *Generalization:*
Through discussion, lead students to conclude that the CV/CV and CVC/C patterns are useful for dividing multisyllable stems into their separate syllables. Record this step on a chart or a chalkboard, or direct students to record it in their notebooks.
1. Locate the prefix.
2. Locate the suffix.
3. Identify the stem.
4. Divide into syllables using the CVC/CVC, CV/CV, or CVC/V pattern.

Word-Pronunciation Lesson 6—Context Clues

A. *Purpose:*
Sometimes a reader can extract a clue to pronunciation from the context surrounding a word. Context clues are phrases, sentences, or paragraphs that provide clues to an unknown word. This lesson acquaints students with these clues.

B. *Instruction:*
1. Write the following two sentences on the chalkboard. Point out that a word is missing, for a reason you will reveal shortly.
    a. To pronounce an unknown word, all learners at all levels must learn how to _____ approach the unknown word. (*systematically*)
    b. The _____ *strategy* being taught with these lessons is a systematic approach for identifying unknown words. (*pronunciation*)
2. Have students silently read the sentences, then write what he thinks is the missing word.
3. Discuss the students' various choices for each sentence. Use discussion to build a logical and meaningful basis for selecting words to fill the blanks.
4. After the class has chosen fill-in words and agreed that they are reasonable insertions, point out that they have proven the value of using context clues. Remind them that context clues consist of all graphics, sentences, and/or paragraphs useful for word pronunciation.
5. From a 500-word selection, delete every seventh word. Duplicate the selection and give each student a copy. Lead students through the process of using graphic, sentence, and/or paragraph context clues to hypothesize and justify choices for the missing words.

C. *Generalization:*
Through discussion, lead students to conclude that context clues are a valuable aid to pronunciation. You can record context clues on the evolving word-pronunciation strategy chart, or on the chalkboard for future reference, or direct students to record this step in

their notebooks under the section reserved for this strategy. Point out that their strategy now has five steps.

1. Look for a prefix.
2. Look for a suffix.
3. Locate the stem.
4. Divide into syllables using the CVC/CVC, CV/CV, or CVC/V pattern.
5. Try it in context.

Word-Pronunciation Lesson 7—Glossary, Dictionary, and Knowledgeable Reader

A. *Purpose:*
This lesson is merely a set of necessary comments to make to your students. They will want to know what to do when the strategy does not work; this lesson will answer that question.

B. *Instruction:*
1. Explain that the five-step word-pronunciation strategy will not help them identify every word they do not recognize in day-to-day reading. The strategy may not lead to correct pronunciation of an unknown word if the word is not in their listening vocabulary or if they do not have sufficient word-pronunciation knowledge to pronounce the word.
2. Tell students that for a nearly infallible strategy, they need two additional steps. Number 6 is the use of a glossary or dictionary; number 7 is merely to ask someone who knows the word how to pronounce it.
3. Be sure students know how to use the glossary and dictionary to pronounce words. Module 6, "Study Skills and Strategies," explains how to teach skills for using the glossary and dictionary. Resist the temptation to tell students to "look it up" before you know whether they have the necessary study skills to do so.
4. Caution students against skipping the last two steps; they are as important as the first five. Words they leave unpronounced return to produce the same frustration on following pages, and the frustration becomes greater as still more new, unrecognized words appear.

C. *Generalization:*
Record the following generalizations on a chart or chalkboard, or have students record them in their notebooks.

1. Look for a prefix.
2. Look for a suffix.
3. Locate the stem.

4. Divide into syllables using CVC/CVC, CV/CV, or CVC/V pattern.
5. Try it in context.
6. Look it up in the glossary or dictionary.
7. Ask someone.

PRACTICUM EXERCISE 3

You have now completed the seven lesson plans. List and describe each step in the three-step organization for every lesson plan.

1.

2.

3.

ANSWERS TO PRACTICUM EXERCISE 3

1. The first step is *purpose*, containing the information teachers need to establish a purpose for the instruction. At this step you tell the student what he will be able to do as a result of acquiring this new learning.
2. The second step is *instruction*, containing the necessary directions and information to teach the specific skills.
3. The third step is *generalization*, with the information and procedures for incorporating the new skill into the larger word-pronunciation strategy. This step shows the relationship of the individual skill to the overall strategy.

Final Comment

Students who use the strategy will find it a valuable tool for pronouncing words. Ensuring that they apply the strategy is your responsibility. If you do not insist they use the strategy, students will soon forget it, and your instructional efforts will have been wasted. To reach the automatic application level, students need instruction, practice, and application opportunities under your direction.

If you have accomplished the three specific objectives in this module, you are ready for the Posttest. If not, complete them as directed. If you are having difficulty, return to appropriate Enabling Elements or see your instructor.

POSTTEST

Directions: Read each of the following statements and complete each Posttest item as directed.

1. You should now be completely familiar with teaching a word-pronunciation strategy. List, in order, the steps for helping students pronounce multisyllable words.
2. Did you prepare and use the Quick Test of Word Pronunciation (Forms A and B), Word-Pronunciation Strategy Test, and Class Record Form to determine students' word-pronunciation skill and strategy needs?
3. List and explain the three organizational steps in the word-pronunciation lesson plans.

POSTTEST ANSWERS

1. The word-recognition strategy in this module is listed in the order its skills should be used or taught.
   a. Look for a prefix.
   b. Look for a suffix.
   c. Locate the stem.
   d. Divide the stem into syllables (CVC/CVC, CV/CV, CVC/V).
   e. Try the word in context.
   f. Look in the glossary or dictionary.
   g. Ask someone who knows how to pronounce the word.
   Your answer need not be in exactly these words, nor do you need to have the same number of steps, but your answer should contain all the information presented in the strategy.
2. If you have *prepared* and *used* the Quick Test of Word Pronunciation (Forms A and B), Word-Pronunciation Strategy Test, and Class Record Form, you have satisfied this objective. If you have not completed all three, you must do so before you can consider yourself to have satisfied the second objective of this module.
3. The major organizational steps for lesson plans for teaching skills and strategy are:
   a. Establish a purpose for learning. Tell the student why she needs this instruction and what she will be able to do as a result of learning the skill.

    b. Provide instruction. This step contains the directions and information necessary to develop competency with a specific skill.

    c. Build a generalization. At this step, the student incorporates the new skill into a word-pronunciation strategy which she will use when attempting to pronounce multisyllable words.

REFERENCES

Burmeister, L.E. "Selected Word Analysis Generalizations for a Group Approach to Corrective Reading in the Secondary School." *Reading Research Quarterly* 4, no. 1 (1968) 71–95.

———. *Words—From Print to Meaning*. Reading, Mass. Addison-Wesley, 1975.

Cleary, D.M. "Reading Without Vowels: Some Implications." *Journal of Reading*, 20, no. 1 (1976): 52–56.

Cheek, E.H., and M.C. Cheek. *Reading Instruction Through Content Teaching*. Columbus, Ohio: Charles E. Merrill, 1983.

Cunningham, P.M., J.W. Cunningham, and C. Rystrom. "A New Syllabication Strategy and Reading Achievement." *Reading World* 20 (March 1981): 208–14.

Dawson, M.A., ed. *Teaching Word-Recognition Skills*. Newark, Del. International Reading Association, 1971.

Durkin, D. *Phonics, Linguistics, and Reading*. New York: Teachers College, 1972.

Elisiak, J. "There is a Need for Word Attack Generalizations." *Reading Improvement* 14, no. 2 (Summer 1977): 100–3.

Hafner, L.E., ed. *Improving Reading in Middle and Secondary Schools*. New York: Macmillan, 1974.

Heilman, A.W. *Phonics in Proper Perspective*. 5th ed. Columbus, Ohio: Charles E. Merrill, 1985.

Ives, J.P., L.Z. Bursuk, and S.A. Ives. *Word Identification Techniques*. Chicago: Rand McNally, 1979.

Johnson, J.H., and E. Parades. "The Longest Tome Begins With a Single Phoneme." *Journal of Reading* 16, no. 5 (1975): 376–79.

Jones, D.R. "The Dictionary: A Look at 'Look It Up'." *Journal of Reading*, 23, no. 4 (1980): 309–12.

Kottmeyer. W. *Decoding and Meaning*. New York: McGraw-Hill, 1974.

Roe, B. D., B.D. Stoodt, and P.C. Burns. *Reading Instruction in the Secondary School*, rev. ed. Chicago: Rand McNally, 1978.

Stauffer, R.G. "A Study of Prefixes in the Thorndike List to Establish a List of Prefixes That Should Be Taught in the Elementary School." *Journal of Educational Research* 32 (February 1942): 453–58.

Thomas, E.L., and H.A. Robinson. *Improving Reading in Every Class: A Sourcebook for Teachers*. Boston: Allyn and Bacon, 1977.

Thorndike, E.L. *The Teaching of English Suffixes*. New York: Teachers College, Columbia University, 1941.

MODULE 8

DIAGNOSING READING
SKILL NEEDS

CONTENTS

PROSPECTUS

RATIONALE

Even when textual material is at the appropriate readability levels, students can still have difficulty understanding material if they do not have all the specialized reading skills required of your subject area. If teachers are aware of the specialized reading skills needed for their content areas, they can help students master these skills and increase the likelihood of success in the subject areas.

To help students become effective readers, you must diagnose their specialized reading skill needs. This module will help you understand the specialized reading skills in your subject area. The module is not designed to make content area teachers into reading teachers. Content teachers are not responsible for teaching beginning reading skills; however, they can and should help students develop the specialized vocabulary, comprehension, study skills, and higher level word pronunciation skills necessary for the subject area. This module describes the specialized reading skills for the various content areas and suggests ways to construct, administer, score, and use the results of reading skills tests.

OBJECTIVES

Terminal Objective

You will use reading skills tests to determine if students have acquired the reading skills related to your content area.

Specific Objectives

1. You will state the four categories of reading skills and identify the major reading skills necessary to read materials in your content area.

2. You will construct reading skills tests to determine the reading skill needs of students in your content area classes.
3. You will administer, score, and use the results from reading skills tests in your content area.

RESOURCES AND TIME REQUIRED

To compete this module, you will need textbooks and other reading materials from your subject area and paper for developing the reading skills tests. If you have completed Modules 1 and 2 concerning readability, you may want to use the Fry or Raygor graph to check and perhaps alter the readability level of test items, but it is not essential to have completed those modules before doing this one. The estimated time to complete the core Enabling Activities is four to six hours.

PRETEST

Directions: For each question, determine the word that indicates your belief regarding your competency. If you are in doubt, choose NO.

1. All content areas require some special reading   YES   NO
   skills because of the nature of the material. Can
   you (a) identify the major categories of reading
   skills and (b) state the reading skills necessary to
   read materials in your subject area classes?

2. Content area teachers are responsible for teach-   YES   NO
   ing the specialized reading skills necessary to read
   subject area materials. The first step in teaching
   is to determine the needs of students. Have you
   constructed a battery of reading skills tests to
   determine the reading skill needs of students in
   your content area?

3. After you develop or obtain reading skills tests,   YES   NO
   you must use them with your students. Can you
   administer, score, and use the results from reading skills tests in your content area?

BRANCHING PROGRAM ALTERNATIVES FOR PRETEST RESPONSES

1. You are ready for Enabling Element 2 if you already know the categories of reading skills and major reading skills needed to read materials in your content area. If you are uncertain of the reading skills required for your content area, Enabling Element 1 will be valuable.

2. Enabling Element 2 will help you construct reading skills tests to determine which students have or have not acquired the skills for reading your content area materials. If you have a battery of reading skills tests, go on to Enabling Element 3. If not, Enabling Element 2 includes specific instructions and many model tests.

3. Suggestions for administering, scoring and using the results of reading skills tests are presented in Enabling Element 3. Do this Enabling Element if you need practical ideas for using the reading skills tests to provide for students' individual needs. If you can already do so, you are ready for the Posttest.

ENABLING ELEMENT 1
SKILLS NECESSARY TO READ CONTENT
AREA MATERIALS

SPECIFIC OBJECTIVE 1

You will state the four categories of reading skills and identify the major reading skills necessary to read materials in your content area.

ENABLING ACTIVITIES

*1. Read Study Guide 1. Determine the reading skills that students need to read successfully in your content area.

2. Read the separate skill lists for the different content areas in Study Guide 1. Are similar skills needed to read in all content areas? What are the differences?

3. Give examples of reading skills needed for success in content areas, then explain why it is impossible for children to develop all the reading skills during the elementary school years (grades one through six).

4. Evaluate your own reading. Do you continue to develop more skill in reading? Discuss the implications with your colleagues.

*5. Look through various textbooks and written materials you use with your students. Find specific examples of the reading skills needed for success in your content area; for example, look for specialized vocabulary and symbols and note tables, diagrams, charts, or illustrations. Consider the skills and knowledge necessary to use specialized reference materials in your content area. You will be able to use some of these materials and ideas as you construct skill tests.

*Core Enabling Activities are marked with an asterisk.

STUDY GUIDE 1

Besides determining whether students can read textbooks and other required reading materials, many content area teachers want to know if students have developed the specific reading skills necessary to succeed in their content areas. Many content area teachers want answers to these reading-related questions:

- Do they understand the meaning of the generic words in my subject area's textual materials? Teachers who ask this are concerned about the prerequisite vocabulary demands of the textual materials. They understand that they need to introduce the technical vocabulary of their subject areas, but want assurance that students can handle the generic vocabulary. Teachers who are unsure about students' understanding of generic vocabulary prepare tests to assess students' readiness for the generic vocabulary demands of textual material.

- Can my students answer the types of comprehension questions I will ask about the textual assignments? Teachers who ask this question are concerned about how well students can answer questions that require them to recognize or recall information, translate information into their own words, apply what they read to a new situation or problem, analyze what they read, synthesize information to form a new communication, and evaluate what they read. Comprehension questions are important in all subject areas, and students must have definite question-answering strategies to answer them. To be sure students have the appropriate comprehension skills to read the textual materials, teachers prepare tests of comprehension skills.

- Do my students have the necessary study skills and strategies to read assigned textual materials independently? Teachers who ask this question are concerned that their students may not know how to use basic study skills to locate information or material, read graphic material, and adjust their reading rates. They are concerned that students may not be aware of or know how to apply study strategies for reading in social science, physical science, and mathematics materials. When teachers are concerned about what study skills and strategies their students have acquired, they prepare study skills and study-strategy tests.

- Do my students know how to pronounce the multisyllable, generic, and technical words in the textual materials I will assign? Teachers who ask this question are concerned that students may not know the higher level word pronunciation skills or have a strategy for applying those skills to the multisyllable words that appear in the textual material. These teachers know there are many two-, three-, and four-syllable words in their students' listening vocabularies that students may not immediately recognize when they read. To help students who lack these skills become independent in reading textual materials, content area teachers must review basic word recognition skills and show students how to incorporate these into a strategy for pronouncing words.

The wise content area teacher asks questions like these about each student at the beginning of each term. The teacher prepares the necessary skills tests to identify specific needs of students who may have difficulty with generic word meanings, answering comprehension questions, applying study skills and strategies, and/or pronouncing multisyllable words. Since you want to be the best content area teacher you can be, this module will show you how to identify the major reading skills in your subject area and prepare appropriate skills tests. In other modules, you will learn how to teach word meanings (Module 4), how to help students comprehend (Module 5), how to teach study skills and strategies (Module 6), and how to teach students to pronounce multisyllable words (Module 7).

Let us first examine the reading skills for the different content areas. Locate and read the list of skills required for your content area.

CONTENT AREA READING SKILLS

Art
Generally, students in art classes must be able to do the following:

Word Meaning

1. Develop an understanding of the technical vocabulary
2. Become familiar with the prefixes, suffixes, and stems common to technical words in art
3. Know how to use context clues to determine word meaning
4. Know how to use the dictionary to determine meanings of technical words in art.

Comprehension

5. Answer various types of questions.
6. Follow directions exactly.
7. Read critically to note viewpoints and/or determine relationships among various aspects of different cultures.

Study Skills and Strategies

8. Locate and use reference materials with information about art criticism and the history of art.
9. Read diagrams and illustrations

10. Adjust reading technique and rate to fit the purpose and nature of the material
11. Use a study strategy such as SQ3R, presented in Module 6.

Word Pronunciation

12. Pronounce multisyllable words.
13. Pronounce common prefixes and suffixes
14. Recognize common compound words
15. Recognize specialized abbreviations, signs, symbols, notations, and the like
16. Read orally using appropriate phrasing, expression, and rate
17. Use the dictionary's long and short pronunciation keys and respellings to pronounce unrecognized words

Business Education

Students in business education classes, such as accounting, bookkeeping, business mathematics, and typing, must be able to do the following:

Word Meaning

1. Develop an understanding of the technical vocabulary
2. Become familiar with the prefixes, suffixes, and stems common to technical words
3. Know how to use context clues to determine word meaning
4. Know how to use the dictionary to determine meanings of technical words.

Comprehension

5. Answer various types of questions
6. Accurately follow written directions
7. Evaluate the accuracy of a written document
8. Evaluate the expertise of the writer

Study Skills and Strategies

9. Read graphs, charts, diagrams, and other visuals
10. Use reference books
11. Use textbook reference aids, such as title page, copyright page, table of contents, index, glossary, bibliography, or references
12. Apply a study strategy such as SQ3R

Word Pronunciation

13. Pronounce multisyllable words
14. Pronounce common prefixes and suffixes
15. Recognize common compound words

16. Recognize abbreviations, signs, symbols, notations, and the like
17. Use the dictionary's long and short pronunciation keys and respellings to pronounce words

English, Language Arts, and Literature

Generally, students in these areas must be able to do the following:

Word Meaning

1. Develop an understanding of the technical vocabulary
2. Become familiar with the prefixes, suffixes, and stems common to technical words
3. Know how to use context clues to determine word meaning
4. Know how to use the dictionary to determine meanings of technical words
5. Develop scope and depth of vocabulary by studying word origins, slang, idioms, denotations and connotations of words, multiple meanings, and word relationships such as synonyms, antonyms, and homonyms

Comprehension

6. Answer various types of questions to identify significant details, central ideas, mood, sensory images, sequence of ideas, and relationships among ideas, and make inferences about characters, settings, and events
7. Critically evaluate by determining the author's purpose, distinguishing facts from opinions, identifying propaganda techniques, and identifying characteristics of good writing
8. Read creatively to respond to an author's ideas

Study Skills and Strategies

9. Use the card catalogue, the *Reader's Guide to Periodical Literature,* and other reference materials to locate information
10. Develop a flexible style and rate of reading appropriate for different types of literature (poetry, drama, fiction, nonfiction, and so forth) and use study strategies as necessary
11. Organize ideas into an outline, summarize, take notes from a book
12. Develop skill in using reference materials such as dictionaries, encyclopedias, and a thesaurus
13. Use a study strategy such as SQ3R

Word Pronunciation

14. Pronounce multisyllable words
15. Pronounce common prefixes and suffixes
16. Recognize common compound words

17. Recognize specialized abbreviations, signs, symbols, notations, and the like
18. Read orally using appropriate phrasing, expression, and rate
19. Use the dictionary's long and short pronunciation keys and respellings to pronounce unrecognized words

Foreign Language
Students in foreign language classes must be able to:

Word Meaning

1. Understand the specialized vocabulary words, such as cognates, tenses, stem-changing verbs, subjunctive, and auxiliary verbs.
2. Associate foreign words with their English counterparts
3. Learn the etymology of words from different languages
4. Become familiar with the meanings of common prefixes, suffixes, and stems
5. Know how to use context clues to determine word meaning
6. Use various language dictionaries to locate words and phrases and their associated multiple meanings

Comprehension

7. Answer various types of questions
8. Recognize likenesses and differences in sentence structure and grammar
9. Comprehend idiomatic expressions

Study Skills and Strategies

10. Use reference books
11. Use textbook reference aids, such as table of contents, glossary, and index
12. Use textbook study aids such as vocabulary lists, practice exercises, and suggestions for studying
13. Apply a study strategy such as SQ3R

Word Pronunciation

14. Pronounce multisyllable words
15. Pronounce common prefixes and suffixes
16. Recognize common compound words
17. Recognize abbreviations, signs, symbols, notations, and the like
18. Use the dictionary's long and short pronunciation keys and respellings to pronounce words

Health
To be successful in health, students must be able to:

Word Meaning

1. Develop an understanding of the technical vocabulary
2. Become familiar with the prefixes, suffixes, and stems common to technical words
3. Know how to use context clues to determine word meaning
4. Know how to use the dictionary to determine meanings of technical words

Comprehension

5. Answer various types of questions
6. Read and follow specific directions
7. Evaluate the expertise of a writer

Study Skills and Strategies

8. Use reference books
9. Use textbook study aids
10. Read graphs, charts, diagrams, and other visuals
11. Use textbook reference aids, such as table of contents, index, glossary, bibliography or references

Word Pronunciation

12. Pronounce multisyllable words
13. Pronounce common prefixes and suffixes
14. Recognize common compound words
15. Recognize abbreviations, signs, symbols, notations, and the like
16. Use the dictionary's long and short pronunciation keys and respellings to pronounce words

Homemaking

Homemaking includes such courses as home economics, clothing, bachelor living, child development, and interior decorating. In these courses, students must be able to:

Word Meaning

1. Develop an understanding of the technical vocabulary
2. Become familiar with the prefixes, suffixes, and stems common to technical words
3. Know how to use context clues to determine word meaning
4. Know how to use the dictionary to determine meanings of technical words

Comprehension

5. Answer various types of questions
6. Read and follow directions, such as those for recipes

7. Read carefully to understand instructions for operating various appliances
8. Critically read newspapers, catalogues, and magazine articles, including advertisements

Study Skills and Strategies

9. Read labels to find ingredients, directions, and cautions
10. Interpret charts, graphs, diagrams, patterns, drawings, and cutaways
11. Use an appropriate study method such as SQ3R to read textbooks, articles, and pamphlets

Word Pronunciation

12. Read specialized abbreviations, signs, and symbols, such as those in recipes and labels
13. Read bills and statements accurately, including the various codes that appear on them.
14. Read such specialized materials as thermometers, meters, invoices, and legal forms
15. Pronounce multisyllable words, such as *decorating, economics,* and *draperies*

Industrial Arts

To be successful in industrial arts, students must be able to:

Word Meaning

1. Understanding such technical vocabulary as *abrasive materials, arc welding, chamfer, bevel, compressed ratio of engines, cotter pin,* and *pumice stone*
2. Become familiar with the prefixes, suffixes, and stems common to technical words
3. Know how to use context clues to determine word meaning
4. Know how to use the dictionary to determine meanings of technical words

Comprehension

5. Answer various types of questions
6. Read and follow safety rules and instructions
7. Read detailed directions
8. Understand explanations and instructions

Study Skills and Strategies

9. Use the aids available in various manuals, such as indexes, glossaries, and manufacturer's listings
10. Read and interpret drawings, blueprints, charts
11. Read detailed diagrams

12. Read tables, illustrations, and charts
13. Use a study strategy such as SQ3R, PQRST, or SQRQCQ

Word Pronunciation

14. Pronounce multisyllable words
15. Pronounce common prefixes and suffixes
16. Recognize common compound words
17. Recognize abbreviations, signs, symbols, notations, and the like
18. Use the dictionary's long and short pronunciation keys and respellings to pronounce words

Mathematics

To succeed in mathematics, students must be able to:

Word Meaning

1. Understand the specialized vocabulary
2. Understand common stems, prefixes, and suffixes
3. Use the dictionary to define technical terms

Comprehension

4. Answer various types of questions
5. Read detailed material slowly to determine significant and insignificant facts
6. Follow directions precisely, as in detailed explanations of various processes requiring step-by-step operations
7. Critically analyze statistical records such as tax data and financial reports

Study Skills and Strategies

8. Locate and read reference materials on topics such as famous mathematicians or the application of a specific mathematical theory
9. Interpret materials that express relationships, such as principles, axioms, formulas, and equations
10. Read tables, such as those of square roots or logarithms
11. Read bar graphs, line graphs, pictographs, and flowcharts
12. Read visual materials such as diagrams and geometric forms
13. Use an index, table of contents, or other aids to locate information
14. Remember the meanings of symbols and abbreviations
15. Use an appropriate study strategy, such as SQRQCQ, for reasoning problems that require reading

Word Pronunciation

16. Pronounce multisyllable words
17. Pronounce common prefixes and suffixes

18. Recognize common compound words
19. Recognize abbreviations, signs, symbols, notations, and the like
20. Use the dictionary's long and short pronunciation keys and respellings to pronounce words

Music

It is no surprise that many reading skills are required in music. The students must be able to:

Word Meaning

1. Understand meanings of technical music terms, such as *adagio, cantata, impressionism, recapitulation, vibrato,* and *timbre*
2. Understand the foreign derivation of many specialized music terms
3. Use the dictionary to determine word meanings

Comprehension

4. Read to answer various types of questions
5. Read different types of literature to appreciate the setting in which music was written
6. Notice the author's bias when evaluating critical reviews of music

Study Skills and Strategies

7. Use a study strategy such as SQ3R
8. Use special reference books such as a dictionary of musical terms and indexes of musical literature
9. Use textbook aids such as an index of songs and classified indexes

Word Pronunciation

10. Pronounce multisyllable words
11. Pronounce common prefixes and suffixes
12. Recognize common compound words
13. Recognize abbreviations, signs, symbols, notations, and the like
14. Use the dictionary's long and short pronunciation keys and respellings to pronounce words
15. Read the words of songs using syllable divisions

Physical Education

Several reading skills are important for acquiring information in physical education classes. To read and understand physical education materials, students must be able to:

Word Meaning

1. Develop an understanding of the technical vocabulary
2. Become familiar with the prefixes, suffixes, and stems common to technical words
3. Know how to use context clues to determine word meaning
4. Know how to use the dictionary to determine meanings of technical words

Comprehension

5. Answer various types of questions
6. Accurately follow written directions
7. Evaluate the accuracy of a written document
8. Evaluate the expertise of the writer

Study Skills and Strategies

9. Read graphs, charts, diagrams, and other visuals
10. Use reference books
11. Use textbook reference aids, such as title page, copyright page, table of contents, index, glossary, bibliography or references
12. Apply a study strategy such as SQ3R

Word Pronunciation

13. Identify specialized symbols.
14. Pronounce multisyllable words
15. Pronounce common prefixes and suffixes
16. Recognize common compound words
17. Recognize abbreviations, signs, symbols, notations, and the like
18. Use the dictionary's long and short pronunciation keys and respelling to pronounce words

Science
An efficient reader of science materials must be able to:

Word Meaning

1. Understand technical vocabulary, such as *angle of reflection, cumulus, electrode, inertia, isotope,* and *ion.*
2. Analyze stems, prefixes, and suffixes to determine the meaning of technical words

Comprehension

3. Read to answer various types of questions
4. Differentiate facts from opinions
5. Read and follow directions for doing experiments

6. Read to test, prove, or predict outcomes
7. Organize ideas from reading and understand the relationships among ideas to draw conclusions or make inferences or evaluations.

Study Skills and Strategies

8. Use library skills to locate and research a topic in various journals, U.S. Government publications, and other reference materials
9. Interpret graphic and visual materials such as weather maps or diagrams
10. Use a study technique such as PQRST

Word Pronunciation

11. Quickly identify symbols, formulas, and abbreviations
12. Recognize common prefixes, suffixes, and stems
13. Pronounce multisyllable words
14. Recognize common compound words
15. Use the dictionary's long and short pronunciation keys and respellings to pronounce words.

Social Studies

Social studies students must be able to:

Word Meaning

1. Develop an understanding of the technical vocabulary.
2. Become familiar with the prefixes, suffixes, and stems common to technical words
3. Know how to use context clues to determine word meaning
4. Know how to use the dictionary to determine meanings of technical words

Comprehension

5. Answer various types of questions
6. Find main ideas and supporting details
7. Recognize cause and effect relationships
8. Read critically to identify propaganda techniques
9. Read to compare and contrast information and situations
10. Read to distinguish fact from opinion

Study Skills and Strategies

11. Be able to use the parts of a book, such as summaries, chapter introductions, vocabulary lists, glossaries, preface, and footnotes
12. Use library resources such as *Reader's Guide to Periodical Literature* and the card catalog

13. Locate information in encyclopedias and almanacs
14. Read maps, tables, charts, graphs, and cartoons
15. Understand time and space relationships
16. Take notes in outline form from a book or other assigned reading
17. Use a study strategy such as SQ3R

Word Pronunciation

18. Pronounce multisyllable words
19. Pronounce common prefixes and suffixes
20. Recognize common compound words
21. Recognize abbreviations, signs, symbols, notations, and the like
22. Use the dictionary's long and short pronunciation keys and respellings to pronounce words

Speech and Drama
Students in speech and drama classes must be able to:

Word Meaning

1. Understand the technical vocabulary
2. Recognize the meaning of specialized symbols and abbreviations
3. Use the dictionary to define technical words

Comprehension

4. Read to answer various types of questions
5. Read for specific directions
6. Identify mood and tone
7. Determine the nature of a setting
8. Critically evaluate and creatively respond to ideas
9. Determine an author's purpose
10. Notice an author's organization of ideas

Study Skills and Strategies

11. Locate and efficiently use reference materials
12. Read to outline and take notes
13. Use a study strategy such as SQ3R

Word Pronunciation

14. Read orally with appropriate expression, phrasing, and rate
15. Pronounce multisyllable words
16. Recognize common prefixes and suffixes
17. Use the dictionary's long and short pronunciation keys and respellings to pronounce words

After reviewing and remembering the major reading skills for your subject area under the categories of word meaning, comprehension, study skills and strategies, and word pronunciation, you are ready for Enabling Element 2, which will show you how to construct skills tests. After you have constructed these tests, you can determine if students have the specific word meaning, comprehension, study skills and strategies, and word pronunciation requirements of your subject area.

ENABLING ELEMENT 2
CONSTRUCTING READING SKILLS TESTS

SPECIFIC OBJECTIVE 2

You will construct reading skills tests to determine the reading skill needs of students in your content area classes.

ENABLING ACTIVITIES

*1. Read Study Guide 2 to identify the procedures and suggestions for making reading skills tests for your content area.

*2. Complete the Practicum Exercise. Select a reading skill necessary for your content area from those listed in Study Guide 1 and prepare a reading skills test. Use sample selections from textbooks (tables, charts, maps, diagrams, symbols) or other appropriate materials you expect students to read. Perhaps you can revise some of your old quizzes to serve as reading skills tests.

3. Look at standardized achievement tests in your content area. Could the tests be scored in such a way that you would learn which reading skills different students need? If so, can you use these to supplement the teacher-made test to identify specific reading skill needs?

4. Many of the newer textbooks include reading skills tests or review tests. Their inclusion may be one of your criteria for evaluating textbooks for possible adoption. If your present books have these skills tests, you will not have to spend as much time constructing them.

5. See Enabling Element 2 in Module 7 for an example of a word pronunciation test. After you complete Module 7, you can add this test to your battery of reading skills tests.

STUDY GUIDE 2

Most content area teachers routinely construct achievement tests. Constructing reading skills tests differs very little from constructing achievement tests or quizzes. Read the three steps, then do the Practicum Exercise.

- Step 1: Determine the Reading Skills for Your Content Area: As in developing other tests, the teacher's first task is to determine the *objectives* that must be tested or evaluated. In constructing skills tests in reading, you must consider the reading skills students need to read your content area material. Refer to the appropriate list in Study Guide 1 to determine what skills you need to test. For example, if reading a graph is a necessary skill in your content area, you may want to construct a test to see which students can read and correctly interpret a graph.
- Step 2: Select the Specific Content for Your Reading Skills Test: After determining the specific reading skills for your content area, select the textual material for preparing the skills tests. If you have decided to test for technical vocabulary words, skim chapters of the textbook or use the glossary to select words. For comprehension skills, you can choose passages and questions from any textual materials. For study skills, you can use the textbook to test understanding of basic textual aids such as preface, table of contents, list of tables, index, appendixes, and so forth. For word pronunciation, survey various textual materials to identify representative multisyllable words for students to pronounce. By the end of Step 2, you should have identified the major reading skills you want to test and selected material for the test.
- Step 3: Prepare the Test: Each test will need a title; a statement of its objective, a statement identifying the materials included in the test or the materials themselves, directions for the students to follow, and an indication of the acceptable level for mastery, as you will see in this sample skills test for Symbols in Mathematics.

Sample Skills Test (Vocabulary)
Symbols in Mathematics

Objective: Given sets of math symbols and their definitions, the student will match each symbol with its definition.

Material: Teacher prepared test

Directions to the Student: Match the definition with the symbol by placing the appropriate letter in the blank.

_____ 1. +	a.	since; because
_____ 2. −	b.	is greater than
_____ 3. =	c.	degrees
_____ 4. <	d.	difference between
_____ 5. >	e.	plus; positive
_____ 6. ≧	f.	pi; equal to 3.14159+
_____ 7. ≠	g.	is equal to

_____	8. ○	h.	is less than
_____	9. ∩	i.	minus; negative
_____	10. ∵	j.	intersection
_____	11. π	k.	is equal to, or greater than
_____	12. −:	l.	not equal to

Acceptable Level for Mastery: 100 percent

Notice that the sample skills test begins with a title, which indicates in a general way what is tested. When you prepare a sample skills test, write a title that generally explains what is being tested.

Next, notice that there is an _objective,_ spelling out precisely what is given to the student and what the student is to do. For this sample skills test, the student is "given sets of math symbols and their definitions," and is to "match each symbol with its definition." Write your objective beginning with "Given. . . ." and end with "the student will. . . ."

The third section of the sample skills test either specifies where to locate the _materials_ for the test, or contains the actual test materials. If actual materials from a textbook or similar source will be used, the title of the textbook, page number, and precise beginning and ending points would be identified. Reproduced material should be contained within the test.

The fourth section, _Directions to the Student,_ contains the precise steps the student must follow to complete the test. The more direct and precise the directions, the more accurate the results. Make your directions as clear as those in the sample skills test. To check their clarity, you may want to share them with colleagues before you use them with students.

The fifth section is the _test_ itself, and/or questions or tasks that go with it. If a source such as a textbook is used for the skills test, only the questions need appear here. This sample includes the test; other examples include only test questions.

The sixth section specifies the _Acceptable Level for Mastery,_ the percentage of items a student must answer correctly to be considered to have achieved mastery. A test sometimes contains information over which a student should have total mastery. When this is the case, the acceptable level of performance is 100 percent, meaning that the student must answer all the items correctly before moving to new material. Analysis of the test results reveals the specific items each student needs to learn before moving to new material. If a test merely samples knowledge the student must have, the student need not correctly answer every question to demonstrate mastery of a certain skill. Usually 80 percent is considered mastery for such a test. As a teacher, you are in the best position to determine the level of mastery your students must achieve. The mastery level for your tests should be no lower than 80 percent and sometimes as high as 100 percent, but determining the exact percentage required for mastery is up to you.

As you examine the following sample skills tests, notice that each has a title, objective, statement of material, directions to the student, and acceptable level for mastery. Sample skills tests are provided for the four areas of word meaning, comprehension, study skills and strategies, and word pronunciation, to show you how to prepare reading skills tests of your own.

Sample Skills Test (Vocabulary)
Science

Objective: Given a set of words and their meanings, arranged in separate columns and random order, the student will match each word to its definition.

Material: Teacher prepared test.

Directions to the Student: Match the words with the definitions by writing the letters from the right column in front of the correct words in the left column.

Test:

1. _____ style
2. _____ amino acids
3. _____ mitosis
4. _____ cell
5. _____ anther
6. _____ hormone
7. _____ muscle
8. _____ coccus
9. _____ instinct
10. _____ pistil

a. The pollen-bearing portion of the male reproduction organ of flowering plants
b. A spherically shaped bacterium
c. Automatic, unlearned behavior
d. Organic compounds that are the building blocks of proteins
e. The basic structural unit of life
f. The female portion of a flower, usually consisting of ovary, style and stigma
g. A secretion of the endocrine gland that controls and coordinates cell and organ functions
h. The process by which the nucleus duplicates before cell division
i. An organ or tissue that can contract to produce motion
j. The slender stalk of the pistil of a flower

Acceptable Level for Mastery: 80 percent

Sample Skills Test (Vocabulary)
Business

Objective: Given a set of words, the student will write their definitions.

Materials: Teacher prepared test.

Directions to the Student: Define the following terms with concise responses.

Test:

1. Assets—
2. Balance sheet—
3. Certified check—
4. Collator—
5. I.T.W.—
6. Excise tax—
7. F.I.C.A.—
8. Liabilities—
9. Net pay—
10. Promissory notes—
11. Voucher—
12. Requisition—

Acceptable Level for Mastery: 80 percent

Sample Skills Test (Comprehension)
Answering Application and
Analysis Questions in Music

Objective: Given an article from a magazine on music, the student will read the article and answer questions that require application and analysis.

Material: Magazine, *Musical Fun,* article on "Vocal Music," pp. 25–28; teacher prepared test questions.

Directions to the Student: Locate the article, "Vocal Music," in *Music Fun* Magazine. Read the article. When you are through, answer the following questions on a separate sheet of paper.

Test:

1. How are the terms *soprano, mezzo-soprano,* and *alto* related to the terms *tenor, baritone,* and *bass*?
2. What facts support the author's conclusion that choral music interest is on the rise throughout the world?
3. What possible effects will the rise in popularity of choral music have on sales of instrumental records?
4. How do Ralph Allen's ideas differ from those of Adele Redford's on the value of music as therapy?
5. How are music symbols like a code?

Acceptable Level of Mastery: 80 percent

Sample Skills Test (Comprehension)
Answering Recognition and Recall Questions in Art

Objective: Given a selection from the textbook *Great American Art,* the student will answer questions requiring recognition and recall of specific information.

Material: Textbook, *Great American Art,* section on "What Made Art Flourish," pp. 137–41; teacher prepared test questions.

Directions to the Student: In your textbook, *Great American Art,* read the section on "What Made Art Flourish in America." (It begins on page 137 and ends on page 141.) Then answer the following questions on a separate sheet of paper.

Test:

1. To what does the author attribute humans' interest in art?
2. How is the word *commemorative* defined in this section?
3. What are some *formal* reasons for our interest in art?
4. What is a *commemorative* reason for our interest in art?
5. What is *nonverbal art?*
6. How does the author relate *beauty* and *significance* to art?
7. What are some of the examples given of *useful arts?*
8. Where are the art centers of America?
9. Who are some of the early American artists?
10. Which art form is most popular in America?

Acceptable Level of Mastery: 80 percent

Sample Skills Test (Study Skills and Strategies)
Using Reference Books in Geography

Objective: Given a common reference book and questions to show how well the student can use the reference, the student will use the reference and answer the questions.

Material: Reference book and teacher prepared questions.

Directions to the Student: Answer the following questions using the current *World Almanac.*

Test:

1. What kinds of information appear in an almanac?
2. Why are almanacs valuable?
3. Where is the index in an almanac?
4. On what page would you find information about New Jersey?
5. What kind of information is given about New Jersey?
6. On what page would you find information about the Catholic religion?
7. What page tells you about telephones in the United States?

Acceptable Level of Mastery: 100 percent.

Sample Skills Test (Study Skills and Strategies)
Using a Textbook

Objective: Given a textbook, the student can explain and use the different parts.

Material: Textbook and teacher prepared test questions.

Directions to the Student: Use your textbook to answer the following questions.
Test:

1. Who is the author? What are her qualifications?
2. When was the book copyrighted?
3. What is the purpose of each part of the book?
4. Is there a list of tables? Figures?
5. Does the book have an index? When will you use this?
6. Are there pictures and diagrams to help you learn?
7. How are the chapters organized?
8. How are definitions of new words presented?
9. What aids are included at the end of each chapter?
10. Are there appendixes? What information is included in the appendixes? How can this information help you?

Acceptable Level for Mastery: 80 percent

Sample Skills Test (Study Skills and Strategies)
Reading Tables and Graphs

Objective: Given tables, graphs, and questions requiring the student to interpret them, the student will answer the questions to demonstrate an understanding of tables and graphs.

Material: Tables, graphs, or diagrams selected from the students' textual materials and teacher prepared questions.

Directions to the Student: Examine this table and answer these questions:
Test:

1. What is the title of the table?
2. What is the unit of measurement?
3. What are the column (vertical) and row (horizontal) headings?
4. What is the significance of the table?
5. How can you use the information from the table?

(Also write five questions requiring the student to read the table or graph.)
Sample questions for graphs:

1. What type of graph is used?
2. What is the unit of measurement?
3. What information is presented?
4. How is the information arranged?
5. What symbols are used? What do these symbols mean?
6. What is the significance of the information presented in the graph?

Acceptable Level for Mastery: 80 percent.

Sample Skills Test (Word Pronunciation)
Recognizing Prefixes and Suffixes

Objective: Given a list of words separated into prefixes, suffixes and base words, the student will pronounce the words to demonstrate recognition of the prefixes and suffixes.

Material: List of words formed with prefixes and suffixes, selected by the teacher from the students' textual materials.

Directions to the Student: Read aloud each of the following words.

Test:

> *ab* strac tion
> *ante* date
> *bi* focal
> *de* form *ity*
> *dis* honest *ly*
> *ir* respons *ible*
> *non* conform *ist*
> *trans* port *able*
> *ultra* modern
> *un* event *ful*

Acceptable Level for Mastery: 80 percent

Sample Skills Test (Word Pronunciation)
Pronouncing Words

Objective: Given a list of multisyllable words typical of a science textbook, the student will examine and pronounce each word.

Material: Ten multisyllable words selected by the teacher from the students' textual materials.

Directions to the Student: Examine each of these words carefully. Using what you know about pronouncing multisyllables, pronounce each word aloud.

Test:

1. motion
2. carbon
3. station
4. shelter
5. planet
6. sensation
7. relation
8. exercise
9. contemplate
10. universe

Acceptable Level of Mastery: 80 percent

PRACTICUM EXERCISE

It is your turn to prepare a skills test for any reading skill important to your content area. You have already identified some of the important reading skills and selected some material for testing the skill. Now you must prepare the test and set the acceptable level of mastery. Include these six components: title, objective (given . . ., the student will . . .), material, directions to the student, test, and acceptable level of mastery. Use the format in the samples.

ANSWERS TO THE PRACTICUM EXERCISE

Check your skills test to see if its title explains what is being tested. Check your objective to see if it *specifically* states what is given to the student and what the student is to do. Check to see that you identified all the materials necessary for completing the test. Did you provide the student with clear and precise directions? The directions should explain what the student is to do to complete the test. Did you remember to have a colleague check the directions to see if they are as explicit as you believe them to be? Finally, you should have included a percentage for the acceptable level of mastery. If the student must have total mastery, you should have indicated 100 percent; if the test only samples the knowledge the student must have, then 80 percent is an acceptable level of mastery.

You are now familiar with the basic reading skills in your subject area and know how to construct reading skills test. You are ready to learn how to administer, score, and use the test results to help students improve reading skills in your content area.

ENABLING ELEMENT 3
ADMINISTERING, SCORING, AND USING THE RESULTS OF READING SKILLS TESTS

SPECIFIC OBJECTIVE 3

You will administer, score, and use the results from reading skills tests in your content area.

ENABLING ACTIVITIES

*1. Read Study Guide 3, which suggests when to administer and score reading skills tests, how to record the results, and the implications for using the results.

*2. Prepare a reading skills test for one skill in your content area and administer the test to a student.

*3. Make a skill chart to record reading needs in your content area, and use this chart to list skill groups. Modules 4, 5, 6, and 7 give suggestions for teaching some of the reading skills.

4. Establish a skill center that includes materials and activities for developing a specific reading skill. Obtain the cooperation of the librarian and other teachers in planning a series of skill centers for the library or media center.

5. Share your skills tests with colleagues in your content area. Encourage them to try the tests and to make tests of their own.

STUDY GUIDE 3

Administering Reading Skills Tests

Now that you have constructed reading skills tests pertinent to your content area, you can try them with students. Some teachers like to administer the tests at the beginning of the course so they can immediately determine students' reading needs. Then they can use this information to help the students throughout the term. Other teachers use the skills tests as pretests before the unit in which the skills are most likely to be needed.

Remember that the purpose of reading skills tests is to determine if students have the prerequisite skills to get the most out of their textbooks and supplemental materials. The general guideline, then, is to administer the tests early in the semester or immediately before the skills are needed so you can provide necessary instruction. Of course, diagnosis is most useful when it is continuous, and an important diagnostic device is observation of students as they read different types of material and respond to questions. Diagnosis is never completed—you continually evaluate students to determine their instructional needs.

When administering the skills tests, tell students you want to see what they have learned in other classes. Indicate that grades will not be given, but the results will help you teach the skills that will help them get more from their reading. After the tests, talk informally with students about what they have learned about various reading skills.

Scoring Reading Skills Tests

Students do not receive grades for performance on reading skills tests. The purpose of reading tests is to help you become aware of the students' reading skills needs. Use the test's Acceptable Level of Mastery to determine if a student's performance is acceptable or unacceptable. Students who perform acceptably should move to other skills tests or other tasks; those who perform unacceptably should be taught the necessary skills to achieve mastery. They should learn these skills with the day-to-day reading materials used in your classroom.

Using Results from Reading Skills Tests

Like the sample in Table 8-1, a *skills chart* is one method of recording results from reading skills tests; it is economical in terms of

Diagnosing Reading Skill Needs

time and valuable for noticing students instructional needs. Skills charts list skills at the top and names of each student on the left. A check mark by a student's name to indicate successful accomplishment of a skill shows at a glance students who need special help developing skills.·

Table 8-1. Sample Skills Chart of Related Skills in Social Studies

Names of Students	Word Meanings	Comprehension Analysis	Comprehension Evaluation	Study Skills & Strategies Interpret Tables	Study Skills & Strategies Use SQ3R	Word Pronunciation Prefixes & Suffixes	Word Pronunciation Strategy
1. Jimmy		✓	✓	✓	✓	✓	✓
2. Alfonso	✓	✓	✓	✓			✓
3. Joseph	✓	✓		✓			✓
4. Jennifer		✓		✓	✓		✓
5. Mykel	✓	✓	✓		✓	✓	
6. Mark		✓		✓	✓	✓	✓
7. Carlos	✓	✓		✓			✓
8. Alice	✓		✓				
9. May	✓	✓			✓		
10. Sally		✓		✓		✓	✓
11. Zody	✓	✓	✓	✓			✓
12. Jesus	✓			✓	✓		✓
13. Odelfia	✓	✓					✓
14. Tina	✓	✓			✓		
15. Susan		✓	✓				
16. Chris	✓	✓		✓	✓	✓	✓
17. David				✓	✓		✓
18. Grant				✓	✓		✓
19. Sandy	✓	✓	✓				
20. Karen		✓		✓			✓
21. Andrea	✓	✓			✓	✓	
22. Miguel		✓		✓	✓		✓
23. Tony	✓	✓					
24. Andy				✓	✓		✓
25. Lynette	✓	✓	✓	✓		✓	
26. Beth	✓	✓		✓	✓		✓
27. Bobby		✓					
28. Tasha	✓			✓	✓		✓
29. Tonya	✓			✓	✓		
30. Liska	✓	✓			✓		

After you identify students' needs, it is time for instruction. If certain reading skills are needed by most of the students, you can have total group instruction; for example, if you want students to know how to read tables and the skills tests show that most are unable to do so, you can develop group lessons to help them learn to read tables. Or, if half the students demonstrated accomplishment of a skill and the others did not, you can design a *skill group.* Skill groups are temporary groups that dissolve when most of the students have accomplished the skill. Scheduling skill groups is flexible, depending upon other demands on the teacher's time.

Since teaching time is limited, you may want to plan *skill centers,* places in the classroom, study hall, or library where you store the materials, equipment, and supplies concerning particular skills. A skill center on how to read tables would include many practice activities and examples for helping students read tables. A skill center does not have to take an entire corner of a room or require a special table for display; it might be a cardboard box to which students come for materials to help them accomplish the skill. The purpose of the skill center is to provide instruction and practice activities to help students develop skills independently. Although some students may need additional teacher or peer instruction, once you have set up the skill center, many students will be able to use the activities independently.

Skill centers are especially valuable when only a few students need to develop a skill. Providing for all the students' individual needs is impossible; thus, you need materials to which you can refer them. Try to include self-correcting activities, and provide opportunities for students to help each other.

There were other suggestions in some of the preceding modules to help you meet the needs of students. Module 7 provided ideas for helping students pronounce words, and Module 4 contained many activities to help students develop specialized content vocabulary. Module 5 provided ideas for helping students comprehend what they read, and Module 6 explained how to teach study strategies. Even with all these ideas, you will have students who are so far behind that they need more help. You are not expected to teach beginning skills, but only the reading skills related to your area. Module 10, "Identifying and Helping Problem Readers," gives suggestions for helping problem readers learn in the content classes and suggests the resource persons to whom you should refer problem readers.

Final Note

You now know how to determine the reading needs of students in your content area classes, but this skill has no value unless you are committed to doing something with the results. Make a commitment to meet students' individual needs by setting up skill centers, meeting with skill groups, and teaching the reading skills as part of your normal instructional activities.

POSTTEST

1. State the four major categories of reading skills and one reading skill for each category from your subject area.
2. List the three steps for constructing a reading skills test in your content area.
3. Write a brief paragraph describing how you plan to administer, score, and use the results from the reading skills test in your content area.

POSTTEST ANSWERS

1. The four major categories of reading skills are word meaning, comprehension, study skills and strategies, and word pronunciation. If you correctly identified these categories and specified for each a major reading skill from your content area, you have accomplished this objective.
2. The three steps in constructing reading skills tests are to:
   a. Determine the reading skills required for your content area.
   b. Select the specific content for your reading skills test
   c. Prepare the test
3. Your paragraph should describe how you will administer, score, and use the results from your reading skills tests. You need to administer the test to one or more students, score the test to determine what reading skills you need to teach, and then prepare a skills chart to summarize the students' reading skill needs. Finally, you must decide how you will organize your students, and begin instruction.

REFERENCES

Allington, R.L. "Improving Content Area Instruction in the Middle School." *Journal of Reading* 18 (1975): 455–61.

Bader, L. A. *Reading Diagnosis and Remediation in Classroom and Clinic.* New York: Macmillan, 1980.

Bormuth, J. "The Cloze Readability Procedure." *Elementary English* 45 (1968): 429–36.

Burmeister, L. E. *Reading Strategies for Middle and Secondary School Teachers.* Reading, Mass.: Addison-Wesley, 1978.

Chance, L.L. "Using a Learning Stations Approach to Vocabulary Practice." *Journal of Reading* 18 (1974): 244–46.

Cheek, M. C. and E. H. Cheek. *Diagnostic-Prescriptive Reading Instruction: A Guide for Classroom Teachers.* Dubuque, Iowa: William C. Brown, 1980.

Derby, T.L. "Informal Testing in Vo-Ed Reading." *Journal of Reading* 18 (1975): 541–43.

Ekwall, E. K. *Locating and Correcting Reading Difficulties,* 4th ed. Columbus, Ohio: Charles E. Merrill, 1985.

Frankel, J. C. "Reading Skills through Social Studies Content and Student Involvement." *Journal of Reading* 18 (1974): 23–26.

Kratzner, R. R., and N. Mannies. "Building Responsibility and Reading Skills in the Social Studies Classroom," *Journal of Reading* 22 (1979): 501–5.

Lamberg, W. J., and C. E. Lamb. *Reading Instruction in the Content Areas.* Chicago: Rand McNally, 1980.

LaRocque, G. E. "Developing Special Skills for Reading Genres." *Reading Improvement* 14, no. 4 (Fall, 1977): 182–86.

Maxwell, M. J. "Developing a Learning Center: Plans, Problems, and Progress." *Journal of Reading* 18 (1975): 462–69.

Palmatier, R., and J. M. Bennett. "Note Taking Habits of College Students." *Journal of Reading* 18 (1974): 215–18.

Pyraczak, F., and M. Rasmussen. "Skills Measured by Selected Reading Tests Designed for High School Use." *Reading Improvement* 13, no. 3 (Winter 1974): 5–8.

Roe, B. D., B. D. Stoodt, and P.C. Burns. *Reading Instruction in the Secondary School,* rev. ed. Chicago: Rand McNally, 1978.

Sanacore, J. "Locating Information: The Process Method." *Journal of Reading* 18 (1974): 231–33.

Viox, R. G. "Evaluating Reading and Study Skills in the Secondary Classroom: A Guide for Content Teachers." *Reading Aids Series.* Newark, Del. International Reading Association, 1968.

Zintz, M. *Correcting Reading,* 4th ed. Dubuque, Iowa: William C. Brown, 1981.

M O D U L E 9

MOTIVATING
RELUCTANT READERS

CONTENTS

PROSPECTUS

RATIONALE

How often have you heard fellow teachers say, "How do I get Alfonso and Marian to read their assignments?" This is a question all teachers have about students at one time or another. Students like Alfonso and Marian, who have some reading ability but lack the motivation to complete reading assignments, are reluctant readers.

As teachers, we have a responsibility to motivate reluctant readers, that is, to manipulate variables in such a way as to entice students to read their assignments.

The ideas in this module will help you accomplish this task. The suggestions for motivation can be implemented as part of a daily routine in any content area course. They require minimal changes in teacher attitude or instructional technique, and they initiate considerable student motivation. Ultimately, they lead to completed reading assignments.

OBJECTIVES

Terminal Objective

You will acquire and use the described strategy for motivating reluctant readers.

Specific Objectives

1. You will write a one-word synonym for *motivation* and list two sources of motivation.
2. You will list the eight major affective and cognitive factors that influence motivation.

Motivating Reluctant Readers

3. You will list the core factors in a motivation strategy and prepare a mnemonic device for retaining the core factors.
4. You will incorporate a motivation strategy into a subject area reading assignment.

RESOURCES AND TIME REQUIRED

In addition to the module, the only other required materials are your student area textbook, paper, and a writing instrument. The estimated time to complete the core Enabling Activities* is three to four hours.

PRETEST

Directions: For each question, determine the word that indicates your belief regarding your competency. If you are in doubt or know only part of the information for which you are asked, choose NO.

1. Many reluctant readers are merely unmotivated readers waiting for a spark. Can you state a one-word synonym for motivation and list the two principal sources of motivation?   YES NO

2. How a student feels and what he thinks are important teacher concerns. Can you list the eight major affective and cognitive factors that influence motivation?   YES NO

3. Every teacher needs a strategy for motivating students. Can you list the core factors in a motivation strategy and prepare a mnemonic device to aid your retention?   YES NO

4. Knowing something about motivation does not guarantee application. Can you modify a subject area reading assignment to incorporate the motivation strategy presented in this module?   YES NO

BRANCHING PROGRAM ALTERNATIVES FOR PRETEST RESPONSES

1. If you can supply a suitable one-word synonym for *motivation* and identify the two major sources of motivation, you are ready for Enabling Element 2. If you are not sure about the correctness of a synonym or of the two sources of motivation, Enabling Element 1 was prepared for you.

---

*Core Enabling Activities are marked with an asterisk.

2. If you can list eight factors that motivate a learner, go to Enabling Element 2. If you cannot name eight factors, Enabling Element 2 will help you complete the list.

3. If you can list the core factors in a motivation strategy and have a mnemonic device to aid retention, you are ready for Enabling Element 4. If not, Enabling Element 3 will help you formulate and remember a motivation strategy.

4. After you devise a motivation strategy, you must incorporate it into a reading assignment. If you have a strategy and can incorporate it into a reading assignment, you are ready for the Posttest. If you are unsure how to do this, Enabling Element 4 explains and demonstrates the procedure.

ENABLING ELEMENT 1
MOTIVATION

SPECIFIC OBJECTIVE 1

You will write a one-word synonym for *motivation* and list two sources of motivation.

ENABLING ACTIVITIES

*1. Read Study Guide 1 to identify a one-word synonym for *motivation* and to discover two sources of motivation.

*2. Using the Sources of Motivation form (at the end of Study Guide 1, see if you can separate the intrinsic from the extrinsic students in one of your classes. Ask yourself what factors influence student motivation in the extrinsic group. You may discover the very factors discussed in Enabling Element 2.

3. Discuss the extrinsically motivated students in your classes with other subject area teachers, and determine if they classify the students in the same way. Could some subject areas *spark* students more than others?

4. Interview five of the highest achieving students on your intrinsic list. Ask them to tell you what motivates them to achieve. Compare their answers to see if high achievers have similar motivation. Compare their answers with the factors listed in Enabling Element 2.

*5. Distribute the Incomplete Sentences form at the end of Study Guide 1. Ask students to complete each sentence to show how they feel about reading assignments. Compile their answers. Do students' perceptions of reading assignments agree with yours?

STUDY GUIDE 1

Motivation often explains why Angela completes reading assignments but Ralph does not. Intelligence, language facility, cultural background, and other such factors may differ insignificantly for the two students; motivational differences may be the significant factor.

Motivation, at one level of understanding, may be considered a *need.* It is an individual need that causes a student to do something that will result in satisfaction. Need comes from within the learner's environment; thus, teachers manipulate factors in an attempt to create needs.

All of us have had students like Angela who complete their assignments seemingly regardless of what we do. No matter how casual we are in making an assignment or how unclear we are about the purpose of the assignment, Angela always gets the job done. Students like Angela are motivated from within. Psychologists call them *intrinsically motivated.* These students have such a strong need to succeed academically that they always complete their assignments. Teachers need to change the environment very little for students like Angela.

Teachers also have students like Ralph, who occasionally complete their reading assignments. Ralph sometimes gets started, but often fails to reach completion. He often seems unconcerned about completing his reading assignment. Students like Ralph demonstrate low-level or nonexistent academic needs. They are not intrinsically motivated like Angela. Occasionally, however, Ralph does complete an assignment when he has a need to do so, although the need is created by someone other than himself. Students like Ralph are *extrinsically motivated,* motivated by something in their environment. For these students, teachers need to be aware of the factors that influence or bring about motivation. Awareness of the factors coupled with planned manipulation is likely to yield more completed reading assignments from reluctant students.

To identify the *intrinsically* and *extrinsically* motivated students in your class, the Sources of Motivation form should be helpful. It contains definitions of *intrinsic motivation* and *extrinsic motivation,* and two columns for students' names. When you have divided students by source of motivation, examine each group to see if you can identify specific intrinsic or extrinsic motivation factors.

For insight into how students perceive your reading assignments, use the Incomplete Sentences form. A compilation of students' perceptions may provide additional clues to their sources of motivation.

You now have a definition of motivation and are aware of two sources of motivation. If you can list the motivational factors classroom teachers must manipulate to interest extrinsically motivated students, go to Enabling Element 3. If you are unsure of the factors, Enabling Element 2 identifies and discusses them.

Sources of Motivation

Intrinsic motivation: self-starter, started from within; moved to complete a task by innate need.

Extrinsic motivation: externally started; start comes from outside the learner; moved to complete a task by outside influences that create need.

Names	*Names*
1.	1.
2.	2.
3.	3.
4.	4.
5.	5.
6.	6.
7.	7.
8.	8.
9.	9.
10.	10.
11.	11.
12.	12.
13.	13.
14.	14.
15.	15.

Incomplete Sentences

Name _____

Class _____ Date _____

Directions: Complete each item to express how you feel about the many reading assignments you get in school each week. Make complete sentences.

1. I complete my reading assignment _____
2. Long reading assignments _____
3. Teachers who assign only page numbers for reading assignments _____
4. What annoys me most about my reading assignments _____
5. Reading _____
6. Reading to find the answer to a question _____
7. People walking around the classroom when I am reading

   _____
8. Reading at home _____
9. Hard books _____
10. Answering the teacher's questions correctly after completing my reading assignment _____

11. Reading about something that interests me _____
12. Reading textbooks _____
13. When I use the information from my reading, _____
14. Teachers make reading assignments _____
15. Easy books _____
16. When the teacher tells me I am wrong, _____
17. Being right _____
18. I would like to help my teacher _____
19. Reading newspapers and magazines _____
20. Reading is fun when _____

ENABLING ELEMENT 2
FACTORS INFLUENCING MOTIVATION

SPECIFIC OBJECTIVE 2

You will list the eight major affective and cognitive factors that influence motivation.

ENABLING ACTIVITIES

*1. Read Study Guide 2 and compile a list of factors that influence motivation.

*2. In *one* of your classes, distribute the What Motivates Me form at the end of Study Guide 2. Ask students to complete the form and turn it in, or distribute the form and have students use it as a basis for a discussion of motivational factors and learning.

3. In another of your classes, discuss motivation individually with several high- and low-achieving students. Ask them to list factors that motivate them to achieve in your classes. Did you acquire any new insight into students' motives?

4. Write a one-paragraph description of one of your most reluctant readers using the motivation factors presented in Study Guide 2. This activity can reveal factors you can change or manipulate to increase the student's output.

*5. Talk with other teachers who have the same student and compare your description. Are there differences in perceptions among the teachers? Might it be that some teachers have the *motivational keys* to some students, while others do not? Were any of the keys identified? You can learn a great deal about reluctant readers from talking with other teachers.

*6. Want to learn something about yourself as a teacher? Distribute the My Teacher form found at the end of Study Guide 2. Ask students to complete the form and return it to you. No names are necessary. Tally and analyze the answers to see how your students perceive you.

STUDY GUIDE 2

The basic factors underlying motivation are well known and understood, but are often not applied. They can be divided into two categories: how students feel (affective factors) and how students think (cognitive factors). Affective factors include interest and attitudes; cognitive factors include purpose for reading, short-term goals, reading level, knowledge of results, success, and usefulness of knowledge. Although we will discuss these factors separately, together they operate to bring about a motivated student.

Affective Factors

The affective factors that influence motivation are *interest* and *attitudes.* These two factors interact to create a good or bad feeling in the learner.

Interest refers to curiosity or concern about something—in this case, subject area. For most students, interest in a subject area does not bloom overnight; rather, it develops after many exposures to intricacies that strike their curiosity. A social studies teacher who compares and contrasts marriage customs and ceremonies in different countries with junior- and senior-high-school girls is appealing to their curiosity. Likewise, a mathematics teacher who deals with consumption and cost of gasoline to determine cost-per-mile of automobile operation is appealing to the curiosity of high-school boys. Teachers develop interest in a subject area by continually relating course content to their students' curiosities. This requires not only knowledge of the content area, but knowledge of students' daily interests. The teacher who builds interest knows both content area and students, and can relate one to the other.

Parents and teachers have the greatest influence on students' attitudes toward education. Parents create the initial attitude; teachers refine the attitude toward school in general and their subject areas in particular. An attitude is a disposition or mental set toward something, and may be either positive or negative. Attitude, like interest, is a pervasive quality that develops only after a long period of pleasurable experiences. Teachers who think positively about their students generally create students who think positively about their teachers and the subjects they teach.

Cognitive Factors

The cognitive factors that influence motivation—purpose, short-term goal, adjustment for reading level, knowledge of results, success, and usefulness of knowledge—interact to stimulate the learner's cognitive, or thinking, processes.

Purpose. To be motivating, assignments must be given with a purpose. The purpose is a teacher's specific direction in an assignment.

A teacher who tells students to read pages 27 through 54 for the next day provides a very unrealistic purpose for learning; the student perceives the purpose as getting to page 54, while the teacher perceives the purpose as being prepared to answer questions about the material. The student will not find out what the purposes are for reading until the teacher begins to ask questions on the following day. Suppose the student completes the assignment by reading pages 27 through 54, comes to class, and the teacher asks a few questions. Suppose also that the student is unable to answer the questions because she did not read the material for those purposes. The teacher will probably assume the student did not read the material, since she could not answer the questions. After a few such assignments, the student quits reading them. A better way to give a reading assignment is to write several questions on the chalkboard directed at the important points in the reading, and tell students to read whatever is necessary to answer the questions. They then have specific purposes for reading and are alerted to precisely what they need to obtain from the reading assignment.

Short-Term Goals. When goals are short-range, students expect them to take very little time, and are less reluctant to do an assignment. When you give students questions for which to read, you are providing short-term goals. Each question becomes a goal in itself, and makes the assignment appear shorter.

Adjustment for Reading Level. You must consider all students' reading levels when making assignments. Assigning the same material to students who read above, at, and below grade level makes the reading assignment nonmotivating for perhaps the above- and surely the below-average reader. One way to avoid this pitfall is to select a number of textual materials with a range of readability levels. Module 3 suggests ways to determine suitability of material for various students; Module 1 suggests ways to determine readability; and Module 2 provides ways to alter reading levels. Given enough time, a school or county librarian can locate many materials at various reading levels.

Knowledge of Results. None of us achieves unless we know what we have done right and *specifically* what we have done wrong. A student who is told he used the right process to determine the latitude and longitude of Chicago on a globe assumes the same process will apply for finding the latitude and longitude of Orlando, Florida. Pointing out a specific error in a process and giving specific instructions to eliminate it help the student obtain the correct answer next time. Some teachers fail to tell students when they are correct, but consistently tell them when they are wrong. Knowing what is wrong tells us how *not* to respond the next time, but gives no clue as to *how* to respond next time. The best way to motivate students is to emphasize the positive and de-emphasize the negative. When you do emphasize the negative, *be specific.*

Success. Most people gravitate toward vocations and avocations in which they meet success. When we meet with repeated failure, we physically and mentally withdraw from the situation. Teachers who make reading assignments without providing a purpose probably ensure that students will meet with failure when the assignment is due. A student may easily read material for one purpose when the teacher has assigned it for another. A few recurrences of this experience creates a subject-area mental dropout; repeated experience across subject areas may produce a school dropout.

Usefulness of Knowledge. Knowledge acquired with no suggested application to daily problems or interests is fleeting knowledge indeed! Every teacher knows it is important to teach students the new vocabulary in a subject area, but if vocabulary is taught with no stress on application and use in the classroom, how long will students remember the vocabulary? And will they be interested in additional vocabulary study? Finding ways to relate content to life is not easy, but it is essential for motivation and retention.

There are other influential factors, including physical and cultural. The condition of the school plant and the home also influence motivation, although these factors often fall outside the realm of a classroom teacher. For the most part, a classroom teacher can only manipulate the affective and cognitive factors discussed in this Study Guide. Manipulating these factors will not bring success with every student, but will increase motivation for many.

The first form at the end of this Study Guide, "What Motivates Me?" consists of questions about motivating factors to which students answer YES or NO, and takes about ten minutes to complete. Analyzing the answers will help you identify important motivational factors from the perception of your students. As an alternative, the statements on this form can be used as focuses for a class discussion of motivation.

The second form, "My Teacher," contains questions about you as a motivator of students and as a teacher. If you wish to learn something about yourself, reproduce copies of this form and distribute them to your students. The form takes about ten minutes for students to complete, and analysis of YES and NO responses will reveal the degree to which you consider motivation factors when you prepare reading assignments and lesson plans.

You are now familiar with a number of factors that affect motivation. If you can create a motivation strategy using the core factors identified in this Study Guide, you are ready for Enabling Element 4. If not, do Enabling Element 3.

Motivating Reluctant Readers

What Motivates Me

Name _____

Class _____ Date _____

Directions: Read each of the following statements carefully and circle YES or NO for each one. Your answers will tell your teacher something about what motivates you to learn.

1. I read my assignments only when the teacher gives class time to do so.   YES   NO
2. I like to know what I am to learn from an assignment.   YES   NO
3. I prefer one long assignment to two short assignments.   YES   NO
4. The more I like a subject, the more likely I will complete my reading assignment.   YES   NO
5. I like to be told if my answers to questions are correct or incorrect.   YES   NO
6. When it is noisy in the classroom, it is difficult to complete my reading assignments.   YES   NO
7. I complete my reading assignments even if the material is difficult for me to understand.   YES   NO
8. I like to read about things I can make or use in my daily life.   YES   NO
9. Other people moving around or talking in the classroom make it hard for me to concentrate.   YES   NO
10. I like to be able to answer questions correctly.   YES   NO
11. When I do something right, someone should tell me so.   YES   NO
12. I like long reading assignments.   YES   NO
13. I like to receive a reward when I complete my reading assignment.   YES   NO
14. When I am right, the teacher can tell everyone; when I am wrong, the teacher should tell just me.   YES   NO
15. I like to help my teachers select my reading assignments.   YES   NO

My Teacher

Name _____

Class _____ Date _____

Directions: Your teacher would like to know more about himself as a teacher. Please read each of the following questions and then circle YES or NO after each question.

1. Does your teacher make fun of you when you are having difficulty reading?   YES   NO

2. Does your teacher often get you so interested in your reading assignment that you talk about the assignment outside of class?   YES   NO

3. When your teacher finishes telling you about your reading assignment, do you sometimes feel you want to go to the library to find out more about the assignment?   YES   NO

4. Does your teacher make material that looks hard to read seem easier to read?   YES   NO

5. Does your teacher tell you what you are to learn from your reading assignment before the assignment is due?   YES   NO

6. Does your teacher ask interesting questions about reading assignments?   YES   NO

7. Does your teacher help you find material you can read for your assignments?   YES   NO

8. Does your teacher give reading assignments from materials that are too difficult to understand?   YES   NO

9. Does your teacher explain or define the new words in reading assignments?   YES   NO

10. Does your teacher tell you when you did a good job on your reading assignment?   YES   NO

11. When you are reading, does your teacher try to keep down the noise level in the classroom?   YES   NO

12. Does your teacher give reading assignments that are too long?   YES   NO

13. Does your teacher help you see the value of reading assignments to your daily life or to daily events?   YES   NO

14. Does your teacher ever ask what you would like to read to complete an assignment?   YES   NO

15. Does your teacher ever let you decide how much reading you need to do to complete an assignment?   YES   NO

16. Does your teacher know what you are interested in reading?   YES   NO

ENABLING ELEMENT 3
A MOTIVATION STRATEGY

SPECIFIC OBJECTIVE 3

You will list the core factors in a motivation strategy and prepare a mnemonic device for retaining the core factors in memory.

ENABLING ACTIVITIES

*1. Read Study Guide 3 to identify the core components of a strategy to motivate reluctant readers.

*2. Read Study Guide 3 to acquire a mnemonic device for remembering the strategy presented in this Study Guide.

3. Examine some of your subject area textbooks to see if they offer any motivation suggestions. If your subject area books are like many others, you will find few suggestions for motivation; however, your textbook may be one in which the authors provide not only suggestions, but also a motivational strategy such as that in this module. If the textbook includes a motivational strategy, you might want to try both strategies to see which is more effective.

4. Discuss with colleagues the strategy in this module. Chances are they use the same strategy. You can learn a great deal from discussions of motivation.

*5. There are many textbooks and popular paperbacks on the topic of motivation. You may find it beneficial to read one to further your understanding and ultimately enhance your techniques for handling students. Look at the references for suggestions.

STUDY GUIDE 3

Study Guide 2 identified a number of factors associated with motivation. All these factors contribute to a student's motivation and are therefore important, but it is probably unreasonable to expect most teachers to keep in mind the eight or more factors mentioned. Therefore, this module presents a brief but powerful four-step motivational strategy.

The four-step motivational strategy, which you can use when making reading assignments, employs a mnemonic device that makes the strategy easier to remember. The strategy was developed by identifying the many major factors that contribute to a student's motivation and reducing them to four core factors. Considering these core factors in lesson planning increases the probability of motivating students. To help you remember the motivation strategy, the first letter of the key word in each core factor has been used to form an acronym.

P *Purpose.* Students acquire more meaning from what they read when they have a purpose for reading. Providing students with purposes for reading defines the specific information and understanding they are to look for as they read, and makes material more meaningful to the reader. Purposeful and meaningful assignments are motivating.

A *Attitude.* Students must acquire a positive attitude toward reading. This quality develops through associations with teachers who have positive attitudes toward their students. Negative attitudes and reinforcement cause students to withdraw from teachers, their subject areas, and their assignments. Eternal optimism is essential to teachers who wish to motivate students and teach important skills.

R *Results.* Students must be made aware of results by the teacher's stipulation of right and wrong responses. Providing students with knowledge of right and wrong is one way to teach them what they should and should not do the next time they face a similar situation.

S *Success.* Students, like teachers, do not repeat experiences unless they meet with some success. Every student needs to find some success in every lesson you teach and in every assignment you make. Accumulation of successes increases motivation for future assignments.

Additional suggestions for implementing the core components appear at the end of this Study Guide.

The acronym formed by the first letter of each key word in the core factors is a familiar word. *Par* is what most golfers hope to score on every hole on the golf course; *pars* are what the golfer accumulates to signify satisfactory performance. Since satisfactory performance is every teacher's goal for every learner, **PARS** is a useful acronym and mnemonic device for remembering the four core factors in this motivational strategy.

You now have a strategy to apply when you make reading assignments to help motivate many of the reluctant readers in your classroom. To further help you implement the strategy, the following suggested activities are listed under the core component descriptors—Purpose, Attitude, Results, and Success.

Activities for Implementing the Motivation Strategy

Purpose provides direction for reading and gives meaning to what is read.

1. Prepare questions for setting a purpose for and guiding students' reading. Write the questions on the chalkboard, and leave them there for the duration of the assignment.
2. Prepare true and false questions over the assignment. Duplicate and distribute the questions and ask students to answer the true–false questions after they read the assignment.
3. Preview the reading assignment with the class. Ask students to create questions based on the preview that they can use to guide their reading. List the questions on the chalkboard or duplicate and distribute them before students read the assignment. Module 6 provides guidelines for creating questions by previewing.
4. Divide the class into small groups and have each group preview the reading assignment and prepare questions. Collect the questions, duplicate the best ones, and distribute them before students read the assignment.
5. Check the teacher's manual of your textbook to see which questions the authors think students should be able to answer at the end of a unit or assignment. After students preview the assignment and create their own questions, share the author's

questions with them. Through discussion, agree upon a set of questions for guiding the students' reading. Assign questions of fact to the less able readers and inferential questions to the more able.

6. Have students preview the reading assignment individually and draw up their own purposes or questions for reading, then have them read the assignment to achieve their own purposes. Afterwards, conduct a class discussion of the assignment and determine agreement on reading purposes. Have students explain their previewing techniques and their interest in the topic. Their interests will probably explain the different purposes.

Teachers have a responsiblity to create positive *attitudes* toward school in general and to their subject matter areas specifically. Positive attitudes develop through teacher-pupil interactions.

1. Demonstrate to students that you are aware of what they know as well as what they do not know, to show your concern for them as individuals.
2. Recognize the many excellent responses students make to build positive attitudes and motivation.
3. Avoid berating and degrading students. Berating students builds negative attitudes toward an individual teacher and ultimately toward education in general.
4. Avoid downgrading the school or your colleagues, which give students negative associations. The negative associations ultimately turn into negative attitudes toward teachers and schools.
5. Speak positively about your subject area. It is difficult for students to become interested in a subject for which the teacher demonstrates no enthusiasm.

Immediate and frequent knowledge of *results* is instrumental to motivation.

1. Prepare answer sheets for students to check their own answers, to give immediate and frequent feedback.
2. Be sure the learning from one assignment adds to previous learning so students can see their overall growth in the subject area.
3. Do not overemphasize right or wrong responses. A student who is right too often is not likely to be challenged, and a student who is wrong too often is likely to become frustrated and give up the task. The teacher should emphasize rights more than wrongs, always keeping in mind that one way students learn is from their errors.
4. When emphasizing what a student has done wrong, be sure to

follow up with instruction that tells the student specifically what to do to be right.

5. Students with poor attitudes toward a subject area need to have teachers recognize their correct responses in the presence of their classmates. Although teacher recognition is always important, peer approval means more.

Success breeds success; without it, there is no motivation.

1. Every day, find a task in your subject area that every student can accomplish successfully.
2. Display the successes of poorly motivated students in the classroom for others to see.
3. Use individual assignments on a contractual basis; this helps ensure that students meet with success in every assignment.
4. Reach an agreement with students as to the purposes of assignments. If you and the student agree on purposes for reading, success for the student is much more likely.
5. Provide students with materials at their reading level.
6. Allow students to read an amount appropriate to their interest in a topic.
7. Contract with students for a certain grade and a certain quality of performance in a reading assignment.
8. Pair a good reader with a reluctant reader to work cooperatively on an assignment.

You have now completed Study Guide 3 and are ready to apply the motivation strategy to a reading assignment. If you already know how to do this, go directly to the Posttest. If you are not sure how to incorporate the motivation strategy into daily reading assignments, go to Enabling Element 4.

ENABLING ELEMENT 4
PREPARING READING ASSIGNMENTS

SPECIFIC OBJECTIVE 4

You will incorporate a motivation strategy into a subject area reading assignment.

ENABLING ACTIVITIES

*1. Read Study Guide 4 to familiarize yourself with the procedure for incorporating a motivation strategy into your daily lesson plan.
*2. Examine the subject area reading assignment example and incorporate the motivation strategy into this assignment to enhance its appeal.

3. Examine the reading assignments suggested by the authors of your textbook. Do these provide any material you can use as a component of the motivation strategy?

*4. Authors sometimes provide discussion questions at the end of a unit. If your textbook has such questions, examine them to see if you can assign them as reading purposes.

*5. Incorporate the strategy in this module into one of your reading assignments and evaluate the effectiveness of the lesson.

STUDY GUIDE 4

This Study Guide explains and demonstrates how the motivation strategy introduced in Study Guide 3 can enhance the appeal of reading assignments. An assignment is an important part of a lesson plan; if the student does not complete it, she will not have the necessary information for the subsequent discussion and will be unable to answer the teacher's questions. Assignments are often not completed because they are not planned and presented in a way that creates a need or motivates the reader.

Teachers' planning books often reveal this kind of reading assignment:

Pages 127–152 for Tuesday. Continue discussion on WWII.

The teachers' manuals for textbooks more often give reading assignments this way:

Pp. 127–152. This chapter describes the events leading up to the involvement of the United States in World War II. Important events, dates, places, and people are brought into perspective.

Neither example is likely to appeal to students. A few changes by the subject area teacher will make the assignment more motivating. Let us incorporate the motivation strategy (PARS) into this reading assignment.

Stating the Purposes

First we will read to establish a *general purpose* for reading the assignment. General purposes are most meaningful and directive when stated as questions, so turn the statements into questions. The general topic is the events leading to United States involvement in World War II; we can state our general purpose as the following question:

General Purpose for Reading
The United States generally does not want to fight others, and yet we were involved in a war. What major events led to the involvement of the United States in World War II?

This is a broad purpose that provides the student with direction for the reading assignment; without a broad purpose, students can become mired in details and lose sight of the overall organization of the assignment.

Second, *specific purposes* help students look for facts they can eventually compile into a list of major events leading to the involvement of the United States in World War II. Specific purposes are also most meaningful and directive when stated as questions. The questions serve as precise teacher directions for reading the textbook, and each question also serves as a short-range goal.

To get the reading assignment under way, all the teacher need do is assign the general and specific purposes along with a *beginning* page number and direct students to read to obtain the necessary information. Do not give a terminal page number. The following sample questions are arranged in the order they are discussed in the reading material and concern the *major events* asked for in the general-purpose question.

Specific Purposes for Reading

1. After World War I, the victorious Allies met in Paris, France, to arrange the terms of the peace treaty to be signed by the defeated Germans. Why were the German people unhappy with the terms of this peace treaty?
2. What was the economic and political situation in Germany following the signing of the peace treaty?
3. What conditions were present that allowed Hitler to come to power in Germany?
4. Why did Germany, Italy, and Japan join forces in World War II?
5. What was the reaction in the United States when Germany invaded Austria? Czechoslovakia? Poland?
6. What was the reaction in the United States when Germany invaded and conquered France and beat the British at Dunkirk?
7. Who were the candidates in the 1940 presidential election?
8. The winner of the 1940 presidential election interpreted his victory as a mandate from the American people to send aid to friendly, war-torn European countries. Why was this a significant event?
9. What did the Lend-Lease Act signal to the Germans, Italians, and Japanese?
10. What single event was responsible for the direct involvement of the United States in World War II?

Teacher Attitudes

The second component in the motivation strategy is *teacher attitudes*. Attitudes toward students and subject area appear in one's actions or disposition. Although attitudes and ensuing actions cannot, like purposes, be written into lesson plans, they are equally important. The teacher who differentiates reading assignments according to knowledge of students' reading levels and interests, emphasizes *right* responses, avoids ridicule and degradation, and demonstrates enthusiasm for the subject area builds motivation and positive attitudes toward school and subject matter.

Knowledge of Results

The third component is *knowledge of results.* As mentioned earlier, immediate and frequent knowledge of results is instrumental to motivation, and is easy to incorporate into reading assignments or lesson plans. After agreeing on questions to define purpose for reading, tell students how they can check their answers. You may want to provide prepared answers to the questions used for setting purposes so students can read the answers immediately after they complete their assignment. If their answers differ, give them an opportunity to reread parts of the assignment to see where they were misled. An alternative procedure for immediate feedback is to pair students or have them form small groups to compare and discuss answers. You can also try individual conferences with students to discuss and clarify their answers; still another technique is the customary class discussion of answers. Reluctant readers should read part of their assignments in class and part outside class. Students who tend not to complete assignments often do so when they have an opportunity to start the assignment in class, especially if the teacher shows reluctant readers how much progress they have made with their assignments in class and assures them they are obtaining the desired information.

Success

The fourth component is *success.* If you have established purposes for reading, demonstrated your belief in the dignity of your students and the value of your subject area, and made arrangements for immediate feedback, you have done most of what is necessary to ensure that every reader will meet with some success. To further ensure success, you may want to include some motivating activities, such as a reading contract, or asking reluctant readers to read for fewer purposes, or assigning only one purpose per period of reading time and keeping the reading unit short. Pairing a good student with a reluctant reader is an additional way to ensure the success of the reluctant reader. Remember, success breeds success and enhances motivation, but the teacher must plan for success; it cannot be left to chance.

You now see how the motivation strategy enhances the appeal of a reading assignment. Often, changes in the nature of reading assignments and in our attitudes are necessary to motivate students.

Using Student Teams to Motivate Reluctant Readers

You may enjoy introducing reading assignments, then have students work on the assignments as teams. Three rather sophisticated plans for using student teams have been developed and field-tested at Johns Hopkins University by members of the Johns Hopkins Team Learning Project. The three plans are (1) Teams—Games—Tournaments (TGT); (2) Student Teams—Achievement Divisions (STAD), and (3) Jig Saw.

The Teams—Games—Tournaments (TGT) approach, developed by David DeVries, divides students into four- or five-member learning teams. Each team has high achievers, average achievers, and low achievers. Students are encouraged to work together to help each other learn. When making reading assignments in the TGT program, the teacher gives each team a list of questions to answer. The team divides the questions among its members, the members answer the questions, and at the end of the week, they compete in games or tournaments against other teams. Each team's scores determine their standings. This form of team competiion enables every student to have an opportunity to contribute a maximum number of points to the team, and students encourage each other to learn since the final product is a team score.

Research shows that teachers who use TGT in the classroom find the students are highly motivated to learn. Research also reveals that students in the TGT classes in grades three through nine learn significantly more in reading vocabulary than students in traditionally structured classes studying the same material. To divide students into teams, list their names in order from highest to lowest achiever, then divide them into teams as shown in Table 9-1. According to this method, each of the six teams would have five members. Team A would consist of members who rank Numbers 1, 12, 13, 24, and 25 and Team D, Numbers 4, 9, 16, 20, and 28. After you determine the teams according to achievement, make sure all team members are not of the same sex or race. Research indicates that mixing the teams promotes friendships among students of different races.

The Student Teams—Achievement Division (STAD) uses quizzes instead of games to check student achievement. Again, students are divided into teams as described previously, then work together to help each other learn. Students take quizzes to earn points for their team. Each student's score is compared to that of another student of similar past performance so that students of all ability levels have a good chance to earn points for their teams. The STAD approach was developed by Robert Slavin.

The final approach to using teams is Jig-Saw, developed by Elliott Arronson. In the Jig-Saw method, students are divided into six-member teams, and the academic material they are to read is broken down into as many parts as there are team members. Each student reads his part and shares the information with the other members. The students take a quiz over the information in the whole assignment, and can only do well on the quizzes by sharing information and paying close attention to what their peers have learned. Jig-Saw encourages students to show interest in each other's work.[1]

---

[1] For more information on using team learning in the classroom, write to the Johns Hopkins University Center of Social Organization of Schools, 3505 North Charles Street, Baltimore, Maryland 21218.

Table 9-1. Assigning Students to Teams

	Rank Order	Team Name
High-Achieving Students	1	A
	2	B
	3	C
	4	D
	5	E
	6	F
Average-Achieving Students	7	F
	8	E
	9	D
	10	C
	11	B
	12	A
	13	A
	14	B
	15	C
	16	D
	17	E
	18	F
	19	F
	20	D
	21	B
	22	C
	23	B
	24	A
Low-Achieving Students	25	A
	26	B
	27	C
	28	D
	29	E
	30	F

PRACTICUM EXERCISE

Now it is your turn to modify a reading assignment. To complete this section, all you need is a sheet of paper and a writing instrument. Answer each question in order, then compare your answers to ours.

Mr. Hernandez, an 11th grade biology teacher, is about to make a reading assignment to his students. The topic presently under discussion is the circulatory system of the human body. Pages 117–131 in the textbook discuss this topic. Mr. Hernandez has many reluctant readers in his class who consistently do not complete their reading assignments.

How would you advice Mr. Hernandez to prepare this reading assignment to enhance motivation?

Write your answers to the following questions, then compare them with the answers provided.

1. What are the key letters in the mnemonic device and key words in the motivation strategy that can be incorporated into this reading assignment?
2. The topic under study is the circulatory system, which includes the heart, blood, and blood vessels. What suggestions regarding *purpose* do you have for Mr. Hernandez?
3. What about the manner in which Mr. Hernandez makes the assignment? What are the important considerations about teacher attitude?
4. After Mr. Hernandez's students have completed the assignment, how can he provide for immediate feedback?
5. Mr. Hernandez has a reluctant reader for whom he wants to guarantee considerable success. What do you suggest?
6. Describe how Mr. Hernandex could use teams to complete reading assignments.

ANSWERS TO THE PRACTICUM EXERCISE

1. The basic mnemonic device is PARS. The key words are Purpose, Attitude, Results, and Success.
2. Mr. Hernandez needs to set one general reading purpose related to the broad topic—the circulatory system. Then he needs about three specific reading purposes, one for each major component of the circulatory system—heart, blood, blood vessels. Reading purposes are probably best stated in question form, which provides specific and clear direction for students.
3. If Mr. Hernandez takes into consideration his students' reading levels and interests, he demonstrates concern for them as individuals. If he is supportive of students' reading efforts (no matter how meager) and emphasizes their growth (no matter how small), he demonstrates his concern. By doing these things and showing enthusiasm for his subject area, he builds positive attitudes toward school, teachers, and subject area.
4. Knowledge of results can be provided immediately after students complete their reading assignments by (a) providing self-correction answer keys, (b) placing students in pairs or small groups to compare and discuss answers, or (c) holding teacher-pupil conferences. You may have thought of additional acceptable techniques for providing immediate feedback.
5. Success can be guaranteed through (a) writing a teacher-student work contract wherein the amount and quality of work is

agreed upon in advance; (b) making a grade contract, which guarantees a certain grade for a specified quantity and/or quality of work; (c) pairing a reluctant reader with a good reader to work together to complete the assignment; (d) assigning material that is at or below the reading level of the reluctant reader and providing a single, short-range purpose for the assignment; (e) providing class time for reading the assignment.

6. Mr. Hernandez could use one of three approaches for having students work in teams. With the Teams—Games—Tournaments, he would divide students into four- or five-member learning teams with members who are achieving at different levels. He would encourage team members to work together to answer specific questions. They would study the answers to the questions, then compete in a game at the end of the week.

If your answers agree with the sample answers in content or intention—congratulations! You have reached the end of this Study Guide and should be ready for the Posttest.

One word of caution about motivation strategies before we close. Motivation strategies, like most other strategies, do not achieve their greatest effectiveness until they have been applied consistently over a long period, because motivation factors are not discrete entities, but interrelated factors. When manipulated by a teacher, each factor interacts with other factors. The ultimate cumulative effect is to create a need in some of even the most reluctant readers. This effect takes time to achieve, so do not be disappointed or give up if you do not see immediate results.

Final Comment

From this module, you have acquired a strategy to help motivate more students in your subject area. Applying this strategy is up to you, but we hope you will feel a professional and ethical responsibility to apply a motivational strategy. If you do, you will accomplish more of your instructional objectives, and many of your students will remember you as someone who cared.

POSTTEST

Directions: Read each of the following statements, and complete each Posttest item as directed.

1. Write a one-word synonym for *motivation*. List two sources of motivation.
2. List the eight major affective and cognitive factors influencing motivation.

3. List the core factors in the motivation strategy presented in this module and write its acronym.
4. List and explain the application of this strategy to enhance the appeal of this subject area reading assignment:

Mr. Davis is a physical education teacher who wants to familiarize his classes with football theory. He is about to assign pages 22–31 from a basic textbook in sports. The topic under study is the Fundamentals of Football, which consists of such subtopics as (a) time and periods of play, (b) kickoff, (c) scrimmage, (d) passing, (e) downs, and (f) scoring.

POSTTEST ANSWERS

1. Appropriate synonyms for *motivation* are *need* and *desire.* Two sources of motivation are intrinsic (from within) and extrinsic (from without).
2. The major affective and cognitive factors are:

Affective	*Cognitive*
Interest	Purpose
Attitude	Short-term goals
	Adjustments for reading levels
	Success
	Usefulness of knowledge
	Knowledge of results

3. The core factors in the motivational strategy in this module are: Purpose, Attitude, Results, and Success and the mnemonic device to aid retention of the core factors is the acronym PARS.
4. The procedure for modifying the "Fundamental of Football" reading assignment is to:
   a. Establish *purposes:* Prepare general and specific purposes in the form of questions for the reading assignment.
   b. Adjust your *attitude.* Consider the needs and interests of individual students, be supportive of individual efforts, and be enthusiastic about your subject area. Be positive!
   c. Provide *results.* Provide immediate knowledge of results through self-correction devices, small group discussions, or teacher-pupil conferences.
   d. Ensure *success.* See that every individual student succeeds on some part of the reading assignment.

If any of your answers and the sample answers disagree in content or intention, review the discussion of the specific components or the reading assignment on U.S. involvement in World War II. If you are still having difficulty, see your instructor.

REFERENCES

Ausubel, D.P. "A Teaching Strategy for Culturally Deprived Pupils: Cognitive and Motivational Considerations." In *Teaching Reading in High School: Selected Articles,* ed. R. Karlin, Indianapolis, Ind.: Bobbs-Merill, 1969.

Bergman, J.R. "A New Tool Designed to Develop Positive Attitudes Toward Reading." *Reading Improvement* 14, no. 2 (Summer 1977): 70–73.

Betts, E. A. "Capture Reading Motivation." *Reading Improvement* 13, no. 1 (Spring 1976): 41–46.

Crisculo, N. P. "Convincing the Unconvinced to Read: 12 Strategies." *Journal of Reading,* 21, no. 3 (1977): 219–21.

Darling, D. "Evaluating the Affective Dimension of Reading," In *Perspectives in Reading,* vol. 8. Ed. T. C. Barrett, Newark, Del.: International Reading Association, 1967.

Estes, T.H., "A Scale to Measure Attitudes Toward Reading," *Journal of Reading* 15, no. 2 (1971): 135–38.

Guerra, C.L., and D.B. Payne, "Using Popular Books and Magazines to Interest Students in General Science." *Journal of Reading* 24, no. 7 (1981): 583–86.

Haimowitz, B. "Motivating Reluctant Readers in Inner-city Classes." *Journal of Reading,* 21, no. 3 (1977): 227–30.

Heathington, B.S. "What to Do about Reading Motivation in the Middle School." *Journal of Reading* 22, no. 8 (1979): 709–13.

Mason, G.E. and J.M. Mize. "Twenty-Two Sets of Methods and Materials for Stimulating Teen-Age Reading." *Journal of Reading* 21, no. 8 (1978): 735–41.

Mueller, D.L. "Teacher Attitudes Toward Reading." *Journal of Reading* 17, no. 3 (1973): 202–5.

Nichols, J.N. "Using Predictions to Increase Content Area Interest and Understanding." *Journal of Reading* 27, no. 3 (1983): 225–28.

Seaton, H.W., and R.L. Aaron. "Modification of Pupil Attitude Toward Reading Through Positive Reinforcement Scheduling." *Reading Improvement* 15, no. 2 (Summer 1978): 96–100.

Shuman, R.B. "Reading with a Purpose: Strategies to Interest Reluctant Readers." *Journal of Reading* 25, no. 8 (1982): 725–30.

Slavin, R.E. *Using Student Team Learning.* Baltimore, Md.: The Johns Hopkins University, 1978.

Smith, C.B., S.L. Smith, and L. Mikulecky. *Teaching Reading and Subject Matter in the Secondary School.* New York: Holt, Rinehart, and Winston, 1978.

Thelen, J. "Preparing Students for Content Reading Assignments." *Journal of Reading* 25, no. 6 (1982): 544–49.

Welker, W. A. "Reading and the High School Student: An Attitudinal Approach to Reading." *Reading Improvement* 13, no. 2 (Summer 1976): 98–100.

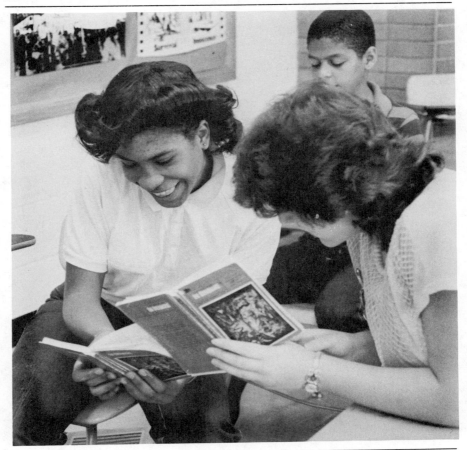

IDENTIFYING AND HELPING PROBLEM READERS

CONTENTS

PROSPECTUS

RATIONALE

A constant frustration for content area teachers is having students who read far below grade level. These students often appear uninterested, rebellious, withdrawn, slow, or unmotivated. Usually, students who are poor readers do not complete assignments, often attempt to copy from other students, and fail to take part in class discussions. You may wonder why these students even come to school.

This module will (1) help you develop a better understanding of these students and (2) provide practical suggestions for identifying, helping, and referring students who have reading problems. Students with reading problems can survive—and learn—in content area classes. Their teachers must understand the symptoms and causes of reading problems, identify factors that may be interfering with students' responses to reading, be aware of sources of help, and have ideas for teaching students who cannot read the typical content materials. These competencies, along with the commitment to help students succeed, will enable students to perform better and learn more in your content area.

OBJECTIVES

Terminal Objective
You will identify problem readers and factors that may be interfering with their responsiveness to reading tasks, and adapt instructional procedures to help problem readers succeed in your content area.

Identifying and Helping Problem Readers

Specific Objectives

1. You will describe characteristics of problem readers and indicate three major responsibilities for helping problem readers succeed in your content area classes.
2. You will list and explain by categories those factors that may cause reading failure.
3. You will use nontesting devices to identify factors that may cause reading failure.
4. You will indicate appropriate referral sources for students who manifest certain symptoms, and state guidelines and techniques for adapting instruction to help problem readers succeed in content classes.

RESOURCES AND TIME REQUIRED

All materials for completing this module are included. It would be helpful for you to talk with the school nurse, librarian, reading specialists, guidance counselor, school psychologist, and assistant principal in charge of curriculum to determine specific support sources. Discussions with the various resource personnel will help you accomplish the objectives in this module. The estimated time to complete the core Enabling Activities* is two to four hours.

PRETEST

Directions: For each question, determine the word that indicates your belief regarding your competency. If you are in doubt, choose NO.

1. You undoubtedly have problem readers in your   YES   NO
   classes. Can you define the term *problem reader*
   and describe your three major responsibilities in
   helping such readers?
2. Many factors determine how well students learn   YES   NO
   to read. Can you state and explain six major factors that influence reading achievement?
3. Content teachers share the responsibility for de-   YES   NO
   termining factors that can interfere with students'
   responsiveness to reading. Do you have an observation checklist, personal inventory, and other
   nontesting devices for identifying possible causes
   of reading failure? Are you using them?
4. All teachers can help problem readers succeed if   YES   NO
   they seek appropriate assistance. Do you know
   the specialists to whom problem readers should

---

*Core Enabling Activities are marked with an asterisk.

be referred? Do you have guidelines and techniques to help problem readers succeed in your classes?

BRANCHING PROGRAM ALTERNATIVES FOR PRETEST RESPONSES

1. A problem reader is a student who is not able to read at grade level and therefore cannot read the usual content area materials in your classes. If you are not sure of typical behaviors of problem readers or your role in identifying, referring, and helping problem readers, complete Enabling Element 1. If you are familiar with these behaviors and know your three major responsibilities for helping problem readers, you are ready for Enabling Element 2, which deals with factors that contribute to reading failure.

2. The six major factors that influence reading achievement are similar to those that influence success in any academic area. If you are familiar with the six factors (physical condition, language development, environment, aptitude, social-emotional problems, and educational background), go on to Enabling Element 3. See Enabling Element 2 if you need to refresh your memory or learn a mnemonic device to help you remember the factors.

3. If you are using your own checklist, personal inventory, and other nontesting devices to identify possible causes of reading failure, go to Enabling Element 4. If you need such nontesting instruments, Enabling Element 3 presents sample devices.

4. Do you know to whom you should refer a student who exhibits certain educationally inhibiting behaviors, and are you aware of guidelines and techniques for helping problem readers in your classroom? Enabling Element 4 is designed to alleviate teacher and student frustration by providing alternative strategies for helping these students. If you want to "make it through the day," as well as actually help students succeed, do Enabling Element 4.

ENABLING ELEMENT 1
CHARACTERISTICS OF PROBLEM READERS

SPECIFIC OBJECTIVE 1

You will describe the characteristics of problem readers and indicate your three major responsibilities for helping problem readers succeed in your content area classes.

ENABLING ACTIVITIES

*1. Read Study Guide 1 to determine typical problem reader behaviors and to learn a general definition of the term *problem reader.*

2. At a departmental faculty meeting or with the entire faculty in your school, discuss who is responsible for teaching basic reading skills to students who read below grade level. Will the English teachers assume this responsibility? Should special developmental reading classes be established? Is there a need for special remedial reading classes? Is there a sufficient number of reading classes to provide for the number of students who do not read at grade level?

3. List the names of ten students you have or have had who can be classified as problem readers. After each name, write two or three adjectives that describe them as students. Analyze your list to determine common characteristics among them. Think about the differences among the students, and list possible reasons for the differences. Why do some students learn to cope better with their problems?

4. Look at your students' achievement scores in reading, if they are available. You would expect one-third of the students to read *below* grade level, one-third of the students at grade level, and one-third *above* grade level. What percentage of your students read below grade level according to the results of a standardized achievement test in reading?

*5. Imagine how problem readers feel in your class. How would it feel to be unable to complete the reading assignments and therefore unable to participate in class discussions? How would it feel to be given a test you could not read? How would it feel to be asked to read in front of your peers? Would you withdraw and say nothing, or try to save face by making fun of a situation or by creating a disturbance so as to avoid the unpleasant situation? Would you be inclined to cheat by looking at someone else's work? Can you begin to feel the frustrations of a problem reader? If so, are you committed to doing something about them?

STUDY GUIDE 1

By the time students enter middle or secondary schools, they should be able to use an appropriate strategy for attacking unfamiliar words. They should be able to comprehend different types of written materials and have an extensive reading vocabulary. Students at this level can use different study strategies and employ a flexible reading rate. They should be developing varied tastes and interests in reading and critically evaluating what they read. Students entering middle and secondary schools will also, we hope, begin to find reading an important source of pleasure and knowledge.

Obviously, not all students exhibit these behaviors when they complete elementary school. Some students are behind even in first grade. You will be able to readily identify problem readers by administering an informal suitability survey. Some students will miss most of the comprehension questions on the survey, which you administer as a group test. When you meet with these students to administer the informal suitability survey on an individual basis, you will find that they are embarrassed to read aloud to you. Some may even refuse to do so, because they are ashamed of being unable to read materials that correspond to their grade level. As a content area teacher, you have a right to be concerned about these students' chances of success in your class, especially if there are frequent reading assignments.

Problem Reader Defined

A reading specialist would define a *problem reader* as a student who is reading two years below *expected* reading level. For example, a student who is expected to read at the ninth-grade level according to his aptitude, but reads at the seventh-grade level, is classified as a problem reader. If this student is in the seventh grade, he is not much of a problem reader to the content area teacher. But if the student is in the ninth grade, he *is* a "problem" to the content area teacher—the student will have difficulty reading some of the common reading materials.

For content area teachers, then, a *problem reader* can be defined as a *student who reads below grade level and is therefore unable to read the materials you commonly use in your content area classes,* even though you implement ideas from the previous modules. These students need remedial reading instruction in a special class in the school or at a private reading clinic. You might wish these students could drop out of your class until they are able to meet the prerequisite reading level, but you realize this is impossible. The problem reader also feels discouraged because he is unable to complete all the course requirements, regardless of his motivation. One of your major concerns as a content area teacher, then, should be to identify and help these students in your classes.

Characteristics of Problem Readers

An array of the characteristics of problem readers will be evident, although one student will not exhibit all the behaviors. In fact, you can lessen their rate of occurrence by assigning materials suitable for students' reading levels. For example, if you use a textbook written at the eleventh-grade level to teach a group of eighth-grade students, many students will manifest characteristics of problem readers. To prevent this situation, determine the readability levels of materials you usually use. Remember that a problem reader is one who does not read at grade level and is therefore unable to read most of your content area materials. You can create many problem readers in your class by using textbooks or other reading materials that are written at too high a readability level for the grade.

The problem reader *has inadequate word-pronunciation skills.* When you ask a problem reader to read orally during an informal suitability survey, you will notice that the student fails to use context clues. Problem readers tend to skip hard words or guess at unfamiliar words, rather than analyze the word to see if there is a prefix, suffix, or stem. These students generally ask someone what the word is, rather than use a word-pronunciation strategy (described in Module 7).

The poor reader usually *has a limited vocabulary.* Problem readers know the meanings of some words in the content area, but most of their definitions could be classified at the specific level. They understand some words at the functional level of understanding, but rarely have conceptual definitions for your content area vocabulary.

A poor reader will also exhibit a *low level of comprehension.* Problem readers have difficulty answering the higher level questions you ask to check comprehension. Frequently, they can answer recall or recognition questions, but fail to answer questions that involve translation, application, analysis, synthesis, or evaluation. A large part of the difficulty results from the lack of vocabulary, but even when they are given the meanings of words, problem readers still have trouble arriving at correct answers.

You will also find that the poor reader *does not apply study skills or strategies.* When teachers make reading assignments, problem readers usually approach the assignment by attempting to read the first page; they do not survey the materials or develop questions as purposes for reading. Problem readers rarely take time to recite, since they did not really have particular questions in mind, nor do they spend much time reviewing material they read. Besides having poor study strategies, the problem reader has not developed the study skills necessary for reading materials in your content area.

A poor reader also often *appears uninterested or lazy.* Problem readers are *not motivated* during class, and frequently make you wonder why they are even in school. No matter how effectively you apply the PARS motivational strategy, the problem reader fails to read the assignment because he finds it too difficult. Some problem readers withdraw and try to "hide" when you ask questions as part of a class discussion; others make fun of the situation. Many problem readers have irregular attendance because they feel inadequate in classroom situations, and of course the irregular attendance continues to hinder their academic progress.

It will not take you long to recognize problem readers. You will identify them early if you use the Informal Suitability Survey described in Module 3. If you do not use assessment devices, you will begin to notice poor readers when you make reading assignments or administer quizzes.

The Content Area Teacher's Responsibilities

Your primary responsibility is to help students achieve the objectives of your particular area. It is not your responsibility to teach children how to read, but rather to teach them how to do math problems, develop concepts in social studies, achieve objectives in physical education, or whatever your particular content area is. There are three responsibilities you can accept, however, to help the problem reader accomplish the objectives in your class.

Your first task is to *identify* those factors that may be causing reading failure. Your students, if given a choice, do not want to be problem readers. They would like to be able to read the materials with ease! Rather than just classifying or describing these students as lazy, uninterested, or "turned-off" to schooling, you must try to identify the factors in their lack of reading achievement. Behavior is *caused;* therefore, you must look for factors influencing a student's lack of response to reading instruction. (Study Guide 2 describes six factors that influence reading achievement and provides nontesting devices to help identify factors that are hindering a student's progress.) If you can identify the factors that are causing a reading problem, you may be able to find help to overcome the problem.

Your second responsibility is to *refer* students to colleagues in specialized areas. The school nurse, guidance counselor, media specialist, administrators, school psychologist, and reading teachers may be able to help eliminate some of the factors causing a student's reading problems. Rather than give oversimplified answers to the student or the parent as to why a student has a reading problem, or say the student will "grow out of it," you must seek the help of colleagues with information or expertise beyond your own. (Enabling Element 4 suggests specific techniques for referring problem readers.)

When you refer problem readers, your responsibility is only beginning. The student will still be coming to your class to accomplish the objectives of the content area. Your third responsibility, then, is to *help* the problem reader achieve these objectives by adapting instructional techniques to help him succeed. You can use low-level reading materials, more audiovisual aids to convey information and ideas, administer oral tests, have students help each other, and/or make differentiated reading assignments. Although the adaptations require extra effort, you will be surprised at the repertoire of ideas and materials you can develop when you are sincere about helping problem readers succeed. Students can achieve many of your objectives when they get information and ideas via some technique other than reading. Problem readers are especially skillful in getting information by listening to tapes, looking at pictures, participating in class discussions, and using audiovisual aids such as films, filmstrips, and overhead transparencies.

Your responsibility is to (1) identify problem readers and the factors that hinder their progress, (2) refer problem readers for specialized help, and (3) adapt instructional strategies to help them achieve content objectives. Now go to Enabling Element 2 to find out why some students are not able to read at grade level.

ENABLING ELEMENT 2
POSSIBLE CAUSES OF READING FAILURE

SPECIFIC OBJECTIVE 2

You will list and explain by categories factors that may cause reading failure.

ENABLING ACTIVITIES

*1. Read Study Guide 2. Identify and be able to explain the six major factors that influence reading achievement.
2. Discuss how emotional problems can cause reading failure and how reading failure can influence emotional problems.
3. Elementary teachers are often blamed for reading failures. Explain why this is unjust.
*4. Reading failure usually results from several interrelated factors. Describe some students who can be classified as problem readers, and indicate the various factors that may be working together to cause their problems.
5. Some reading specialists believe environment is the most important factor in reading achievement. Do you agree? Can parents of middle-school and secondary-school students help their children with reading? In what ways? How can these suggestions be communicated to parents?

STUDY GUIDE 2

Content teachers can offer valuable assistance if they know some of the reasons students fail to read at grade level. Using this information, they can help problem readers succeed. As you read about the possible causes of reading failure, think about ways to identify these factors in your students. Remember that problems often result from interrelated factors rather than one isolated factor.

Physical Condition

Several physical factors correlate with failure in reading. Disabilities in vision and hearing can produce reading problems. A student may have difficulty seeing the chalkboard or the textbook clearly. Reduced visual acuity, fusion difficulty, and weak eye muscles are a few of the visual disabilities that correlate with reading failure. Students with inadequate hearing or discrimination usually have problems in reading because they misunderstand oral directions and explanations.

The student's general health is also important in learning to read. Students who do not have a proper diet or sufficient rest may experience difficulty, because reading is an abstract task that requires a high degree of concentration. These students generally have poor attendance, and may have had many childhood illnesses that caused extended absences. Sometimes specific illnesses such as glandular disturbances or thyroid dysfunctions can hinder academic achievement, or students may take drugs or other substances that affect hearing, vision, and general health.

Language Development

The relationship between language development and reading success is obvious. Students who have a meager vocabulary, poorly developed sound–symbol relationships, and a weak grasp of the language's grammar base have considerable difficulty with reading.

Not all students grow in height and weight at the same rate, nor do they all develop language facility at the same rate or have excellent language models. Students who mature slowly are likely to arrive at school too immature for the academic task of reading; likewise, students who have not heard standard English will experience difficulty when they encounter unfamiliar language patterns and words. Some students thus fall behind in reading—and remain behind—because of maturational factors and nonstandard language models.

Environment

Reading requires students to bring meaning to printed symbols. To find meaning is only possible, however, when students have had experiences that relate to what they are reading. Students who have not had many real or vicarious experiences are at a disadvantage; if a student is reading a selection about a country he has visited, he is likely to get more meaning from the material than the student who has never been out of the city in which he was born.

Parents are part of their children's environment and set an example for them. Parents who read frequently and enjoy reading as a source of information and pleasure are likely to convey these attitudes to their children; students who come from homes where there are no reading materials may have difficulty learning to read because they have not learned to value this task.

Aptitude

There is a high positive correlation between reading achievement and intelligence among high-school students and adults because many of the factors measured by intelligence tests are the same factors required for success in reading. Most intelligence tests measure visual memory, auditory memory, the ability to make judgments, and general information and vocabulary, which are all important in learning to read. A student who does not seem to have an aptitude for learning to read as well as other students usually falls behind; however, students with below average intelligence can still learn to read when instructional methods are adapted to their aptitudes.

Social-Emotional Problems

Social-emotional factors also influence reading achievement. Some students fail in reading because they are overwhelmed by personal problems brought on by unhappy relationships with parents, siblings, and peers. Symptoms associated with social and emotional problems, such as short attention span, preoccupation, and lack of desire to stay with a task, are the same behaviors associated with academic failure.

Educational Background

Schools have also caused many reading problems. Previous teachers may have used unsuitable materials or methods, or may have neglected students who attended irregularly and seemed unmotivated. In large classes teachers find it impossible to provide for all the individual differences and cannot do as much as they would like or need to do to help each student. The result is that students' reading levels and needs for specific skills have often not been properly determined and/or remediated.

PLEASE Remember the Factors

These factors work together to help or hinder reading progress, and teachers must consider all of them to determine why some students fail to learn to read as well as expected.

A mnemonic device to help you remember these factors is the acronym PLEASE. Each letter represents a major factor that influences reading achievement:

P—physical condition—health, hearing, vision, nutrition
L—language development—vocabulary, grammar, sentence structure
E—environment—home, attitudes toward reading, motivation
A—aptitude—visual memory, auditory memory, judgment, general information
S—social-emotional problems—relationships with peers, family, and self
E—eduational background—quality of teaching, appropriateness of materials, class size

Perhaps you will remember this acronym because it is the plea made by problem readers—Please! Your task is to *PLEASE identify*, *PLEASE refer*, and *PLEASE help* problem readers. The other study guides in this module will help you perform these task.

ENABLING ELEMENT 3
USING NONTESTING DEVICES TO IDENTIFY
POSSIBLE CAUSES OF READING FAILURE

SPECIFIC OBJECTIVE 3

You will use nontesting devices to identify factors that may cause reading failure.

ENABLING ACTIVITIES

*1. Read Study Guide 3. Compare the advantages and disadvantages of the different devices for identifying possible causes of reading failure.

*2. Try the Observational Checklist with problem readers in your class. Can you identify some explanations for their reading failures? Remember, the more you use the checklist, the more automatic your observations will become. Periodically reread the checklist to refresh your memory.

3. Duplicate the Incomplete Sentences and Personal Inventory forms and have students complete them. Think of ways to use this information for adapting instruction.

4. Talk with teachers in your building to determine who will use the different devices. It is suggested that all teachers use the Observational Checklist as a guide to observing and talking with students, and that others who have major responsibility for certain students use the Personal Inventory and Incomplete Sentences. Adapt these suggestions to your school.

5. Share results of the personal inventories with the school librarian. Responses to items 7, 9, 13, and 20 can yield valuable information for selecting books, magazines, and other materials for the library or media center.

STUDY GUIDE 3

If factors that seem to interfere with students' responsiveness to reading can be identified, then students can be given appropriate help. Even though content area teachers are not expected to provide remedial reading instruction, they can help determine factors that hinder progress. This module includes four useful devices for identifying PLEASE factors.

Because students are different, teachers need to employ different techniques for gathering information about problems. Some students are eager to talk with teachers; others avoid talking about themselves, so teachers must be able to observe or use paper and pencil inventories to gather information. This Study Guide presents an Observational Checklist, guidelines for interviewing students, and two paper and pencil inventories.

Using an Observational Checklist

The observational checklist in Table 10-1 provides guidelines for observing students who are experiencing reading difficulties. If you read the checklist periodically, you will keep these factors and specific behaviors paramount in your mind as you observe. Remember the mnemonic device in Study Guide 2—PLEASE; each of the letters in the acronym refers to a major reasons for reading failure: P-physical factors; L-language development; E-environmental factors; A-aptitude; S-social-emotional; E-educational factors. The checklist includes observable behaviors for each factor.

You are not expected to complete the checklist for each student; its purpose is to guide your observations as you try to identify possible causes of reading problems. Your observations are often the key to identifying the causes of reading problems.

Table 10–1 Observational Checklist for Identifying Possible Causes of Reading Failure

Directions: Which areas seem to be interfering with students' responsiveness to reading? Underline specific behaviors you observe; add comments as necessary.

Factor   Comments

_____ *Physical Factors*
When the student reads, does she
  Lose her place?
  Rub her eyes?
  Blink excessively?
  Tilt her head so as to use only one eye?
  Complain of blurred print, headaches, or watering eyes?
When you speak to the student, does she
  Tilt her head?
  Cup her ear?
  Appear inattentive?
  Ask you to repeat directions?
Does she appear well rested and generally healthy?
What is her attendance record?

_____ *Language Factors*
When she speaks, does she
  Have a meager vocabulary?
  Use poor sentence structure?

Does the student make frequent spelling errors that indicate lack of knowledge of sound–symbol relationships?

Does she have a past history of poor performance in
language-related courses?

If you have had occasions to talk with parents and siblings, did you notice anything helpful for interpreting
the student's language background?

_____ *Environment Factors*

Does the student talk about experiences, or places she
has visited?

Does the student have books, magazines, or other reading
materials of her own?

Do her parents seem interested in her and accept her?

Is education valued by the family?

_____ *Aptitude Factors*

Does the student ask questions?

Does she have a fairly good background of information?

Is she able to draw conclusions and make sound judgments based on facts?

Does she learn rapidly and remember what she has
learned?

Is she able to see similarities and differences in concepts?

_____ *Social-Emotional Factors*

Is the student accepted by family and peers?

Is she able to get along with others?

Does she have a positive self-concept?

Is she able to control her emotions and concentrate long
enough to complete a task?

_____ *Educational Factors*

Does the student have positive or negative attitudes
toward school?

Does she have purposes for learning?

Has the student met with success or failure in most
academic areas?

Has the student been enrolled in any remedial reading
programs?

Are the appropriate materials available for the student?

Using a Personal Inventory

Consider using or adapting this Personal Inventory if you want to
gather more information about your students quickly. You can administer a Personal Inventory to the students for whom you have the major
responsibility. As you read the items, notice that they are geared toward the six major factors that influence reading achievement and
general academic progress.

Notice that the directions tell the student to leave blank the items
he does not wish to answer. You should make note of these items, then

use observation to gather more information about them. As with all devices, remember that the responses indicate a student's feelings on that particular day. The answers must be combined with other samples of behavior before making any conclusions or judgments.

After administering the inventory, use the guidelines for interpreting the information. Keep in mind, however, that some responses may provide information about more than one factor.

Personal Inventory

Name _____ Date _____
Address _____ Age _____
Telephone _____

Directions: The following questions are designed to help me get to know you. Write your answers in the blanks. If you are not sure of an answer, or do not want to answer some question, leave it blank.

1. What other schools have you attended? _____
   _____

2. Are you supposed to wear glasses? _____ If yes, when did you first get them? _____

3. Do you read your eyes bother you when you read or write?_____In what way?_____

4. Is your hearing (circle one) excellent, good, fair, or poor?

5. Is your health (circle one) excellent, good, fair or poor?

6. How many hours do you sleep each night? _____

7. Do you read for pleasure? _____ If yes, name some recent books or magazines you have read. _____
   _____

8. Is your reading (circle one) excellent, good, fair, or poor?

9. What is the most interesting topic you like to study? _____
   _____

10. What is the least interesting topic you must study? _____
    _____

11. How much time do you usually spend each day studying outside school? _____

12. List some of the places you have visited outside of (city) ___
    _____

13. What interests do you have outside of school? _____
    _____

14. What school activities do you enjoy? _____
    _____

15. How do you get along with your parents? _____
    _____
    _____

16. Circle the word that shows how most teachers think of you as a student: excellent, good, fair, or poor.
17. Is your vocabulary: excellent, good, fair or poor?
18. Is your spelling: excellent, good, fair, or poor?
19. Do you have a place to study at home? Please describe it. _____
20. What kinds of responsibilities would you like to have as an adult? _____
21. How do you get along with the other students in this class? Do you know these students well? Who are your favorite students? _____ _____ _____
22. Why do some people like you? _____ _____
23. Are there some people who do not like you? _____ Why? _____ _____
24. What is your father's occupation? _____ What is your mother's occupation? _____
25. What language is usually spoken in your home? _____
26. Do your parents talk with you about school? _____ If so, what kinds of things do they ask? _____ _____

Table 10–2 Guide to Interpreting Information from the Personal Inventory

Major Factor	Questions Designed to Provide Information
Physical Condition	2, 3, 4, 5, 6
Language Development	8, 17, 18, 25
Environment	12, 19, 24, 26
Aptitude	9, 10, 13, 20
Social-Emotional Problems	15, 21, 22, 23
Educational Background	1, 7, 11, 14, 16

Incomplete Sentences

Some teachers like to use incomplete sentences like the following to gather information about students. The teacher who has the major responsibility for certain students may be the one to administer the incomplete sentences. When interpreting responses, remember that the student's responses represent feelings only on a particular day. Before making rash judgments, you should gather more information by consulting the guidance counselor, cumulative records, personal inventory, other teachers, and information from talks you have with the student.

Identifying and Helping Problem Readers

Name _____ Date _____

Directions: Quickly complete the following sentences. Write down the first thing that enters your mind. There are no right or wrong answers.

1. Reading is_____
2. I like to _____
3. My friends _____
4. I feel _____
5. The best magazine _____
6. Elementary school was _____
7. My eyes _____
8. My ears _____
9. My parents _____
10. Education is _____
11. I have been to _____
12. I wish I could _____
13. When I read to others _____
14. I am liked by _____
15. School is _____
16. My teachers _____
17. Books are _____
18. I sleep _____
19. When I finish school _____
20. My home _____
21. I need help in _____
22. My best subject is _____
23. Spelling is _____
24. Teachers usually _____

Although responses vary, you will find the following guidelines useful for analyzing the responses. Certain responses will necessarily fit more than one classification; however, we have tried to make them as discrete as possible. For example, one student may complete item 4 with "I feel tired"; another student may say, "I feel lonely." In the first case, the response refers to a physical factor; the second response concerns social-emotional factors. You will need to adapt the guidelines to students' responses in Table 10-3.

Table 10–3 Guidelines for Analyzing the Incomplete Sentence Responses

Factor	Number of Sentence That May Provide Information
Physical	4, 7, 8, 18
Language	1, 13, 17, 23
Environment	5, 10, 11, 13, 20
Aptitude	12, 19, 21, 22
Social-Emotional	2, 3, 9, 14
Education	6, 15, 16, 24

Talking and Listening to Students

Some students are eager to share information with teachers if the teachers seem genuinely interested. Talking to and listening to students can be a useful technique to gather information about the six factors influencing reading achievement. All teachers have some responsibility to listen to students, because different students relate better to different teachers. If all the teachers on the staff are aware of the importance of listening to students and hold perceptive conversations with students, the staff will be better able to help students. A student may relate to the physical education teacher on the field, but not relate at all to the English teacher in the classroom; another student may relate better to the English teacher and avoid face-to-face encounters with the physical education teacher.

Many of the questions in the Personal Inventory form can be used in conversations with students. Of course, you will phrase the questions differently and ask them in a natural sequence as the conversation develops. A teacher who is aware of the six major categories, however, can organize student responses into meaningful categories for interpretation.

When talking to students, you must be sincere and concerned. Ask questions in such a way that students realize you are not "meddling," but are trying to help. You will want to help students accept themselves as they are, yet provide hope for improvement. Help students realize that reading and success in academic areas are important, but that there are other important things in life, too. Here are sample questions you can use during a *natural* conversation with the student.

- *Physical Condition:* Have you ever had any trouble seeing or hearing? What illnesses have you had? How many hours do you sleep in a day?
- *Language:* What language do your parents speak? Did they graduate from high school? College? Did you have any problems learning to spell, read, or write?
- *Environment:* What places have you visited on vacations? How do your parents feel about your school activities? Can you study at home?
- *Aptitude:* What things do you do best? Do you want to do better in school? Why? Do you think you can learn to read better?
- *Social-Emotional:* Who are your best friends? How well do you get along with your family? What kinds of things make you happy? Frustrated? Sad?
- *Education:* What kind of student were you in elementary school? Have you ever been in a special reading class? Do your teachers generally like you?

Final Comment

Besides these nontesting devices to determine possible causes of reading failure, you can also use some of the reading skills tests in Module 8 to help you further identify special reading difficulties that can be remediated. And, if you use an Informal Suitability Survey, you will be doing your part to help find appropriate materials for problem readers. One testing or nontesting device is insufficient; you need a battery of devices to enable you to gather enough information to help students. For practical ideas on using the information you have gathered, go on to Enabling Element 4.

ENABLING ELEMENT 4
REFERRING AND HELPING PROBLEM READERS

SPECIFIC OBJECTIVE 4

You will indicate appropriate referral sources for students who manifest certain symptoms, and you will state guidelines and techniques for adapting instruction to help problem readers succeed in content classes.

ENABLING ACTIVITIES

*1. Read Study Guide 4 to identify possible resource persons to whom problem readers can be referred and note ways you can help such students in your classes.

*2. Talk with the school nurse, psychologist, and guidance counselors to determine the specific services they offer and the procedures for initiating referral. Ask about professional services that are free to low-income families.

*3. Talk with the reading specialist and developmental reading teachers to determine what reading services are offered in the school. What other types of reading instruction should be offered?

4. Discuss guidelines for referring students for special help. What are the school and county guidelines for referring problem readers? You should not refer students to specialists outside the school without the advice and consent of the appropriate person. Often the guidance counselor, assistant principal, school psychologist, or some other resource person is able to use more elaborate screening devices to determine if referrals are necessary.

5. Talk with your colleagues about ways to involve parents in home–school tutoring programs for problem readers.

6. Read the Teacher's Daily Dozen Checklist. Note one item you would like to improve. Brainstorm with colleagues and review previous modules to determine specific ways to implement the behavior.

STUDY GUIDE 4

There are two additional ways content teachers can help problem readers. First, you need to refer students to the proper sources of help. You are not expected to teach beginning reading skills, diagnose or prescribe glasses or hearing aids, or act as a full-time guidance counselor. You need and must have the help of specialists. Second, even though you are not expected to teach primary-grade reading skills, you can make some adaptations in instructional strategies to help problem readers. You have some responsibility to help students reading two or more years below grade level to succeed in your content area while they try to overcome their reading deficiencies. Problem readers can succeed in content areas if you use the following suggestions.

Helping Students with Physical Problems

- Refer the student to the school nurse for further screening. Perhaps a visual, hearing, or health problem has been overlooked or has developed recently. If drug or substance abuse is evident, refer the student to the school counselor.
- Encourage the student to wear prescribed glasses or hearing aid. Help the student with self-acceptance by being honest about any physical limitations.
- Suggest short periods of work for close work such as reading and writing. Direct the student to set a time limit for studying.
- Have the student sit near the chalkboard, screen, or close to the action. Do not pay too much attention to her, so she won't feel awkward and unusual.
- If necessary, contact the librarian to see if books with larger print are available. You might also see if cassettes are available or could be made for students who have a difficult time reading, yet are able to listen and comprehend.
- Remember not to turn your back on students when speaking or to put your hands in front of your face. Teachers are often not conscious of habits that interfere with their effectiveness. Evaluate yourself continuously to see if you are articulating clearly and maintaining good eye contact.
- It might be helpful to write key vocabulary words on the chalkboard and discuss the meanings and pronunciations of words using the suggestions in Modules 4 and 7.
- If the student is having health problems that hinder attendance,

you might ask the visiting teacher to contact the parents. It may be necessary to adjust assignments and number of credits according to the student's capabilities.

Helping Students with Language Problems

- Refer the student to a remedial reading specialist or remedial English classes. Share with the specialist the information you have gathered about the student's reading skills and habits.
- If possible, give oral tests. You can often administer tests orally while other students are taking written exams. If this is not possible, see if a parent volunteer can help.
- Provide information on cassettes or have others read to students for whom suitable materials are not available. Students can often listen and understand what they are not able to read.
- Repeat the student's responses using correct grammar and sentence structure. Realize that you alone are not going to change the student's use of language overnight; however, if all teachers make conscientious efforts, and if the student wants to improve, it is possible to change language patterns.
- Use many visual materials to expand concepts. The old saying "a picture is worth a thousand words" may be trite, but it is true.
- Correct spelling errors by going over the frequently missed words. Point out sounds that may be confusing.
- To help students increase vocabularies at higher levels, use the ideas in Module 4. Many problem readers only have specific understandings of words.
- Suggest self-study books for improving spelling, reading, or writing. These books frequently include practical exercises and information.

Helping Students with Environmental Problems

- Use many visual and auditory aids to develop concepts. Students can develop many concepts through vicarious experiences when direct experiences are not possible.
- Refer the student to the guidance counselor if physical abuse is evident. Child abuse agencies rely on teachers for referrals; however, you should talk with the appropriate school authority before making referrals to outside agencies.
- Praise the student sincerely for ideas, suggestions, and so forth. Do not overdo praise so as to appear insincere.
- Be available to parents when they express concern.
- Have confidence in the student. Expect the best and show disappointment when you do not get her best efforts.

- Make students aware of the resources available at school and public libraries. If you use many reading materials in your classes, arrange visits to libraries to show students what materials are available and how to locate them. Provide opportunities for students to browse and use some of the materials that interest them.
- Help students realize the value of having a place for study and good study habits. Provide specific suggestions on how to study in your content area. Suggest places in the school or community where they can study and at the same time enjoy the company of other people.
- Read or tell stories about famous people who have become successful even though they came from disadvantaged environments. You cannot change attitudes in one day; however, if you take advantage of teaching opportunities on a daily basis, the change will occur.

Helping Students with Social-Emotional Problems

- Refer the student to the guidance counselor or school psychologist. Some students have problems that require special analysis and guidance. After the student has met with the guidance counselor and/or school psychologist, discuss their recommendations for helping the student in the classroom.
- Avoid antagonizing the student. Avoid behavior that tends to "set off" the student.
- Determine the student's strengths and praise her sincerely. At the same time, help the problem reader face her weaknesses and set goals for improvement.
- Be ready to listen to the student. Not all students are ready to talk, but when they want to, they are generally seeking advice even if they don't say so.
- Give responsibilities that interest the student. Differentiate assignments according to interests and abilities.
- Accept the student as she is. You may not like the behavior, but you can still like the person.
- Use discussion groups and group dynamic techniques to help students develop skill in working with and accepting others. Students often form stereotypes and cliques that hinder social development. It is important for teachers to help students appreciate differences among their classmates.
- Help students plan schedules that allow time for social activities as well as studying. Help students understand that most students enjoy socializing yet must spend some time studying if they are to succeed academically. Plan flexible schedules with the students.

Helping Students with Less Aptitude for Reading

- Refer the student to the school psychologist for an individual intelligence test to determine special aptitudes. An IQ score is not as meaningful as the scores for the intelligence factors the test measures. Determine special areas in which the student might have better aptitude, such as visual or auditory memory, then capitalize on these strengths.
- Use many visual materials, first-hand experiences, and concrete objects. Remember that reading is a highly abstract task; it requires one to form mental images from printed symbols. Students who demonstrate low aptitude often have not had as many experiences as others.
- Adjust materials to capabilities according to results of the Informal Suitability Survey.
- Grade according to individual progress, if at all possible.
- Encourage students by creating pride in achievement. Help students realize the value of a job well done.
- Help students develop confidence in what they can do and be, rather than emphasizing what they cannot do or become. Remember, there are aptitudes for many different types of skills.
- Remember the importance of repetition and practice. Most students, especially those with low aptitude for reading, need many practice and reinforcement activities to learn new concepts or skills.
- Identify the most important concepts, attitudes, and skills for your content area and concentrate on these objectives.
- Divide students into teams to complete some assignments. Make sure each team has students of different achievement levels and aptitudes. You can have teams, rather than individuals, compete with one another to complete certain assignments.

Helping Students with Educationally Poor Backgrounds

- Make sure you provide materials the students are capable of reading. Apply some of your newly developed skills in administering and interpreting Informal Suitability Surveys.
- Use the different teaching strategies suggested for word meaning and word pronunciation skills. Since vocabulary is important to comprehension, identify the most important specialized words in your content area and emphasize these. Have students keep a record of new words as they learn them.
- If you need to use many materials that require reading, have one of the best readers put the most important sections of the materials on cassettes to keep in the library or classroom for use by poor readers. Use audiovisual aids to help students develop concepts without reading.

- Summarize the most important material on a handout written at a low reading level. Review Module 2 for specific suggestions on writing materials at specified reading levels.
- Ask the librarian or department chairman for books or other supplemental materials written at lower reading levels that contain the concepts and skills you are trying to teach. You can establish centers that focus on interesting topics or skills.
- Introduce assignments with a purpose so students can look for specific information. Discuss with them how the assignments will help them learn study strategies.
- Use involvement activities during class. Students can learn from each other while they do group research and have discussions. Simulation activities in which students actually apply newly acquired skills or concepts are especially appropriate for problem readers. Role playing and dramatization also make class sessions come alive.
- Use the textbook illustrations, pictures, and charts to explain content. Graphic aids, accompanied by your comments or questions, can convey the essential information in the text. Supplement this material by inviting resource people to your classroom.
- Outline, or teach students to outline, the most important information in the course. Comprehension is easier when thoughts are well organized, as is required when outlining. A skill group might help teach this skill or other important skills problem readers have not developed.

You are not expected to change problem readers into mature readers in the short time they are with you; however, a positive attitude toward problem readers, belief that they can succeed in your classes, and effective teaching techniques will enable problem readers to develop better concepts through success, and this, too, will help them grow in reading achievement.

Putting It All Together
A combination of factors usually influences reading achievement. A student may be plagued by social-emotional problems triggered by physical problems, which in turn result in educational problems. The following checklist will help "put it all together" as you try to help problem readers; it is not a series of steps to follow for helping problem readers. The emphasis is on *continual* effective teaching. Use the checklist to continually evaluate yourself to make sure you are not contributing to students' reading problems.

Identifying and Helping Problem Readers

Teacher's Daily Dozen Checklist

_____ 1. Am I using materials the students are capable of handling? Do I use my department chairman and librarian as resources for getting such materials?

_____ 2. Have I identified the most important concepts for my students? Am I teaching the concepts, skills, and attitudes that will make their lives better?

_____ 3. Am I using a variety of activities in the classroom? Do I use activities such as simulation, role playing, resource people, discussions, and audiovisual aids?

_____ 4. Do I differentiate assignments according to the needs of the students? After administering Informal Suitability Surveys, am I using the information to provide appropriate materials? Do I suggest to the students how to read the materials?

_____ 5. Do I accept my students as they are? Do I avoid labeling them? Have I determined their strengths, and do my instructional techniques maximize them?

_____ 6. Do I refer students who need specialized help? Do I know what support services are available in the school and community?

_____ 7. Do I identify and demonstrate enthusiasm for my content area? Am I stimulating students' interests and curiosity?

_____ 8. Am I continually observing students to determine factors that are helping or hindering their academic achievement? Have I used this information to help the students?

_____ 9. Do I take time for myself? Am I able to enjoy many experiences outside school that will make me a better teacher in the classroom?

_____10. Am I helping students increase their vocabularies and develop appropriate strategies for word pronunciation, comprehension, and study?

_____11. Am I aware of the reading skills required for the materials in my content area? Do I help students learn to read these specialized materials, or do I just assume that anyone can read them? Do I use skill groups and skill centers to provide for individual differences?

_____12. Am I implementing the PARS (Module 9) strategy for motivating reluctant readers? Will my attitude influence students to succeed in my classes? Do I have faith in students?

POSTTEST

Directions: The following questions are designed to measure your accomplishment of the objectives in this module. Read each item and respond as directed.

1. Describe the characteristics of problem readers and list your three major responsibilities for helping problem readers succeed in content area classes.
2. List the six major factors that influence reading achievement. After each factor, give a specific example of how it can help or hinder reading achievement.
3. Read the following description of a fifteen-year-old problem reader and identify two factors that may be causing his reading failure, then indicate two possible referral sources and two ways you could help Tom in your class.

When Tom comes to your class, he seems to want to "goof off." He does not pay attention when you talk and never completes assignments. When you provide time for him to begin his textbook reading assignment in class, he doesn't even open the book. When you surveyed the suitability of the textbook for students, you found the major textbook was too difficult for him, yet when you read the textbook, he is able to understand with 100 percent accuracy.

According to Tom's cumulative record, he received a prescription for glasses when he was in the fourth grade, but you have never seen him wear them. As you think back, you have noticed that he squints when looking at the chalkboard.

Even though Tom fools around in class, once in awhile he does ask good questions. He is friendly and outgoing; however, you noticed he does not have many close friends in this class. He is always courteous when you talk with him individually.

When Tom's homeroom teacher administered the Incomplete Sentences (Study Guide 3) to the class, Tom was one of the first to complete the sentences. Read his responses to the Incomplete Sentences:

1. Reading is a rip off.
2. I like to watch television.
3. My friends are OK.
4. I don't like these questions.
5. The best magazine is *Popular Mechanics.*
6. Elementary school was fun.
7. My eyes are OK.
8. My ears are on my head.
9. My parents work.
10. Education is a drag.
11. I have been to New York.
12. I wish I could find a job.

13. When I read to others I get nervous.
14. I am liked by my dog.
15. School is a drag.
16. My teachers are smart.
17. Books are hard.
18. I sleep in on Saturdays.
19. When I finish school I will make more money.
20. My home is near the expressway.
21. I need help in math.
22. My best subject is shop.
23. Spelling is OK.
24. Teachers usually like me.

POSTTEST ANSWERS

1. A problem reader can be defined as a student who reads below grade level and is therefore unable to read common content area materials. Although the characteristics of problem readers vary, these behaviors are typical:
   a. Lacks systematic method for pronouncing unknown words.
   b. Has limited vocabulary in speaking, writing, listening and reading.
   c. Experiences difficulty comprehending materials.
   d. Has not developed study strategy or specialized study skills necessary for success in content areas.
   e. Displays negative attitude toward reading assignments.

2. The six factors that influence reading achievement are:
   a. Physical Condition
   b. Language Development
   c. Environment
   d. Aptitude
   e. Social-Emotional Problems
   f. Educational Background

   Physical factors can help or hinder reading achievement in many ways. Excellent visual and auditory skills are prerequisites for the reading task, and good physical health enables a person to learn. If a student has visual, health, and/or auditory problems, chances for success in reading are limited.

   Language development can also influence reading achievement. Students who were generally slow in developing language skills, or who do not have adequate models to learn standard English, fall behind during the early school years. Concentrated efforts to improve language can help the student become a better reader.

   The environment is one of the most important factors in reading achievement. The student whose home does not have books or other reading material, or a place for him to study, is hindered. Reading progress is made more difficult by parents who do not support the schools or the student. Conversely, overprotective parents or those who put too much pressure on the child can hinder achievement, too.

Reading correlates highly with intelligence as measured by academic aptitude tests. A student who is below average in factors that influence reading—visual memory, auditory memory, and vocabulary—has difficulty learning to read.

Social-emotional factors can help or hinder reading achievement. Reading requires a great deal of concentration and thinking, and a student plagued by social-emotional concerns will not be able to concentrate. A student who feels incapable of learning will also have a more difficult time learning to read.

Students with enthusiastic, dedicated teachers, who diagnose to determine appropriate objectives and activities, have a better chance for success in reading. Teachers who neglect the problem reader contribute further to the problem.

3. A visual defect may be influencing Tom's responsiveness to instruction. Glasses were prescribed when he was in the fourth grade, but he does not wear them. According to his response to item 7, he seems to avoid accepting this limitation. According to the description, Tom does not have friends in your class. Likewise, his responses to items 4 and 14 may indicate possible social-emotional problems. It could be he is "goofing off" to gain acceptance from peers. Also, he may not be wearing his glasses because he does not want to appear different from his peers. The interaction effects of poor vision and lack of appropriate peer relationships could be contributing to his lack of responsiveness to instruction.

4. At this time Tom should be referred to the school reading specialist to determine the extent of his reading disability and to suggest instructional materials that would be most beneficial for him. You might also refer Tom to his counselor, who might provide some insights to his "acting-out" behavior and negative self-concept. The school nurse could screen his vision again and talk with him about the visual defect. Try to give attention to Tom and motivate him by using the questions he asks in class. Involve him in activities that do not require reading. Perhaps you might have Tom listen to some tapes that include sections of the textbook you would like him to understand. If possible, relate some of your content area objectives to Tom's interest in cars, math, and industrial arts.

Final Comment

This module explains why certain students are problem readers and outlines the techniques for adapting instruction for those students.

These techniques will enable you to help the problem reader develop the skills and knowledge for your content area. Simply because a student is a problem reader does not mean he or she cannot succeed in school, but the student's success depends upon the most important factor in the educational process—you!

If you have correctly completed all Posttest items, you are finished with the module. If not, see your instructor for help, or go back through the Enabling Elements as necessary.

REFERENCES

Aukerman, R.C. *Reading in the Secondary School Classroom*. New York: McGraw-Hill, 1972.

Brooks, B.D., and S. Merino. "Strategies for Teaching Within a Bicultural Setting." *Reading Improvement* 13, no. 2 (Summer 1976): 86–91.

Colwell, C.G. "Humor as a Motivational and Remedial Technique." *Journal of Reading* 24, no. 6 (1981): 484–86.

Cushenbery. D.C. *Remedial Reading in the Secondary School*. West Nyack, N.Y.: Parker, 1972.

Davey, B., and S.M. Porter. "Comprehension-rating: A Procedure to Assist Poor Comprehenders." *Journal of Reading* 26, no. 3 (1982): 197–202.

Early, M. and D.J. Sawyer. *Reading to Learn in Grades 5 to 12*. San Diego, Calif.: Harcourt, Brace, Jovanovich, 1984.

Forgan, H. *Help Your Child Learn to Read*. Toronto: Pagurian Press, 1975.

Hafner, L.E. *Improving Reading in Middle and Secondary School*, 2nd ed. New York: Macmillan, 1974.

Karlin, R. *Teaching Reading in High School*, 2nd ed. Indianapolis, Ind.: Bobbs-Merrill, 1972.

Mangieri, J.N. "A Secondary Reading Program That Worked." *Reading Improvement* 15, no. 1 (Spring 1978): 10–12.

Mercer, C.D. *Children and Adolescents with Learning Disabilities*, 2nd ed. Columbus, Ohio: Charles E. Merrill, 1983.

Otto, W., and R.J. Smith. *Corrective and Remedial Teaching*. Boston: Houghton-Mifflin, 1980.

Ramsey, W.Z., ed. "Organization for Individual Differences." *Perspectives in Reading*, vol. 9. Newark, Del.: International Reading Association, 1967.

Rossman, J.F. "Remedial Readers: Did Parents Read to Them at Home?" *Journal of Reading* 17 (1974): 622–25.

Strang, R. *Reading Diagnosis and Remediation*. Newark, Del.: International Reading Association, 1968.

——, C.M. McCullough, and A.C. Traxler. *The Improvement of Reading*. New York: McGraw-Hill, 1967.

Wilson, R. M. *Diagnostic and Remedial Reading for Classroom and Clinic*, 5th ed. Columbus, Ohio: Charles E. Merrill, 1985.

INDEX

ABOUT THE AUTHORS

Harry W. Forgan is currently a Professor of Education at the University of Miami, Coral Gables, Florida. He earned his Bachelor of Education, Master of Education, and Doctor of Philosophy at Kent State University. He has written nine books concerning reading methods and has coauthored four books. He has written a book for parents, *Help Your Child Learn to Read*, and several practical handbooks: *The Reading Corner, Phorgan's Phonics, Getting Ready To Read*, and *The Reading Skill Builders*. Dr. Forgan has been a classroom teacher and serves as a consultant to many school systems, teacher centers, and professional reading associations. He continues to work with students in elementary, junior high, and high schools in Dade County, Florida.

Charles T. Mangrum II is Professor of Education and Chairperson of the Graduate Reading Area at the University of Miami, Coral Gables, Florida. Dr. Mangrum did his advanced graduate work at Indiana University. He has taught in both elementary and secondary schools and served as a Reading Consultant for an elementary and junior high school district. He served as Editor of the *Reading Aids Series* published by the International Reading Association and Editor of the *Florida Reading Quarterly* published by the Florida Reading Reading Council. He is past President of the Florida State Reading Council and coauthor of three textbooks and six instructional programs. He contributes to journals, presents at conferences, and is a consultant to numerous schools.